Careers in Applied Anthropology in the 21st Century: Perspectives from Academics and Practitioners

Carla Guerrón-Montero, Volume Editor

Satish Kedia and Tim Wallace, General Editors

NAPA Bulletin (1556-4789) is published in March and September on behalf of the American Anthropological Association by Blackwell Publishing, Inc. with offices at (US) 350 Main Street, Malden, MA 02148-5020, (UK) 9600 Garsington Road, Oxford OX4 2ZG, and (Asia) 155 Cremorne Street, Richmond VIC 3121, Australia.

Mailing: Journal is mailed Standard Rate. Mailing to rest of world by IMEX (International Mail Express). Canadian mail is sent by Canadian publications mail agreement number 40573520. POSTMASTER: Send all address changes to NAPA Bulletin, Blackwell Publishing, Inc., Journals Subscription Department, 350 Main Street, Malden, MA 02148-5020, USA.

Publisher: NAPA Bulletin is published by Blackwell Publishing, Inc., 350 Main Street, Malden, MA 02148-5020, USA. Blackwell Publishing, Inc. is now part of Wiley-Blackwell.

Information for Subscribers: NAPA Bulletin is published in two one-issue volumes per year. Subscription prices for 2008 are: Premium Institutional: £27 (Europe), US$54 (The Americas), £27 (Rest of World); Customers in the UK should add VAT at 7%; customers in the EU should also add VAT at 7%, or provide a VAT registration number or evidence of entitlement to exemption. Customers in Canada should add 5% GST or provide evidence of entitlement to exemption. The Premium institutional price includes online access to the current and all online back files to January 1st 1997, where available. For other pricing options, including access information and terms and conditions, please visit www.blackwellpublishing.com/napa.

Delivery Terms and Legal Title: Prices include delivery of print journals to the recipient's address. Delivery terms are Delivered Duty Unpaid (DDU); the recipient is responsible for paying any import duty or taxes. Legal title passes to the customer on despatch by our distributors.

Copyright and Photocopying: © 2008 American Anthropological Association. All rights reserved. No part of this publication may be reproduced, stored or transmitted in any form or by any means without the prior permission in writing from the copyright holder. Authorization to photocopy items for internal and personal use is granted by the copyright holder for libraries and other users registered with their local Reproduction Rights Organization (RRO), e.g. Copyright Clearance Center (CCC), 222 Rosewood Drive, Danvers, MA 01923, USA (www.copyright.com), provided the appropriate fee is paid directly to the RRO. This consent does not extend to other kinds of copying such as copying for general distribution, for advertising or promotional purposes, for creating new collective works or for resale. Special requests should be addressed to: journalsrights@oxon.blackwellpublishing.com.

Back Issues: Single issues from current and recent volumes are available at the current single issue price from Blackwell Publishing Journals. Earlier issues may be obtained from Periodicals Service Company, 11 Main Street, Germantown, NY 12526, USA. Tel: +1 (518) 537-4700, Fax: +1 (518) 537-5899, Email: psc@periodicals.com.

Journal Customer Services: For ordering information, claims and any enquiry concerning your journal subscription please contact your nearest office:
UK: Email: customerservices@blackwellpublishing.com; Tel: +44 (0) 1865-778315; Fax: +44 (0) 1865-471775
USA: Email: customerservices@blackwellpublishing.com; Tel: +1 (781) 388-8599 or 1 (800) 835-6770 (Toll free in the USA & Canada); Fax: +1 (781) 388-8232 or Fax: +44 (0) 1865-471775
Asia: Email: customerservices@blackwellpublishing.com; Tel: +65 6511-8000; Fax: +44 (0) 1865-471775

Associate Editor: Michelle S. Sathan
Production Editor: Sarah McKay, Email: napa@bos.blackwellpublishing.com
Advertising: journaladsUSA@bos.blackwellpublishing.com

Print Information: Printed in the United States of America by The Sheridan Press. This journal is printed on acid-free paper.

Online Information: This journal is available online at Blackwell Synergy. Visit www.blackwell-synergy.com to search the articles and register for table of contents e-mail alerts.
Access to this journal is available free online within institutions in the developing world through the AGORA initiative with the FAO, the HINARI initiative with the WHO and the OARE initiative with UNEP. For information, visit www.aginternetwork.org, www.healthinternetwork.org, and www.oarescience.org.

Aims and Scope: The NAPA Bulletin series is dedicated to the practical problem-solving and policy applications of anthropological knowledge and methods. NAPA Bulletins are peer reviewed, and are distributed free of charge as a benefit of NAPA membership. The NAPA Bulletin seeks to:
facilitate the sharing of information among practitioners, academics, and students.
be a useful document for practitioners.
contribute to the professional development of anthropologists seeking practitioner positions.
support the general interests of practitioners both within and outside the academy.
The Bulletin is a publication of NAPA produced by the American Anthropological Association and Wiley-Blackwell. Through the publication of the NAPA Bulletin, the AAA and Wiley-Blackwell furthers the professional interests of anthropologists while disseminating anthropological knowledge and its applications in addressing human problems.

Submission Instructions: For submission instructions, subscription and all other information visit: www.blackwellpublishing.com/napa

Disclaimer: The Publisher, American Anthropological Association and Editors cannot be held responsible for errors or any consequences arising from the use of information contained in this journal; the views and opinions expressed do not necessarily reflect those of the Publisher, American Anthropological Association and Editors, neither does the publication of advertisements constitute any endorsement by the Publisher, American Anthropological Association and Editors of the products advertised.

ISSN 1556-4789 (Print)
ISSN 1556-4797 (Online)

Contents

PART 5: FURTHER RESOURCES

INTRODUCTION: PREPARING ANTHROPOLOGISTS FOR THE 21ST CENTURY

Carla Guerrón-Montero

University of Delaware

With its sustained emphasis on creating, implementing, and maintaining positive impacts on issues of local, national, and global importance, applied anthropology continues to be a crucial and relevant field of study. Its practitioners demonstrate their engagement in multifarious ways both in and outside the academy, showcasing their commitment not only to the tenets of academic rigor, but also to challenges shaped by real-world situations. This unique volume of 14 articles by 16 academics and practitioners provides specific advice to students on both the tangible benefits and potential disadvantages of careers in applied anthropology in the national and international arenas. Contributors offer practical, step-by-step advice on practicing anthropology with an M.A. degree, careers in national and international consultancy, small consulting business development, executive leadership, combining careers in applied anthropology and the academy, field school training, collaborative research and public engagement, applied anthropology in nonanthropological settings, among others. Although most draw on their personal life histories and careers as illustrations, their focus is on reflection, analysis, and recommendations that result from their experiences. The contributors to this volume stress the contemporary relevance of anthropology, the advantages of obtaining training in anthropology, and the plethora of opportunities to put anthropology to use in the real world with exceptional results. Keywords: applied anthropology, career advice, practicing anthropology, mentorship, theory and praxis

In his lecture entitled "The Anthropology of Trouble," prominent anthropologist Roy Rappaport called for the repositioning of engaged research (i.e., of "the application of anthropology to the solution of real world problems") toward the center of anthropological inquiry (1993:295). In today's increasingly complex and interconnected world, this invitation has become even more relevant.

The boundless vigor that has characterized applied anthropology worldwide continues and flourishes in the 21st century, and the United States is clearly no exception. Nowadays, more anthropology graduates in the United States find work outside the academy. The current trend began in the 1970s and has accelerated since the late 1980s. At the present time, it is estimated that from 42 to 60 percent of Ph.D. anthropologists and virtually all M.A. anthropologists work outside the academy (Fiske this volume; Kedia and van Willigen 2005; Nolan 2003). As this tendency is likely to continue resulting from factors internal and external to the discipline (Baba 1994; Kedia this volume), anthropology

NAPA BULLETIN 29, pp. 1–13. ISBN 9781405190152. © 2008 by the American Anthropological Association. DOI:10.1111/j.1556-4797.2008.00001.x

departments, organizations, and societies have the responsibility to effectively prepare and aid future generations of practicing anthropologists. The strengthening of what Johnsrud calls "a strong market niche" outside academia is critical if anthropology is to be recognized for its potential to have a positive and sustained impact on local, national, and global issues and programs (2001:95). Likewise, an anthropology more engaged with pressing social issues is nowadays a more present demand in the minds of students and the society at large (Hemment 2007).

The current volume responds to this demand, by offering practical, step-by-step advice from both academics and practicing anthropologists. I am fortunate that outstanding academics and practicing anthropologists in cultural anthropology accepted my invitation to contribute to this volume and address the most salient issues regarding careers in practicing anthropology.

In line with Goldschmidt's (2001) assertion that applied and theoretical anthropology should be mutually supporting, the volume also addresses the theoretical and applied implications of the anthropological enterprise outside the academy. Throughout its history, anthropology has traditionally merged practice and theory successfully and fruitfully (Goldschmidt 1979, 2001). Applied and academic anthropology developed together and share methods and personnel (Ferraro 1996). Nonetheless, although practicing anthropologists have been recognized and supported through robust applied organizations and in spite of the complexity of the intellectual demands of anthropological praxis (Moran 2000),[1] practicing anthropology has not received the same recognition and esteem as 'pure,' academic anthropology. In addition, "the relationship of theory to practice has been a source of continued anguish for anthropology since its very beginning" (Moran 2000:132; Hill 2000; Hymes 1999). As Stocking (2000), among others, notes, in the United States, this divide is the result of the Cold War. Thus it is necessary to stress that the artificial divide that has prevailed between practice and theory (and by erroneous extension, between applied and academic anthropology) has changed over time and space (Baba 2005; Kedia and van Willigen 2005), is confined mostly to the subdisciplines of cultural anthropology and linguistics (Ferraro 1996; Greenwood 2000), and is out of touch with contemporary practice in anthropology and the social sciences (Greenwood 2000; Lassiter this volume; Rylko-Bauer et al. 2006).

Such disjuncture is also more prevalent and evident in the United States and other western countries (Pink 2005). Anthropologists in many industrialized and developing nations learn to be well versed in—and to hold in high esteem—practice and theory within anthropology's subdisciplines and beyond, and to navigate between practicing and academic settings as a natural result of the inbuilt interdisciplinary character of training programs and job markets (Baba 2005; Chambers 1987; Greenwood 2000; Guerrón-Montero 2002a; Hill and Baba 2006; Nader 2000). In my experience as an anthropologist initially trained in Ecuador, the disconnection between applied and academic anthropology found in the United States is not present in Latin America. During my first year in graduate school in the United States, even though I was studying in a program with an applied focus, I became aware that students were not sufficiently informed about how to obtain employment in the nonacademic world, nor were they privy to the tension between applied and academic anthropology in many departments or to the obstacles to tenure and promotion that applied work presents within the academy at many universities. These circumstances motivated me to organize and coorganize sessions for nine consecutive years at the Society for Applied Anthropology (SfAA) annual meetings, in order to make available information about careers in applied anthropology to undergraduate and graduate students. This collection represents a summing up of much of the advice and guidance provided at those sessions.

OVERVIEW OF THE VOLUME

This unique volume of 14 articles by 16 academics and practicing anthropologists provides specific advice to students on the benefits and challenges of careers in applied anthropology in the national and international arenas. This is the first collection in one volume of experience-based advice from anthropologists practicing anthropology both outside and inside the academy, and it complements previous National Association for the Practice of Anthropology (NAPA) publications on related topics.[2]

The contributors represent a broad spectrum of professional and personal experiences, and are located at different points in their careers. They also come from diverse backgrounds in terms of ethnicity, class, gender, and age. Although most draw on their personal life histories and careers as illustrations, their focus is on reflection, analysis, and recommendations that result from their experiences. Despite their different backgrounds, experiences, and specialty fields within applied anthropology, there is remarkable convergence of the advice being given. It is worth noting that, although the analysis and recommendations provided by the contributors to this volume can be applied to any subdiscipline of anthropology, the volume centers on professional careers in cultural anthropology. The last section of the volume includes a list of job boards, professional organizations, literature, and other resources pertinent to specific subfields of anthropology (Shaffer this volume).

The volume is divided into four sections. Following this Introduction, the first section includes a chapter that frames the volume, "Changes and Recent Trends in the Practice of Applied Anthropology," by Satish Kedia. Kedia discusses transformations occurring in the 21st century that will affect the way we do anthropology in the coming decades. Some of these transformations are external in nature (economic and demographic shifts) and some are internal (interdisciplinary work, changing relations with study subjects). These changes "have significantly altered the ways anthropologists examine and affect the human condition, from roles and tasks to goals and methods, from application priorities to guidelines for practice" (Kedia this volume). Kedia addresses these external and internal forces at length. He also assesses the current job market and the prevailing and versatile roles fulfilled by anthropologists in the market. Kedia concludes with a discussion of rising trends in the discipline, particularly in regard to research philosophies and technologies, as well as discipline priorities and guidelines. In addition to new areas of study, emerging technological advances have fostered the development of sophisticated methodological approaches that will become commonplace in the future. These changes represent a challenge for anthropologists. "In preparation, applied anthropologists must hone their skills in diplomacy, collaboration, and oral and written communication to raise the stakes for disciplinary and scholarly recognition of applied work and, particularly, their community engagement" (Kedia this volume).

The second section, Graduate School in Applied Anthropology, includes two chapters. Terry Redding's chapter, "Mastering the Art of the M.A. Program and Beyond," centers on advice for those who are seeking to enter, are already enrolled in, or are just completing an M.A. degree program in applied anthropology. The chapter provides a comprehensive discussion of essential aspects in regard to finding the appropriate M.A. program, building a fitting graduate school experience, and making the transition into the work place. Through his experiences and those of his colleagues, Redding highlights the need to be flexible, creative, and open-minded about one's career choices and outcomes. This discussion should be taken as a warning against the assumption of the existence of one linear path for a person's career. The U.S. ideology of "a linear career, a quest in which the end goal is visible from the start [. . .] still holds a powerful sway over many of our students" (Wasson 2006:16). Redding's career experiences and choices remind us that improvisation and unpredictability should be acknowledged and even welcomed. "I have not yet worked in 'typical' applied anthropology contexts, although I do use my training in subtle or unconscious ways. I learned to never assume anything, to never be satisfied that the way things appear were the way they were, and to watch people's actions rather than their words" (Redding this volume).

In her chapter, "Small Fish in a Big Pond: An Applied Anthropologist in Natural Resource Management," Jennifer Gilden provides a candid account of her experiences as an applied anthropologist working in fisheries management. Gilden emphasizes that the nature of her work has demanded flexibility and constant learning. As an applied anthropologist working in a field dominated by biologists (that of fisheries management), Gilden's job "has involved many types of education: educating myself about fisheries biology, educating managers about the contributions of social science, educating the public about the fisheries management process, and, perhaps most importantly, educating myself about the role and limitations of social science in this particular field" (Gilden this volume). In addition, Gilden discusses the challenges and rewards of being an applied anthropologist (or social scientist) working in a natural science field. Finally, complementing Redding's discussion, this chapter also addresses the topic of practicing anthropology with a M.A. degree.

Gilden notes that a Ph.D. in anthropology ensures the possibility of accessing research networks that are sometimes difficult to reach otherwise. In addition, Gilden states that the length, intensity, and demands of Ph.D. programs can lead to "a more solid sense of identification as an 'anthropologist' than might be achieved in M.A. programs" (Gilden this volume). Redding argues that Ph.D. roles tend to be more clearly defined in position descriptions, while M.A. graduates might need to be particularly flexible in performing a variety of tasks and trying many new roles. Finally, Gilden calls for more networks available for anthropologists with M.A. degrees, and for those with M.A. degrees to be properly familiar with current theories and ideas in the field.

Four chapters in the third section of the volume offer advice from the academy to budding anthropologists. As an academically based applied anthropologist, Philip D. Young addresses the topic of combining careers in the academy with (part-time) practicing anthropology outside the academy. In his chapter, "Practicing Anthropology from within the Academy: Combining Careers," Young notes that this endeavor is both challenging and rewarding, for the premises and outcomes of both sectors differ. As Young states, "you will likely find yourself living in two parallel worlds that only touch tentatively here and there" (Young this volume). Young notes that, although many of the skills learned in the academy are transferable to the practicing world of international development, flexibility to learn new ways of performing tasks and analyzing and communicating information are essential. Young stresses the importance of immersing oneself in managerial culture (incl. participation and careful attention to meetings, use of acronyms, negotiation and presentation skills), and addresses the seldom discussed issue of ethical dilemmas faced by practicing anthropologists in the field.

In the chapter, "Moving Past Public Anthropology and Doing Collaborative Research," Luke Eric Lassiter addresses collaborative research. In this chapter, Lassiter discusses the importance of moving past the debates regarding applied–practicing vs. public anthropology to the development and strengthening of collaborative research as a special opportunity to conduct publicly engaged anthropological work. The author understands collaborative research (or community-based research, action research, participatory action research, or participatory community research) as work that is conceived, produced and enacted by the researcher and the social actors involved in the process. Lassiter's scholarship and practice lies within collaborative ethnography, "a very specific kind of ethnography that builds on the cooperative relationships already present in the ethnographic research process (i.e., between ethnographers and informants/consultants) and endeavors to engender texts that are more readable, relevant, and applicable to local communities of ethnographic collaborators (i.e., local publics)" (Lassiter this volume). Additionally, Lassiter provides recommendations for students interested in engaging in collaborative ethnography as an applied and public practice.

The topic of collaborative research is further discussed by Geraldine Moreno-Black and Pissamai Homchampa, who focus on collaboration and cooperation—particularly international collaboration—among applied anthropologists within the academy. As Van Arsdale (this volume) notes in regard to ethnographic field schools and the emphasis placed on individualized rather than group field research experience, Moreno-Black and Homchampa state that collaborative work is discouraged, and sometimes even penalized, in the academy. An indication of this discouragement is precisely how little has been written about collaboration among researchers (with the exception of feminist and anticolonialist scholarship and interpretative anthropology). The authors contrast this standard with that of other disciplines in the natural and social sciences, and center on the area of health sciences, the purview of a significant portion of their collaborative work. Moreno-Black and Homchampa address collaboration from different angles, based on their experiences as professors, research assistants, graduate students, cross-disciplinary colleagues, and program directors.

The section ends with the chapter "Learning Applied Anthropology in Field Schools: Lessons from Bosnia and Romania," by Peter Van Arsdale. Field experience that is required of students of anthropology can be obtained through individualized experiences (the traditional "Lone Ranger" approach of conducting ethnographic fieldwork) or group experiences. Van Arsdale notes that ethnographic (or "cultural") field schools are a very suitable approach to acquire these experiences, and he provides illustrations based on field schools he has organized in Bosnia and Romania. These field schools are unusual in their approach, as they combine elements of more traditional study-abroad programs and more recent service-learning programs. One of the most important outcomes of these programs is the incorporation of the concept of "pragmatic humanitarianism." "Tied to an emerging theory of obligation, this notion of humanitarianism features hands-on training with at-risk populations" that respects humanitarian intervention and acknowledges the positive outcomes of individual and group efforts (Van Arsdale this volume).

Young, Moreno-Black and Homchampa address the challenges of being a (part-time) applied anthropologist in a nonapplied academic anthropology department and engaging in cross-disciplinary collaboration. Young also notes that applied anthropologists tend to be better received in departments or programs where applied work in general is more highly valued (i.e., international studies programs). In the context of applied work in academic departments, anthropologists are able to advance praxis by engaging traditional research and applied work in a dialogue. In fact, academic–practicing anthropologists can "bridge the gap between academics and practice" by bringing the insights and theory development that results from applied work into the academic arena, while also offering solutions to real human problems through knowledge gained in traditional research (Jordan 2001:85).

The fourth section of the volume centers on advice from practicing anthropologists, some of whom are also active academics or scholar–practitioners (Wasson 2006). Shirley Fiske offers a discussion of careers for anthropologists in the U.S. federal government. Fiske reminds us that the federal government is the single largest employer of anthropologists outside universities, particularly at the present time with at least five agencies employing in-house anthropologists. She provides a detailed explanation of the varied and complex world of careers in the federal government, emphasizing that generalizing about them is challenging. She describes careers in the federal government for a number of specialty areas including international development, both as a consultant and as a full-time permanent government employee, cultural resource management, the legislative branch, forensic and physical anthropology, natural resource management, and defense and security sectors (Fiske this volume). In order to both demystify and exemplify these career paths, the author offers illustrations from her 22-year experience in the field and from interviews conducted with accomplished senior anthropologists in five agencies. In addition, Fiske provides advice on how to go about finding, applying for, and obtaining a job in the federal government.

In her chapter, "Applied Anthropology and Executive Leadership," Barbara Pillsbury narrates her experiences forging a path as an executive leader and the ways in which anthropology assisted her in this endeavor. "In today's world, to be an effective executive means connecting [one's] vision and values to a position of responsibility for *executing* a program—that is, managing personnel, time, budgets and ideas to achieve, and better yet surpass, expected objectives" (Pillsbury this volume). Based on her career and that of two other anthropologist executive leaders, Pillsbury focuses on pivotal management and decision-making skills, and discusses how anthropological theory and methodology—such as the emphasis on the concept of culture broadly understood, the holistic approach, or the understanding of diverse worldviews—can become invaluable tools for executive leadership positions. This is particularly true in international and intercultural work. However, the author also warns us about some characteristics of the anthropological approach that may constitute hindrances in the context of executive leadership, namely emphasis on cultural difference and resistance to generalization, prominence of participatory methods (which might be viewed as too time consuming), and lack of management and budget skills (see also Young this volume).

From the world of high level executive leadership, the volume moves to a discussion of creating and running a small-business operation. Carla Littlefield and Emilia González-Clements address this topic in their chapter, "Creating your own Consulting Business." They provide a detailed account of the basic principles of business startup as well as specific illustrations about running a consulting business based on their extensive experience. The authors also answer the question: "What makes anthropologists good consultants?" by pointing out that

> as anthropologists, we are trained in data collection, analysis, and interpretation. We may also receive instruction on research design and how to conduct fieldwork and research. . . . Our anthropological training in observing and understanding the beliefs and behaviors of groups, to see things from their unique perspective gives us an edge as consultants. Our training helps us work in other cultural settings, and to work with different groups and sub-groups. [Littlefield and González-Clements in this volume]

In addition, the authors highlight the key nature of networking as a fundamental promotion strategy that can take place at professional meetings (local, regional, or national) or at community organizations relevant to one's business (organizations, foundations, or coalitions).

The last two chapters of this section are specifically dedicated to international issues in the practicing world, issues that are also addressed by Young, Fiske, and Pillsbury in the volume. In "Using Anthropology Overseas," Riall Nolan notes that anthropologists commonly find work in the international arena, particularly in the areas of international development and humanitarian assistance. In this chapter, Nolan advises students on how to prepare for and secure anthropological employment in the international arena. The author reminds us that anthropologists excel at development work, and that "by using what we know as anthropologists, and by working in collaboration with others around the world, we can achieve far more than any of us could manage to do on our own" (Nolan this volume). Nolan recommends that students of anthropology interested in working overseas make sure they obtain some basic qualifications including the necessary academic background (M.A. or Ph.D., depending on the position desired), workplace skills (incl. self-management, functional, and technical skills), cross-cultural experience, and language proficiency. Nolan also discusses the types of jobs available to anthropologists in international development work.

Gisele Maynard-Tucker focuses more specifically on the process and challenges of becoming an international consultant. Echoing the words of other contributors to this volume (Gilden, Littlefield and González-Clements, Nolan, Redding, and Young), Maynard-Tucker asserts that becoming a consultant is a challenge "that is both exciting and intimidating," and it requires acquiring general anthropological knowledge *and* mastering a specialization. "Becoming a consultant is not easy and one has to be willing to tough it out, to be flexible and adapt to various situations, to make decisions on short notice, to be pragmatic and focused" (Maynard-Tucker this volume). The author provides a detailed discussion of the solid academic background and international experience necessary for a student of anthropology considering international consulting work. Maynard-Tucker defines consultations and describes the types of consultations and clients and how to contact development agencies. The author includes illustrations deriving from her experience in international development. Maynard-Tucker concludes by reflecting on the benefits and constraints of the profession, and offers lessons learned during more than 20 years of international consultancy work in the field of global health.

The last section of the volume consists of a chapter by Scarlett Shaffer, a graduate student at the School for International Training (Brattleboro, Vermont). Shaffer identifies several resources on career-building, networking, and job opportunities for applied anthropologists within the four subfields of anthropology.

GENERAL TRENDS AND RECOMMENDATIONS

The contributors to this volume stress the contemporary relevance of anthropology, the advantages of obtaining training in anthropology, and the plethora of opportunities to put anthropology to use in the real world with exceptional results. Contributors also speak of a trend toward more flexible, less traditional, and linear careers, even for those anthropologists mostly based in academic settings (Wasson 2006). The contributors note the holistic nature of anthropology, its emphasis on a broad conception of culture and on ethnography, the ability to communicate and understand other cultures and worldviews and to translate this knowledge into comprehensible terms. As Nolan (this volume) articulates, "We are inductive in our methods and our thinking, good at building a picture of reality from the ground up. We are very good at eliciting local data, making sense of it, and using it, rather than relying on theoretical constructs from outside. And in the process, we are not threatened by ambiguity, contradiction, or discrepant information."

Many of the contributors also address some of the limitations of our training when working in nonacademic areas: our general fixation on research, and more specifically, long-term research, on detailing the complexities of phenomena when simpler, less elaborate answers and solutions are needed, or the stress placed by the discipline on individual research, the "Lone Ranger" or "lone-wolf" approach. Results of a recent survey covering the past 25 years sponsored by NAPA and conducted by Harman et al. (2004) with M.A. graduates in anthropology indicate that there is a general discrepancy between skills used at work and skills taught in their training programs (4).[3] Contributors to this volume remind us that anthropologists need to be entrepreneurial in their approach toward a career outside the academy. Johnsrud also makes this point:

> Most practitioners today must be extremely entrepreneurial in development practitioner careers. This requires several skills, including an appropriate degree of assertiveness, excellent fieldwork skills to interpret organizational contexts and recognize opportunities when they arise, the ability to communicate in non-anthropological terms, tenacity, and the ability to project an image, especially in the private sector, of willingness to learn. [2001:97]

A student interested in working in the professional world of anthropology as a practitioner needs to acknowledge the assets and recognize the limitations, so that anthropology does not become an "interesting but irrelevant" field (Johnsrud 2001:98).

Recommendations provided in this volume are especially useful in structuring academic programs to train practicing anthropologists. These recommendations apply both to institutions and individual students, and they can be summed up in the need to develop an elastic anthropological curriculum. In this regard, one major difference between applied and nonapplied anthropology programs tends to be focused on methodological approaches. In nonapplied anthropology programs, methods are oftentimes less emphasized than theory, whereas applied programs that specifically train students in applied work stress the importance of sound methodological approaches (Hemment 2007), although engagement with the public sector beyond the academy has also become more common in traditional academic programs and settings (Borofsky 1999; Lassiter et al. 2005).[4] The curriculum in applied anthropology should involve a combination of theory and methods. However, some specific areas should be stressed when training future practicing anthropologists (Ervin and Holyoak 2006). In theoretical terms, this curriculum should include an interdisciplinary approach and accentuate both critical thinking and problem solving skills. Contributors recommend adding one or more specialization(s) to one's general anthropological knowledge (health, business, environmental studies, law, etc.). In practical terms, this curriculum should offer innumerable opportunities for teamwork, interaction with practitioners, case studies and simulations that replicate to the extent possible the experiences of practicing anthropologists (Van Arsdale this volume). In terms of methodology, there should be a strong combination of quantitative and qualitative research methods, and emphasis on language and computer skills. In other words, merging theory and practice in the curriculum becomes essential to prepare well-trained practicing anthropologists.

Mentoring has been a crucial topic discussed directly or indirectly in several chapters of this volume. The importance of mentoring cannot be overstated, especially in the case of women (Stone and McKee 2000) and minorities. Aspiring practicing anthropologists need to find creative ways to access mentors throughout their studies and, later on, their careers. In connection with mentoring, networking is addressed in several chapters. Networks provide anthropology with visibility and a "presence" outside the academy (Johnsrud 2001:96). It is essential for fledging anthropologists inside and outside the academy to actively participate in network development. However, as Nolan warns, "to network, you will need a story; a story about who you are and what you are seeking. Since networking is a professional activity, and not simply chitchat, craft this story carefully" (Nolan this volume).

Several authors in this volume mention the importance of being affiliated with one or more active professional organizations, such as the SfAA, the NAPA, Local Practitioner Organizations (LPOs), and other formal or informal organizations (see also Bennett 1988). Kedia (this volume) points out, "anthropologists early in their careers should take advantage of the opportunity to join professional associations and attend and participate in meetings, forums, and conferences to help establish themselves in their field and remain abreast of the latest trends in the discipline." In addition to the information provided by several authors, Shaffer's chapter provides an extensive list of sources of this information (Shaffer this volume). Students should also participate in conferences as early and often as possible; participating in and attending conferences specifically organized by or intended for nonacademic anthropologists should be essential for the development of larger networks (Johnsrud 2001:96), and more importantly, for the development of more acceptance and more collegiality among academic and practicing anthropologists.

As more and more anthropologists find employment as practitioners in the private sector as well as the nonacademic public sector, their successes will continue to highlight the value of applying anthropological methods, analysis, and interpretation to humanity's problems. The contributors and I sincerely hope that the readers benefit from the generous and careful discussions offered in this volume.

NOTES

Acknowledgments: This volume is the result of nine years (1997–2005) of organized sessions (14 workshops, panels, and roundtables) sponsored by the International and Membership Committees of the SfAA and held at the society's annual meetings. The sessions were designed specifically to provide information about careers in applied anthropology to undergraduate and graduate students. Sessions ranged from workshops on international career opportunities for students, workshops on CV and resume development, to one-on-one career counseling, mentorship, practice job interviews, and networking. Articles containing summaries of these workshops were published in the SfAA newsletter (Guerrón-Montero 1997, 1998a, 1998b, 2000, 2001, 2002b). I would like to express my gratitude to the SfAA Board of Directors, officers, and program chairs who supported the organization of the sessions from which this *NAPA Bulletin* derives. I especially thank Gisele Maynard-Tucker, Jeanette Dickerson-Putnam, and Carla Littlefield, cochairs of some of these sessions. My sincere appreciation goes to the panelists and audience of the aforementioned sessions, and especially to all the contributors to this volume. I have learned from your wisdom and grown professionally and personally as a result of this experience. I also thank Philip D. Young, Satish Kedia, Pamela Puntenney, and the anonymous reviewers of this introduction and the volume for their insightful suggestions. Last, but not least, I offer my appreciation to Tim Wallace and Satish Kedia, NAPA coeditors, for their support, enthusiasm, and confidence on the importance of this project.

1. I understand praxis as a combination of theory, practices, and ethical and civic values that become embodied in the anthropological (and social science) project (Greenwood 2000; Kozaitis 1999).

2. These publications include John van Willigen 1987, Paula L. Sabloff 2001, and Christina Wasson 2006.

3. Some of the necessary skills recommended by the M.A. graduates included supervision, organizing, workplace public interaction, management skills (management, budget, training, time management, etc.). In addition, it was recommended to add emphasis on writing, especially that of reports and grant proposals, survey preparation, statistics, and qualitative analysis (Harman et al. 2004:4).

4. Applied visual anthropology is not discussed in this volume; however, the value of applied visual anthropology theory and methods (art, drawing, photography, video, digital and visual media, multimedia technologies, etc.) in training practicing anthropologists is worth noting (Pink 2004).

REFERENCES CITED

Baba, Marietta
  1994 The Fifth Subdiscipline: Anthropological Practice and the Future of Anthropology. Human
      Organization 53(2):174–186.
  2005 To the End of Theory-Practice Apartheid: Encountering the World. Epic 2005:205–217.
Bennett, Linda, ed.
  1988 The Place of LPOs in American Anthropology of the 1980s. Theme issue, "Bridges for Changing
      Times: Local Practitioner Organizations in American Anthropology," NAPA Bulletin 6(1):1–6.
Borofsky, Robert
  1999 Public Anthropology. Anthropology News 40(1):6–7.
Chambers, Erve
  1987 Applied Anthropology in the Post-Vietnam Era: Anticipations and Ironies. Annual Review of
      Anthropology 16:309–337.
Ervin, Alexander, and Lorne Holyoak
  2006 Applied Anthropology in Canada: Historical Foundations, Contemporary Practice and Policy
      Potentials. NAPA Bulletin 25(1):134–155.
Ferraro, Gary
  1996 Applied Anthropology: A Mid-Decade Assessment. Teaching Anthropology: Society for Anthropology
      in Community Colleges Notes 4(1):11–14.
Goldschmidt, Walter
  1979 Introduction: On the Interdependence between Utility and Theory. In The Uses of Anthropology.
      Walter Goldschmidt, ed. Pp. 1–13. Washington, DC: American Anthropological Association.
  2001 Malinowski Award Lecture. Notes Toward a Theory of Applied Anthropology. Human Organization
      60(4):423–429.
Greenwood, Davydd J.
  2000 Theory-Practice Relations in Anthropology: A Commentary and Further Provocation. NAPA Bulletin
      18(1):164–175.
Guerrón-Montero, Carla
  1997 Student Open Forum a Success. SfAA Newsletter 7(2):12.
  1998a Student Column: Careers Workshop "Applied Anthropology Outside the Academy." SfAA
      Newsletter 8(2):11–13.
  1998b The 1999 Annual Meetings and Student Activities. SfAA Newsletter 8(4):12.
  2000 SfAA Workshops: A Positive Learning Experience for Students. SfAA Newsletter 11(4):14.
  2001 Career Counseling Workshops in Mérida. SfAA Newsletter 12(2):11.
  2002a Introduction: Practicing Anthropology in Latin America. Practicing Anthropology 24(4):2–4.

2002b "Many Journeys and Many Paths": Careers Workshop in Applied Anthropology. SfAA Newsletter 13(2):8–10.

Harman, Robert C., Jim Hess, and Amir Shafe
2004 Report on Survey of Alumni of Master's Level Applied Anthropology Training Programs. Arlington, VA: American Anthropological Association. NAPA. Electronic document, http://www.practicinganthropology.org/departments/, accessed January 15, 2007.

Hemment, Julie
2007 Public Anthropology and the Paradoxes of Participation: Participatory Action Research and Critical Ethnography in Provincial Russia. Human Organization 66(3):301–314.

Hill, Carole
2000 Strategic Issues for Rebuilding a Theory and Practice Synthesis. *In* The Unity of Theory and Practice in Anthropology: Rebuilding a Fractured Synthesis. NAPA Bulletin 18(1):1–16.

Hill, Carole, and Marietta Baba
2006 Global Connections and Practicing Anthropology in the 21st Century. *In* The Globalization of Anthropology. NAPA Bulletin 25(1):1–13.

Hymes, Dell
1999 Reinventing Anthropology, with a New Introduction by the Editor. Ann Arbor: University of Michigan Press.

Johnsrud, Cris
2001 Integrating Anthropologists into Nonacademic Work Settings. NAPA Bulletin 20(1):95–98.

Jordan, Ann T.
2001 Building a Bridge between Academics and Practice. NAPA Bulletin 20(1):85–86.

Kedia, Satish, and John van Willigen
2005 Applied Anthropology: Context for Domains of Application. *In* Applied Anthropology: Domains of Application. Westport, CT. Greenwood Press.

Kozaitis, Kathryn
1999 The Rise of Anthropological Praxis. *In* The Unity of Theory and Practice in Anthropology: Rebuilding a Fractured Synthesis, Carole E. Hill, and Marietta L. Baba, eds. NAPA Bulletin 18(1):45–66.

Lassiter, Luke Eric, Samuel R. Cook, Les Field, Sjoerd R. Jaarsma, James L. Peacock, Deborah Rose, and Brian Street
2005 Collaborative Ethnography and Public Anthropology. Current Anthropology 46(1):83–106.

Moran, Emilio
2000 Theory and Practice in Environmental Anthropology. *In* The Unity of Theory and Practice in Anthropology: Rebuilding a Fractured Synthesis, Carole E. Hill and Marietta L. Baba, eds. NAPA Bulletin 18(1):132–146.

Nader, Laura
2000 Preface. *In* The Unity of Theory and Practice Anthropology: Rebuilding a Fractured Synthesis, Carole E. Hill and Marietta L. Baba, eds. NAPA Bulletin (18):v–vii.

Nolan, Riall
2003 Anthropology in Practice: Building a Career outside the Academy (Directions in Applied Anthropology). Boulder, CO: Lynne Rienner.

Pink, Sarah, ed.
2004 Applied Visual Anthropology: Social Intervention, Visual Methodologies and Anthropology Theory. Visual Anthropology Review 20(1):3–16.

2005 Applications of Anthropology: Professional Anthropology in the Twenty-First Century. New York: Berghann.

Rappaport, Roy A.
1993 Distinguished Lecture in General Anthropology: The Anthropology of Trouble. American Anthropologist 95(2):295–303.

Rylko-Bauer, Barbara, Merrill Singer and John van Willigen
2006 Reclaiming Applied Anthropology: Its Past, Present, and Future. American Anthropologist 108(1):178–190.

Sabloff, Paula L.

 2001 Introduction. *In* Careers in Anthropology: Profiles of Practitioner Anthropologists. NAPA Bulletin 20(1):1–4.

Stocking, George

 2000 Do Good, Young Man: Sol Tax and the World Mission of Liberal Democratic Anthropology. *In* History of Anthropology, vol. 9. Pp. 171–264. Madison: University of Wisconsin Press.

Stone, Linda, and Nancy P. McKee

 2000 Gendered Futures: Student Visions of Career and Family on a College Campus. Anthropology and Education Quarterly 31(1):67–89.

van Willigen, John

 1987 Becoming a Practicing Anthropologist: A Guide to Careers and Training Programs in Applied Anthropology. NAPA Bulletin 3(1):1–28.

Wasson, Christina

 2006 Making History at the Frontier. *In* Making History at the Frontier: Women Creating Careers as Practicing Anthropologists. NAPA Bulletin 26(1):1–19.

RECENT CHANGES AND TRENDS IN THE PRACTICE OF APPLIED ANTHROPOLOGY

SATISH KEDIA
University of Memphis

The emergent global economy of the 21st century will create an ever greater need for research-based information and pragmatic utilization of social science skills, creating new work opportunities for applied anthropologists in a variety of settings. However, anthropologists may need to adjust their traditional roles and tasks, approaches and methods, and priorities and guidelines to practice their craft effectively. Anthropological training and education must be based in sound ethnographic techniques, using contemporary tools, participatory methods, and interdisciplinary knowledge in order to accommodate faster-paced work environments and to disseminate their findings efficiently to a diverse audience while fulfilling the goal of empowering and enabling humans around the world to address social, economic, and health issues, along with other pressing concerns facing their communities. Keywords: applied anthropology, practicing anthropology, changes, trends, and guidelines for practice

As Rylko-Bauer and colleagues (2006) and a host of other writers (Basch et al. 1999; Borofsky 2002; Hill and Baba 2006; van Willigen and Kedia 2005) have noted, the application and practice of anthropology has been much affected in the 21st century by external forces, in particular economic, political, and demographic shifts. These transformations have created new work contexts and thus new employment opportunities for anthropologists. At the same time, internal changes such as cross-fertilization with other social sciences and especially changing relations with study subjects have significantly altered the traditional ways anthropologists examine and influence human conditions, from roles and tasks to goals and methods, from application priorities to guidelines for practice. This article critically reflects on some of these changes and trends that are influencing the practice of applied anthropology.

EXTERNAL FORCES

Contemporary anthropology has been most indelibly marked by rising population fluxes, development projects, public health crises, environmental problems, natural catastrophes, political strife, and transformations driven by a global economy. These fluxes have led to migrations, both forced and voluntary, and associated problems such as increases in poverty, morbidity, crime, and drug abuse. Economic development has led to increased use of natural resources and intensified exploration into remote regions for the extraction of oil or natural gas and hydroelectric power. These activities have resulted in displacement

NAPA BULLETIN 29, pp. 14–28. ISBN 9781405190152. © 2008 by the American Anthropological Association. DOI:10.1111/j.1556-4797.2008.00002.x

of indigenous groups by private entities and sometimes their own governments; at the same time, the global sharing of information aided by the Internet and satellite feeds have made international audiences more keenly aware of the kinds of privation such development projects often perpetrate on these disempowered communities. By and large, however, new technologies have become a commodity of those in power benefiting the technically skilled class far more than local populations.

A number of recent health crises and natural disasters, including the worldwide HIV/AIDS pandemic, the 2004 Indian Ocean tsunami, and 2005's Hurricane Katrina, have demonstrated that the expertise of practicing anthropologists is needed in First World as well as in Third World societies. Of ongoing concern to anthropologists is the global spread of AIDS, which has left its mark on populations across the globe from sub-Saharan African to Cambodia to the Caribbean. For example, from 1985 to 1990, sub-Saharan Africa saw typically higher death rates for the very young (birth–4 years) and very old (60+), but these rates dramatically shifted as the epidemic spread in the subsequent decade and affected the usually most productive members of society, those ages 20 to 49 (UNAIDS: The Joint UN Programme on HIV/AIDS 2006:4). AIDS has impacted entire national economies, crippling already poverty-stricken regions by depleting the adult work force and increasing responsibilities for grandparents and public agencies to accommodate orphans. This in turn has kept children from taking advantage of educational opportunities because they often must act as caretakers for sick parents and breadwinners for entire families, most commonly as sex trade workers who frequently become HIV infected themselves, thus perpetuating the downward cycle.

Confronting these issues not only requires trained personnel who understand the dynamics of multiple cultures, societies, and economies, but also the mechanics and imperatives of funding that must be in place to support such research. Anthropologists can inform programs and policies affecting local communities and the activities of funding agents by helping ensure best practices through advocating proper considerations, precautions, and follow-up measures. As with HIV/AIDS programs, funding for research, healthcare, and relief related to the 2004 tsunami and Hurricane Katrina has come from governmental and private sources as well as local, national, and international charitable organizations. However, while billions of public dollars have been directed toward improving efforts to detect and respond to tsunamis, very little has been devoted to victim relief. In fact, only $300 million of the $3.4 billion formally committed in response to the Indian Ocean tsunami disaster had actually been pledged to victim relief a month after the deadly wave hit (UN News Service 2005). With regard to Hurricane Katrina, much attention in the national press has been given to questionable allocations, ranging from mishandling to outright fraud, of both public and private monies. Vast private funds were poured into Katrina relief, as well as significant amounts from many government and nongovernmental organizations, but a number of reports made public have demonstrated that these funds have not yet reached their intended targets. Inadequate and ill-informed policy and planning have actually led to money being spent to store supplies that were never delivered to, or used by, the victims who sorely needed them in the months following the disaster (O'Hara 2006). These unfortunate results may well have been avoided had applied anthropological practitioners been employed to preemptively establish proper measures to ensure the accountability, sustainability, and effectiveness of funded programs.

Indeed, there are a number of ways in which anthropologists might apply their knowledge to address societal issues. For example, of much current interest is the sustainability of natural resources as they dwindle or become more difficult to access. A greater understanding of environmental and ecological impacts is necessary as development increasingly pervades every continent. Applied anthropologists can contribute to environmental dialogues by evaluating current practices and offering recommendations, as well as evaluating responses to those recommendations within both the public and private sectors. Another growing field for practitioners is gerontology/aging as a sociocultural and biological phenomenon, particularly as the baby boomers in the United States reach retirement age. They are leaving urban locales to retire in rural settings, necessitating reassessments of healthcare availability and resources that the evaluative research and community involvement of applied and medical anthropologists can provide.

A rapidly developing subject of interest includes diet, nutrition, and related health issues, along with their relation to a proliferating commercialized mass culture dominated by marketing. Junk and fast food are replacing healthy food choices around the world, thereby advancing concerns about *globesity,* the global trend toward greater body fat indexes. Finally, media communications is reemerging as a domain in which anthropologists can play a significant role by developing prosocial campaigns targeted at specific populations and relevant stakeholders. The public's increasing need for greater accessibility and availability of new venues for information dissemination has helped provide more efficient means for communicating research results.

Perhaps the best demonstration of the range of nontraditional work settings now available to those trained in anthropology is found in the projects funded by the David Rockefeller Center for Latin American Studies (DRCLAS). DRCLAS provides nearly 100 grants for graduate and undergraduate students in several fields, including applied anthropology. In 2001, DRCLAS supported community development work on education programs in Chile, research by the Socios en Salud (Partners in Health) organization in Peru on the successful treatment of patients with multiple drug-resistant tuberculosis, human rights advocacy by the Instituto de Defensa Legal (Institute for Legal Defense) nonprofit group in Peru, investigation of converging medical systems in Latin America, analysis of state mediation of visual forms in Cuba, exploration of tourism's impact on women in social contexts in Honduras, and studies in Bolivia on the potential and actual sociopolitical consequences of the racialization of *campesinos* (subsistence farmers in Latin America countries often subject to exploitation; Harvard Gazette 2001).

INTERNAL FORCES

Two decades ago, Robert H. Hinshaw (1980) and Erve Chambers (1985) noted the increasing necessity of collaboration in practitioners' knowledge transfer and decision making. Today, applied anthropologists are expected to work in tandem with others even more frequently because of greater interdisciplinary efforts and increased community involvement. In particular, they are required to act as members of a team because of the changing nature of applied work, which dictates that anthropologists can no longer operate wherever or whenever they wish, particularly without local input (Wolf 2002). Their collaborators can include other scientists or professionals; national, regional, and local officials; government agency representatives (at home and abroad) and their constituents; members of the community being studied; translators; medical personnel or public policymakers; and statisticians and market researchers.

Working with such a wide array of partners requires effective communication and diplomatic skills in sharing with and accepting input from others and for negotiating competing interests and stakes (Wolf 2002). In addition, this greater interdisciplinary exchange has resulted in transformations in the assumptions and procedures within nearly all of the social sciences. Networks of individuals working in both applied and academic realms are influencing each other, although their training may be in different fields. The boundaries between the type of knowledge produced by anthropologists and those in other areas are becoming blurred, as ideas from various disciplines influence the concepts and methodologies in others.

In the contemporary, information-driven government and corporate world, job classifications and requirements are being broadened beyond a specific skills set. This means that the interdisciplinary nature of anthropologists' nonacademic work will entail not only collaboration, but also competition for jobs from other anthropologists and those with whom they often work, such as sociologists, psychologists, statisticians, market researchers, and even computer professionals. Consequently, practitioners will need to expand their skills by mastering methodologies and technical terminology from a variety of cognate fields in order to most effectively articulate what value they specifically bring to the various settings in which they might be employed, in the face of an expanded field of competition.

Successful applied anthropological work in the private sector also requires effective communication of information to nonspecialists. For example, most funding agencies—the source of nearly all anthropological inquiry—require researchers to document the pertinence, scope, and impact of their proposed activity in practical terms. Practitioners will also need to communicate their goals and make their knowledge accessible to laypeople and participate even more in public discourse, as such work will entail both a far greater community outreach and circulation of research results to new audiences. No longer are study and project results relegated solely to scholarly academic journals, but are increasingly included in policy reports, press releases, websites, brochures, fact sheets, newspaper articles, speeches, and countless other types of documentation with a variety of readerships.

The relationship between applied practitioners and the people they study has also changed substantially, reflecting the transformation throughout the discipline of anthropology of a power dynamic from that of control to a more equitable exchange. In the late 1960s and 1970s, many anthropologists in the United States began questioning the involvement of social scientists in the Vietnam War. There was also growing concern that invasive and environmentally hazardous development projects were adversely impacting people's health and regional ecologies, which added to desire within the discipline for more proactive involvement with study subjects. This created a demand for adjustments in methods and guidelines and greater innovations in inquiry. Anthropologists began to act as advocates for marginalized cultures and communities rather than simply offering recommendations for policy change. Today, they more often work with local communities as partners; those studied are not only subjects but also individuals with the ability to affect and control what is being done in their communities. The growing public anthropology movement reflects this heightened involvement of subjects in the planning and implementation of research, as practitioners understand the importance of participation and empowerment of the local community. Such collaborations have in many cases helped provide communities with the tools they need for political mobilization, to gain state recognition of indigenous rights, and to protect biodiversity. In fact, applied practitioners are developing professional relationships with public constituencies to an extent that has not been previously seen in our discipline. This in turn has meant greater critical reflection by applied practitioners on the underlying structures causing certain problems, particularly ongoing concerns about sustainability and viability of environments, cultures, programs, and livelihoods.

Moreover, as Western researchers focus on and more closely address the perspectives of a partnering community rather than operating from a strictly "objective" anthropological or academic perspective, they also benefit greatly from opportunities to collaborate with Third World scholars. Distinctions among theory, method, and practice are less pronounced in non-U.S. settings as a result of an often more direct involvement by native scholars in effecting socioeconomic and political changes.

THE JOB MARKET AND PREVAILING ROLES

Partly as a result of the emergent and exciting variety of fields described above, a growing number of anthropologists have chosen careers outside academia. Demographic shifts within the profession have contributed to the migration of anthropology Ph.D.s to employment outside postsecondary settings. While the demand for professionals able to analyze and interpret increasing volumes of data for government, business, and nonprofits has been escalating in the past few decades, the market for academic anthropologists has remained relatively small (Kedia 2005). Although a growing number of anthropologists of the baby boom generation are retiring, the economic and social realities of the contemporary academy have resulted in the hiring of more part-time rather than full-time, tenure-track faculty.

In fact, according to a 1999 American Anthropological Association (AAA) survey of U.S. anthropology departments only half of all faculty were in full-time, tenure-track positions, and a U.S. Department of Education study reported that only slightly more than one third were tenured, further evidence that anthropologists are increasingly pursuing practicing opportunities outside academia rather than teaching positions. Slightly higher levels of satisfaction have been reported by anthropologists in nonacademic jobs than those in teaching positions (Kedia and Bennett 2005). The private sector also offers attractive features not characteristic of a university position, including limited or no teaching, less pressure to publish, and—generally speaking—better compensation. Although dependent on the individual's experience and the specific employer, salaries offered for nongovernmental and private sector work are usually higher than those offered in academia.

At the same time, it is common in the United States for anthropologists to move back and forth between academic and nonacademic settings, with a substantial number of university faculty holding adjunct or nontenured positions or both. As Hill and Baba (2006:11) stated concerning academic versus applied anthropology, "we find that the discipline is developing a more integrated and whole model." As much as applied work has demanded a more complex skills set and greater collaboration, many academics' work have in turn taken on a more applied dimension. They face added tasks as investigators on large research projects and are expected to produce more scholarly publications derived from institutional involvement with the local community, governments, and other entities as a means to bolster the pursuit of sponsored research.

Today, practicing or applied anthropologists are employed in a wide variety of roles, working for domestic and international organizations; municipal, state, and federal agencies; philanthropic and consumer groups; grassroots and advocacy groups; and private consulting firms and corporations (van Willigen and Kedia 2005). Government agencies such as the World Bank and the International Monetary Fund, nonprofits and nongovernmental organizations (NGOs) such as Oxfam-UK and UNICEF, and transnational corporations require greater accountability and evaluation, as well as a deeper understanding of diverse cultures to compete for resources and maintain sustainability as never before. They need to draw on applied anthropologists' abilities to inform policy and program development and to evaluate program efficacy in order to support funding requests. As researchers in postsecondary institutes dedicated to applied anthropological endeavors, practitioners advance university goals and scholarly activity by recruiting students, obtaining funding, and maintaining a local community presence, while also serving the region through the many projects, programs, and policies impacted by their work. Private consulting firms employing applied practitioners are mainly contracted by governmental divisions and other groups whose needs may not require a permanent anthropologist. Likewise, many corporations hire anthropologists as consultants to perform a wide variety of tasks, such as facilitating labor and community relations, building resource and economic development, designing products, increasing productivity, and training employees.

Applied anthropologists also work directly with grassroots movements and consumer groups to seek social justice for people with a limited voice in social, economic, and political arenas or to more effectively change inequitable policies of governmental agencies and industries. Practitioners may choose an area of practice based on with whom they would like to work, whether their skills and experience as well as personal and professional values would allow for such research or practice, and if the role matches where they would like to be "on the continuum from critical outsider to activist insider" (Trotter and Schensul 1998:694). An anthropologist might pursue various levels of community engagement: (1) generating research to inform others, (2) assessing efficacy and weaknesses in projects as an evaluator or monitor, (3) developing interventions geared specifically to a certain population and using a culturally appropriate method, (4) assisting marginalized groups as an advocate who actively removes barriers to equity and social justice, or (5) imparting communities and individuals with a sense of self-determination and empowerment through long-term partnership with the study population (Trotter and Schensul 1998).

Anthropologists may also combine roles, taking positions for which a broad social science background is necessary: policy researcher or research analyst; evaluator, impact assessor, or needs assessor; culture broker; public participation specialist; and administrator or manager. In a 2000 NAPA survey of anthropologists with master's degrees, 30 percent reported working as researchers and another 22 percent as data collectors. The researcher role naturally lends itself to analyst, as evidenced by the survey results showing 20 percent of positions taken by the applied anthropologists required quantitative data analyses and 18 percent ethnographic skills (Harman et al. 2005).

While informing policy through such research and analyst roles, anthropologists may become a part of the policy development and implementation process by having more input in the decisions made based on their work (Chambers 1985). In so doing, practitioners may become involved in program monitoring and outcomes or impact assessments, gauging the successes, failures, and indications of a need for change in a program or project, perhaps by determining how a community or population may be impacted by a given program or policy. Such assessments can take place before, during, or after a program or project is implemented. As planners, applied anthropologists form program designs by determining the social, health, economic, and educational needs of a population. As community advocates, anthropologists may serve as cultural brokers, bridging the gap between those in power and a community, perhaps as a public participation specialist who organizes public education initiatives like town hall meetings or media coverage. While many anthropologists take roles that are auxiliary to community leadership, others have occupied positions of authority; of respondents to the NAPA survey, 15 percent were planners; 10 percent, administrators; and 22 percent, managers (Harman et al. 2005).

Because the most common job titles held by applied anthropologists reflect multiple responsibilities, it is important for future practitioners to understand not only the various roles they might occupy but also the terminology common to these areas and the desirability of gaining some level of technical competency in other fields. An agricultural anthropologist, for example, would benefit from having a working knowledge of agricultural economics and plant biology related to food productivity and a familiarity with crop and livestock production, commodity markets, and policy/regulation in the field of agricultural development. Anthropologists working in the private sector often have administrative or managerial responsibilities that require basic business skills such as handling budgets and staff, negotiating contracts, and understanding marketing.

Taking on other roles such as counselor or therapist would require developing connections to other disciplines—psychology or psychiatry in this case—and receiving additional education. Many similar roles requiring more training might include human resources specialist, curator, historic preservationist, marketing expert, housing director, international development officer, development or environmental consultant, diplomat or local government official, criminal justice specialist, substance abuse counselor, human ecologist, forensic specialist, fundraiser, or cross-cultural trainer. The discipline's expansion into new arenas has resulted in truly novel roles for many practitioners, referred to by Marietta Baba (2005) as "hybrids."

More and more anthropology graduates are employed in government and private sector jobs, partially the result of policy research required by the escalating volume of federal and state regulations. A greater spotlight on accountability and cost-effectiveness has led to more demand for program evaluation as well, now required as a precondition for most, if not all, grant-funded projects (Ervin 1999). In addition, the latter part of the 20th century saw a rise in multinational corporations, which often conduct business in multiple regions at the same time. This growth intensified the need for applied work, with particular emphasis on anthropologists' expertise in culture and ethnographic methods, which helps facilitate improved understanding of workplace, labor operations, and consumer behavior, and thus improved access to crucial markets and consumers. These developments have resulted in a general refocusing of research toward client-specific groups rather than a particular culture, the traditional domain of anthropological practice. In addition to employment with corporations or private firms, there has been a proliferation of new work settings for practitioners in government, state, or municipal agencies; international research groups or policy institutes; and nonprofit, international aid, or charitable organizations.

EMERGING APPROACHES TO RESEARCH

Applied anthropological work is usually conducted by request from an organization that requires a thorough, albeit expeditious, understanding of a situation or problem in order to make important decisions about programs and funding. As a result, the nature of practicing anthropology, including scope and length of study, is generally decided by the funding agent rather than the researcher.

An applied anthropologist must already be equipped with a variety of methodological tools conducive to the work that, as noted above, is becoming interdisciplinary and more fully engaged with the study subjects, while at the same time constrained by time and often fairly rigid deadlines. Correspondingly, practitioners will need to employ more innovative approaches while adhering to the foundational ethnographic method, which involves the systematic and holistic documentation of cultures in action. Such approaches require the practitioners to use direct observation and interview subjects, become accustomed to local languages and customs, and properly record and interpret data. Still, as with applied work in general, ethnography has changed over the last 30 years or so from the independent enterprise it once seemed to its contemporary incarnation entailing work in interdisciplinary teams and with various stakeholders. Practitioners are often required to adjust professional practices in the field by taking into account the social realities, histories, and lives of the local people as well as those of the project collaborators, who may include other stakeholders such as the funding agent and members of that community. Traditionally, anthropologists have understood ethnography as a research process that takes months or years of observation and collection of data; however, because of the time sensitivity of applied work, a faster turnaround is often necessary. In the last several decades, practitioners have developed approaches using new methodologies and technologies that allow for more efficient practices.

Building on the tenets of participatory action research (PAR), which was designed to elicit the greatest level of community engagement, more time-sensitive and issue-focused ethnographic approaches have been developed, including rapid assessment procedures (RAP) and collective interviewing strategies, such as focus groups; streamlined surveys, spatial mapping, role playing, and other innovative forms of direct observation; population participation groups, such as rapid ethnographic assessment procedures (REAP); semistructured, dynamic, and iterative interviews, as well as selective sample interviews and surveys; subjects' self-assessments and self-definition; decision-making modeling; sorting and ranking; ethnocartography; social network analysis, and so on (Cernea 1992; Kedia 2005; Scrimshaw and Hurtado 1987; van Willigen and Finan 1991).

As with any research endeavor, to ensure the most effective and appropriate use of new methodologies, the researcher must be properly trained—experience is no substitute. Care must be taken when employing PAR methods such as RAP because these approaches do not use random sampling to yield statistically significant quantitative data, and thus, typically, generalization of results to wider populations cannot be made. It is possible, however, to improve the reliability of RAP data through triangulation, using multiple methods such as combining easy-to-analyze sampling techniques with streamlined surveys and focus groups in order to substantiate findings.

Practitioners must also be familiar with field-specific methods, because techniques can vary by area. This is the case with rapid rural appraisal (RRA), which uses swift and reliable ethnographic practices and survey methodologies such as iterative and dynamic interviewing to obtain information from those working in agricultural settings. A participatory research appraisal (PRA) gives the local population more involvement in the research project rather than making them an object of the research (Dunn 1994; Rhoades 2005). It might be noted that, despite the speed with which such work is conducted, PRA—like PAR—still necessitates sustained partnerships with local communities in order to ensure their self-determination and empowerment, which can lead to a collective action benefiting the members of that community or group (Smith et al. 1993).

The use of new technologies can be crucial in employing more time-sensitive methodologies. Speedier survey methods and more user-friendly access to quantitative data are provided by statistical software such as SPSS and by computer-aided analysis through aerial photographs, satellite imagery, and Geographic Information Systems (GIS). To address the wide spectrum of issues arising from the transformation of local actions to large-scale transnational operations, which have become so common in the global economy and with applied work, practitioners may integrate computer-based approaches with indigenous knowledge, as is done in multiscalar research (Rhoades 2005).

DISCIPLINARY REQUIREMENTS

Innovative practices and new branches of study with which applied anthropologists engage in order to meet the demands of the 21st century will challenge the discipline and practitioners alike. In preparation, applied anthropologists must hone their skills in diplomacy, collaboration, and oral and written communication to raise the stakes for disciplinary and scholarly recognition of applied work and, particularly, their community engagement.

While experience in applied work settings is important, for a professional anthropological career an individual must pursue an advanced degree such as a master's or a doctorate. Achieving a doctorate in anthropology can take as long as eight to nine years, with as many as 12 to 30 months spent on a field project, which usually becomes the basis for a dissertation. Despite this necessarily lengthy commitment, an increasing number of students are choosing to enroll in doctoral programs, demonstrating a strong recognition of all that anthropology has to offer (Doyle 2003).

The skills set acquired by undergraduate and graduate anthropology students affords much flexibility in developing a professional career. Such students are trained in "careful record-keeping, attention to details, analytical reading . . . social ease in strange situations, [and] critical thinking," as well as a "range of social, behavioral, biological and other scientific research methods [that supplement] statistical findings with descriptive data gathered through participant observation, interviewing, and ethnographic study" (AAA 2000). Quantitative skills including facility with statistical analysis software, such as SPSS or SAS, remain critical for practitioners.

As mentioned above, the collaborative aspect of applied work requires that practitioners be adept in working with others and conversant in the specific technical languages of related fields or other associated disciplines, as well as the *lingua franca* of the cultures or people studied. Students should be encouraged to gain additional training or take coursework in a field related to their career objectives, such as health, nutrition, agriculture, environment, administration, law, economics, education, writing, communications, computers, and public speaking.

While the foundation of effective practice is mastery over a broadly diverse set of research skills and disciplinary knowledge, the ability to advocate is the key way in which applied anthropologists build long-term collaborative relationships with communities. Effective advocacy involves being a consistent proponent of a particular set of goals, advancing the interests of public beneficiaries and stakeholders over personal gain or discipline-specific rewards. Participatory research continues to be in demand, which coincides with the shift toward a more user-focused approach across varying types of development (program, policy, product, marketing, business). Community engagement also mandates effective communication of project results to increasingly diverse audiences (clientele and study subjects), who may have different competencies and who require more accessible exposition than scholarly journal articles (e.g., press releases and websites). This means that graduate training should be expanded to equip students with the communication skills needed to convey research findings to an audience wider than the anthropological discipline and its limited community of practitioners (Lamphere 2004). To meet the requirements of a college course, most students usually develop and submit variations on the term paper, which may provide a structural template for good argument but not the succinctness needed for professional reports or briefs. Training should continue to foster the writing skills necessary for strong on-the-job performance, because clear exposition of research results is critical to securing funding and achieving program objectives. Conference presentations and workshops can serve to enhance these skills, as will additional coursework in technical writing or rhetoric.

Gaining experience in actual applied settings also helps students develop a variety of abilities and learn how to apply them in a real-world context, wherein they can obtain feedback on methodologies employed and see the connections between research and policy decisions and the impact of those actions on individuals and communities. Students have a number of opportunities for practical application, including enrolling in a master's practicum, conducting research with university faculty, and securing paid or unpaid work or relevant internships with cooperative education programs such as the Peace Corps or community or local human service agencies.

During their progress toward an advanced degree in the discipline, applied anthropologists should join professional associations and attend and present papers at meetings, forums, and conferences to help establish themselves in their field and remain abreast of the latest trends in the discipline. Nationally, organizations that provide such opportunities include the American Anthropological Association (AAA); the Society for Applied Anthropology (SfAA); the National Association of Practicing Anthropologists (NAPA); along with Local Practitioner Organizations (LPOs) such as the Washington Association of Professional Anthropologists (WAPA) and the High Plains Society for Applied Anthropology (HPSfAA), among others.

In 1993, anthropological groups from several countries developed the Commission on Anthropology in Policy and Practice within the International Union of Anthropological and Ethnological Sciences (IUAES) to establish a network among professionals in the rapidly growing number of applied and practicing fields. Networking is still an essential component of advancing as a practitioner. In fact, online networking forums such as AnthroTECH.com's AnthroDesign or anthropological association websites such as AAA (http://www.aaanet.org), SfAA (http://www.sfaa.net), NAPA (http://practicinganthropology.org), and WAPA (http://smcm.edu/wapa) are the primary resources anthropologists utilize to find job postings and potential venues for further practice.[1] Additionally, employment prospects are often posted on websites of those employers commonly requiring anthropologists, such as governmental agencies (e.g., http://USAJobs.gov) and international organizations (e.g., http://unicef.org) or consultants (e.g., http://baesystems.com). Various publications associated with the discipline, including the AAA's *Anthropology News* and the SfAA's *Newsletter* (http://www.sfaa.net/newsletter/newsletter.html), also provide information on job openings and forums for research, as do numerous anthropology listservs and discussion groups such as Anthro-L (http://danny.oz.au/communities/anthro-l/) and the "From An Anthropological Perspective" blog (http://www.marcusgriffin.com/blog/).

ETHICAL ISSUES

Ethics, the discernment of moral duty and obligation given a particular situation and setting, is very important, and indeed absolutely central, to applied anthropological work. The very reputation of the field depends on adherence to a strong ethical policy (Chambers 1985). Applied anthropologists must consider the ethical import of major actions to be taken as well as minor utterances, both their own and those of relevant stakeholders. There are instances in which anthropologists experience conflicts related to sponsors' demands and, subsequently, fall into the role of social technician or engineer, without much input from the study population. However, these conflicts can be mitigated or resolved by making clear the understanding that ethical considerations must be part of any professional decision. Practitioners must use existing ethical guidelines—especially from professional associations such as the AAA, SfAA, and NAPA—as well as established laws and policies to make sound professional judgments by relying on a framework that can help balance the requirements of positivistic science, morality, and the client, especially as the perceptions and goals of those involved can be quite varied. Such a professional framework, built on a strong foundation of well-developed skills, is essential to cultivating the sound judgment needed to successfully pursue a career in anthropology.

This is especially crucial because the history of anthropology as a discipline has seen a number of controversies over the ethical/moral responsibilities of the researcher with regard to the study population. The SfAA developed the first professional code of ethics in anthropology in 1949 in response to social scientists' misuse of subjects during WWI and WWII (Mead et al. 1949; Wax 1987). Further national safeguards were developed such as Institutional Review Boards (IRB), initiated by the 1974 National Research Act to help ensure protection of human subjects in research. The maelstrom precipitated by events related to the Vietnam War resulted in more frequent and often heated discussions about the ethical responsibilities of applied anthropologists. Such controversies within the discipline, sparked by the potentially improper roles taken by researchers, led to the formation of the AAA Committee of Ethics in 1970. As a result, a number of guidelines to best practices are now in place to help ensure contemporary applied practitioners are operating within the realm of appropriate standards and behaviors.

The most common ethical issue within anthropology is probably that of informed consent. This may go beyond simply having study subjects submit signed agreements to participate in research that has been thoroughly described to them, because the scope of the proposed research may not be immediately apparent. Inductive research, the kind most often conducted by anthropologists, creates multiple possibilities and a host of ideas that might be investigated. Given the breadth of issues that surface in such work, researchers often find it difficult to determine to what, exactly, the subject should agree. If a researcher knows from the start that a study subject will deny a research request, should the researcher obtain a general consent and then pursue the desired work once rapport is developed with the subject?

Another ongoing ethical issue concerns maintaining the privacy and confidentiality of study subjects. Only with the redirection of the anthropological eye toward the cultural operations of modern societies in the last several decades have social scientists begun to insist on more stringent protection of informants, mostly because subjects in the industrial world (unlike those in Third World populations, the traditional subjects of anthropological inquiry) would be more likely to have access to published research findings (Chambers 1985). This is especially pressing, because today study records in applied work are often largely out of the researcher's control and are subject to public purview. Realizing that the potential for exploiting the researcher/informant relation is high, the anthropologist must always be on guard for any hint of infringement and should always honor the ethical contract with all stakeholders.

CONCLUSION

Applied anthropology as a discipline has carved out a place for itself as a relevant, much needed component in public policy, program development, program evaluation, interventions, and a number of other areas critical to the health of the public sphere. Still, in order to establish themselves as an important voice in such issues, anthropologists must compete with professionals from a number of other disciplines. Students of applied anthropology, then, must be keenly cognizant of the shifting functions and possibilities of their field and must be readily able to articulate the many services it has to offer a changing world.

Collaboration has emerged as a major facet of modern applied anthropology, as practitioners work with members of other disciplines, program staff and stakeholders, and their subjects. Gone are the days when anthropology functioned as an isolated science, housed primarily in the halls of academia while those in the field kept a guarded distance from other anthropologists and, to some degree, from their own subjects. As anthropology becomes increasingly practical, shifting from academia to real-world involvement, today's students have inherited a discipline that is as all-encompassing as it is fluid, adapting to meet changing needs and manifesting itself differently in myriad situations. Interestingly, as the complexity and diversity of contemporary society has grown, anthropology has become a much more domestic endeavor, with anthropologists gravitating more toward study of their own communities, rather than to fieldwork in other parts of the world.

As lifeways continue to change and globalization becomes more of a reality, applied anthropology will no doubt continue to evolve. The practitioners and academicians of tomorrow must remain keenly up-to-date with changing methodologies, technologies, and research strategies. It is their responsibility to usher the discipline into the coming decades, to harness the potential roles the discipline could play while also remaining true to the original mission of applied anthropology, offering ethical, relevant assistance to peoples in need.

NOTE

1. Several website URLs are listed in this article. Over time their accuracy will diminish, so readers will need to turn to search engines to find the resources noted.

REFERENCES CITED

American Anthropological Association
  2000 Anthropology: Education for the 21st Century. *In* Anthropologists at Work: AAA's "Careers in Anthropology." Electronic document, http://www-personal.umich.edu/~bhoey/Applied%20Anthropology/articles/non-academic_aaa_article.htm, accessed February 6, 2007.

Baba, Marietta L.
  2005 To The End of Theory-Practice "Apartheid": Encountering The World. Ethnographic Praxis in Industry Conference Proceedings 1:205–217.

Basch, Linda G., Lucie Wood Saunders, Jagna Wojcicka Sharf, and James Peacock, eds.
  1999 Transforming Academia: Challenges and Opportunities for an Engaged Anthropology. Arlington, VA: American Anthropological Association.

Borofsky, Robert
  2002 The Four Subfields: Anthropologists as Mythmakers. American Anthropologist 104(2):463–480.

Cernea, Michael M.
  1992 Re-Tooling in Applied Social Investigation for Development. Planning: Some Methodological Issues. *In* Rapid Assessment Procedures—Qualitative Methodologies for Planning and Evaluation of Health Related Programmes. Nevin S. Scrimshaw, and Gary R. Gleason, eds. Boston: International Foundation for Developing Countries (INFDC). Electronic document, http://www.unu.edu/unupress/food2/UIN08E/uin08e00.htm, accessed November 12, 2007.

Chambers, Erve
  1985 Applied Anthropology: A Practical Guide. Prospect Heights, IL: Waveland Press.

Doyle, W. R.
  2003 A Report on the Field of Anthropology in the United States. New York: Wenner-Gren Foundation. Electronic document, http://www.wennergren.org/news-doyle-report.pdf, accessed February 4, 2005.

Dunn, T.
  1994 Rapid Rural Appraisal: A Description of the Methodology and Its Application in Teaching and Research at Charles Sturt University. Rural Society 4(3–4). Electronic document, http://www.csu.edu.au/research/crsr/ruralsoc/v4n3p30.htm, accessed Nov. 7, 2007.

Ervin, Alexander M.
  1999 Applied Anthropology: Tools and Perspectives for Contemporary Practice. Boston: Allyn and Bacon.

Harman, Robert C., Jim Hess, and Amir Shafe
  2005 Report on Survey of Alumni of Master's Level Applied Anthropology Training Programs. Electronic document, http://www.practicinganthropology.org/docs/surveys/masters_survey_results_2005.pdf, accessed November 27, 2007.

Harvard, Gazette
  2001 Rockefeller Center Awards Nearly 100 Grants. Electronic document, http://www.hno.harvard.edu/gazette/2001/05.24/10-rockefeller.html, accessed November 27, 2007.

Hill, Carol E., and Marietta L. Baba
  2006 Global Connections and Practicing Anthropology in the 21st Century. Theme issue, "The Globalization of Anthropology," NAPA Bulletin 25 (1):1–13.

Hinshaw, Robert H.
  1980 Anthropology, Administration, and Public Policy. *In* Annual Review of Anthropology 9:497–522.

Kedia, Satish

    2005 Careers in Anthropology. *In* Encyclopedia of Anthropology. H. J. Birx, ed. Pp. 138–141. Thousand Oaks, CA: Sage.

Kedia, Satish, and Linda A. Bennett

    2005 Applied Anthropology. *In* Anthropology, Encyclopedia of Life Support Systems (EOLSS). Developed under the Auspices of the UNESCO, EOLSS Publishers, Oxford, UK. Electronic document, http://www.eolss.net, accessed December 17, 2007.

Lamphere, Louise

    2004 The Convergence of Applied, Practicing, and Public Anthropology in the 21st century. Human Organization 63(4):431–443.

Mead, Margaret, Eliot D. Chapple, and G. Gordon Brown

    1949 Report of the Committee on Ethics. Human Organization 8(2):20–21.

O'Hara, Carolyn

    2006 Money for Nothing. Electronic document, http://www.foreignpolicy.com/story/cms.php?story_id=3575, accessed November 27, 2007.

Rhoades, Robert E.

    2005 Agricultural Anthropology. *In* Applied Anthropology: Domains of Application. S. Kedia and J. van Willigen, eds. Pp. 61–85. Westport, CT: Greenwood.

Rylko-Bauer, Barbara, Merrill Singer, and John vanWilligen

    2006 Reclaiming Applied Anthropology: Its Past, Present, and Future. American Anthropologist 108(1):178–190.

Scrimshaw, Susan C. M., and Elena Hurtado

    1987 Rapid Assessment Procedures for Nutrition and Primary Health Care: Anthropological Approaches to Improving Programme Effectiveness. Los Angeles: UCLA Latin American Center.

Smith, Susan, Timothy Pyrch, and Arturo Ornelas Lizardo

    1993 Participatory Action-Research for Health. World Health Forum 14(3):319–324. Electronic document, http://whqlibdoc.who.int/whf/1993/vol14-no3/WHF_1993_14(3)_p319-324.pdf, accessed December 4, 2007.

Trotter, Robert T., and Jean J. Schensul

    1998 Methods in Applied Anthropology. *In* Handbook of Methods in Cultural Anthropology. H. Russell Bernard, ed. Pp. 691–735. Walnut Creek, CA: AltaMira Press.

UNAIDS: The Joint UN Programme on HIV/AIDS

    2006 The Impact of AIDS on People and Societies. Electronic document, http://www.unaids.org/en/HIV_data/2006GlobalReport/default.asp, accessed December 4, 2007.

UN News Service

    2005 Highlights of Press Briefing by UN Emergency Relief Coordinator Before Donor Meeting on Humanitarian Assistance to Tsunami-Affected Communities—Geneva. Electronic document, http://www.un.org/apps/news/infocusnewsiraq.asp?NewsID=847&ID=, accessed November 27, 2007.

van Willigen, John, and Timothy J. Finan, eds.

    1991 Soundings: Rapid and Reliable Research Methods for Practicing Anthropologists. Theme issue, NAPA Bulletin 10.

van Willigen, John, and Satish Kedia

    2005 Emerging Trends in Applied Anthropology. *In* Applied Anthropology: Domains of Application. Satish Kedia, and John van Willigen, eds. Pp. 341–352. Westport, CT: Greenwood.

Wax, Murray L.

    1987 Some issues and sources on ethics in anthropology. *In* Handbook on Ethical Issues in Anthropology, AAA Special Publications 23. Joan Cassell and Sue-Ellen Jacobs, eds. Washington, DC: American Anthropological Association.

Wolf, Margery

    2002 Future of Anthropology: An Ethnographer's Perspective. Anthropology News 43(6):7.

MASTERING THE ART OF THE M.A. PROGRAM AND BEYOND

TERRY REDDING

Beta Social Research

This chapter provides advice and ideas to those who are seeking to enter, already enrolled in, or, just completing an M.A. program in applied anthropology. The chapter first addresses the topic of finding an M.A. program, and includes information on funding, meeting individual student needs, and anecdotal information from several graduate programs. Next, the chapter briefly explores building an appropriate graduate school experience as well as strategies for successfully balancing academic and interpersonal lives. The last and most detailed section covers the transition from graduate school into the workplace, particularly in regards to job searches, the importance of networking, and the application and enhancement of skills learned in school. Thoughts on the benefits of an internship, what to do with a completed thesis, and how and where to find jobs are included. Relevant resources available for further reference are noted throughout the text, including an informative survey of M.A. graduates and their current status. The author uses his personal experiences and those of his associates to illustrate trends in the field for future professionals aspiring to practice anthropology with a master's degree. On completion of the chapter, the reader should have a realistic and practical notion of where an M.A. in applied anthropology might lead, and how best to achieve the outcome desired. Keywords: M.A. program, graduate school, applied anthropology, networking, job search

This chapter is designed especially for those who are seeking to enter, already enrolled in, or, in particular, just completing a master's degree program.

Three sections are presented: finding an M.A. program that meets your needs and desires, building a graduate school experience that sends you in the right direction, and making the transition into the workplace (the job search, networking, and application of skills). Along the way the author will shamelessly interject his own experiences and those of associates, as well as information gleaned from others. Not surprisingly, the M.A. path is broad and divergent and this will be reflected in the text.

FINDING A PROGRAM

If you are just starting to explore graduate school, you will be asking two key questions: "Where should I study?" and "How will I fund it?" If your direction is still somewhat general or flexible, attend a program that has the faculty capacity and coursework you need.

NAPA BULLETIN 29, pp. 29–40. ISBN 9781405190152. © 2008 by the American Anthropological Association. DOI:10.1111/j.1556-4797.2008.00003.x

The Consortium of Practicing and Applied Anthropology Programs (www.copaa.info) has detailed information on two dozen member programs; many other programs exist as well. Visit websites and pay attention to any outside funding the department might be currently granted (e.g., National Institutes of Health [NIH], National Science Foundation [NSF]).[1]

If your direction of study is tightly focused, consult the discipline's journals (e.g., *Practicing Anthropology, Human Organization, NAPA Bulletin,* and the American Anthropological Association's [AAA] *Anthropology News*) and review the associations' annual meeting schedules (AAA and SfAA) to find instructors who are working on your specific topic. On finding relevant papers or journal articles, consult the bibliography to see who else is publishing on the subject.

"Well, that's all well and good," you may grumble, "but I have a mortgage and two kids, and my option is my local university or nothing." If your mobility is limited, enroll locally and work with a professor who is flexible and who can help you chart an academic course that meets your desires. Consider taking coursework outside the department or getting a dual degree, if available. After all, anthropologists embrace a multidisciplinary approach. For many of us, a second specialty has proved instrumental in getting a job.

If you live on a remote outpost with no access to higher education, you have a new option. The University of North Texas (UNT) launched the first online master's program in applied anthropology in the fall of 2006. Students in UNT's three-year M.A. or M.S. program need to present themselves on campus in Denton, Texas, just twice, at the start and finish of their studies; the program is designed to work around the lives of students unable to attend a traditional program.

Of course, the reality of funding your education may bring the idealism train to a shuddering stop. Finding the perfect program will be useful only if you can afford it.

Fortunately, many funding mechanisms are available. Start your search within the department(s) you hope to attend. Graduate assistantships (GAs), research assistantships (RAs), and teaching assistantships (TAs) are available in some quantity through most departments, although the latter two are often designed for Ph.D. students. Financial aid resources may be listed on department websites or in the office, although department willingness to work with individual students to find specific funding will vary. During your inquiry process, do not be shy about asking the department how many students receive funding of one sort or another. Ask about possible tuition waivers or stipends. Ask whether any professors have received or expect to receive research grants that will allow them to hire graduate students.

Information about external grants or fellowships can be found on the web. For example, the University of Washington has an 11-page website list called "Funding Sources on the Internet" (www.grad.washington.edu/fellow/hotlist.htm). The Council of Graduate Schools (www.cgsnet.org) has information under the "Programs and Awards: Resources for Students" link, and the Foundation Center (www.foundationcenter.org) has a dizzying array of information, although it requires digging to find relevant links. The University of California–Riverside also has a list of grant-giving organizations (www.graddiv.ucr.edu/

Admiss/HowFindMoneyNew.html), including minority and subject-specific grants, although the resources are aimed at domestic students.

Student loans are easier to obtain, but the catch is that they have to be paid back someday. Your program should be able to provide application information. Visit the Sallie Mae website (www.salliemae.com) for additional planning and application information. There is also the pay-as-you-go option. In my case, as a standard issue 30-something white male with average undergraduate grades, I did not readily qualify for grants or scholarships. The idea of compiling a mountain of loan debt offered little appeal, so I first attended school part time while working full time off campus. (Fortunately I worked in construction, so my school brain and work brain used different, shall we say, levels of intellectual capacity.) In my final year of school, I had a part-time graduate assistantship and took a full course load. While it took longer to finish, I left school with the flexibility possible by not having a looming loan payment. Other students also benefited from the welcome that our program at the University of South Florida, a largely urban commuter school, gave to part-time attendees.

In preparing this chapter, I obtained information from seven departments about their M.A. enrollees.[2] Most showed steady or growing numbers; the largest department had 68 students, the smallest had 25. All had at least two part-time students; South Florida had about 30 percent of their students attending part time.

Funding from within these departments or universities varied widely, with anywhere from 10 to 80 percent of students receiving some type of local assistance. The number of assistantships also varied greatly, from two or three to 30 or more annually per department. Those that had an idea of student financial aid said that from 50 to 100 percent of students had at least some student loans.

The average age of students was just under 30 years, although many departments had students well into their 50s. Following a trend throughout anthropology for many years, there were many more female than male students, although the two largest programs queried (Northern Arizona and South Florida) had a more balanced ratio. Most program durations were from two to three years.

The most important lesson from this, while anecdotal and not scientific, is that programs and their universities vary in the amount of funding they are able to provide to students, and in the number of positions for which students can be hired. Clarify any assistance you are expecting from a program before you officially accept.

Before we move on, there are other graduate school resources to note. The well-known academic press, SAGE Publications, produced a series of five books in the late 1990s on Surviving Graduate School. The titles include *Surviving Graduate School Part Time, The Women's Guide to Surviving Graduate School,* and *The African American Student's Guide to Surviving Graduate School.* The NIH website offers an indexed list of links titled "Surviving Graduate School" on their site (www.training.nih.gov/careers/careercenter/survgrad.html), and Peterson's (www.petersons.com) provides a well-organized and valuable body of information, including an enlightening timeline and international student information.

Selecting a chair may be your single most important decision in graduate school, and will affect everything you do until graduation and even beyond. In some cases your choice will be clear, but when you have a choice, resist taking the easy path. Select a chair who responds quickly and accurately to your needs, who is proficient and connected in the field, and who takes the role seriously.

My chair was renowned in the department as a curmudgeon, but as the founder of the program he was fully capable. He brooked no foolishness and took his advising seriously. As I was an older student no longer energetic enough to undertake foolishness (at least intentionally), this worked for me. While some in my cohort fumed that their chairs delayed in meeting with them or took many long weeks to comment on their theses, my chair quickly turned around any submissions with thoughtful comments and valid suggestions. Having the nicest, friendliest, or most popular professor will not benefit you if that person cannot be accessed.

Take full advantage of your student status. SfAA and NAPA offer discounted memberships and meeting attendance fees. Invest in memberships to both, as well as a local practitioner organization (LPO) if one exists in your area. All organizations and their committees welcome student volunteers and input as well, and they provide excellent networking opportunities. While the demands of grad school are understandable, it is nonetheless regrettable that relatively few students get involved with their local or national associations.

SfAA is a good venue for students to make professional presentations for the first time, although I find NAPA is much more relevant for practitioners once they graduate. In any case, it is a relief to get that first presentation over with while still a student. If you are working on a topic for which a panel might not be available, try a poster session. That was how I first presented at SfAA, and it was an ideal opportunity to provide in-depth information and chat with those interested in what I was doing in a more informal setting.

Look for student awards and prizes to apply for, and join the National Association of Student Anthropologists (a section of AAA, as is NAPA). Find a mentor outside of your department; NAPA offers a mentorship program, as does the Washington Association of Professional Anthropologists (WAPA).

Along with choosing the right chair, structuring your priorities will be critical to success. Naturally, if you have family or inflexible workplace considerations, you may have limited options for distributing your time. There are no easy solutions for priority setting, but you are the only one qualified to make the potentially difficult choices. Conflicts between intellectual, physical, and mental health are common, as are difficulties in balancing home, work, and school life. Your peers may have strategies to share, or simply an understanding shoulder to lean on.

In my case, I worked full time, had a girlfriend, a dog, and a social life, and was remodeling a house when I started school. Over time, the girlfriend went away, the house stayed largely unrepaired, and the dog hung out with the neighbor's pooch. Weekends and many evenings were spent in the library, and attending classes became something of a social activity. The year I attended classes full time with a part-time assistantship was actually a relief, because the outside, full-time work component was gone.

If you have done remote fieldwork, you probably know how to live frugally; this seems to be a strength of most anthropologists. Your peers can also offer creative solutions to getting by in the local economy.

Your available course selection will depend on the capacity of your program. Choose courses that best suit your needs, including those from outside the department, rather than simply taking the easiest or most popular courses. (This admonishment comes from regretted personal experience.) As we will read later, skills revealed by an M.A. survey to be needed, but that were not a part of curricula, included management (program and human resources), analysis, finance, evaluation, and planning. Classes in quantitative and additional methodologies, other data analysis and management, computer applications and technologies, and related quantifiable skills are useful. You might be surprised in the advantages of real proficiency in the Microsoft Office program suite (effective use of Word, as well as Excel, PowerPoint, and Access).

MAKING A SUCCESSFUL TRANSITION INTO THE WORKPLACE

If you are ready to graduate, you should have already presented at an annual meeting, been in contact with various movers and shakers in your specialty or area of greatest interest, thought about where you want to live, and have several employment feelers out. You should also be considering how to leverage your thesis and internship (if you had them), and any additional skills in order to find your dream job or position.

By the way, that thesis was a lot of work, wasn't it? And now, are you content to have it take up a chunk of the shelf space in the library and let it go at that? Admittedly, I was not, and so I contacted NAPA about turning my thesis into a *NAPA Bulletin.* To my surprise, then-president Nathaniel (Niel) Tashima turned me over to then–*NAPA Bulletin* editor Dennis Wiedman, who was very supportive of my idea.

By way of context, I had entered graduate school thinking I would combine my past careers (I have dual B.A. majors in journalism and sociology) into some sort of mass media and anthropology study. In the midst of my coursework, however, the World Wide Web and user-friendly browsers began to flourish, and I wrote my thesis instead on ways applied anthropologists could apply this new technology in their work. I was unwilling to allow this endeavor to simply languish in obscurity, as I thought perhaps there were lessons suitable for a broader applied audience. Six contributors provided case studies, and James Dow (creator of the ANTHAP listserv) wrote a section on the dawn of the Internet. We decided to publish the work solely online (I was told this was AAA's first-ever wholly online publication) and it became *NAPA Bulletin* 19, "Applied Anthropology on the Internet: Communication and Innovation" (Redding 1999).

Your thesis is the result of a great deal of toil, thought, research, and agony. Perhaps it can be molded into a chapter for a book, especially something outside of the world of anthropology. Maybe it makes a great case for a grant application. Or maybe it is perfect to be all or part of a *NAPA Bulletin.* Any of these will serve as a resume enhancer, and will also aid in your networking efforts by broadening your pool of collaborators and contacts.

Ah, networking; there is that word. You have heard many permutations of the expression, "It is not what you know, but who you snow." The ability to thrust oneself on others, extolling your virtues and soliciting their connections, comes naturally to some. For the rest of us introverted types, networking is a necessary if not arduous process (although research apparently shows that humans are naturally gregarious and learn shyness as young children). The good news is that anthropologists are great networkers, and I have always found colleagues receptive and helpful in making human connections.

One case in point is a members' survey conducted by WAPA in 1987, which showed that some 98 percent of members found their jobs via networking, and the other two percent found theirs through job postings (e-mail from WAPA past president Charity Goodman, November 19, 2006). While the Washington, D.C., area may present a special case, the lesson is important for practicing anthropologists.

From your class literature reviews, you should already know the players in your field of interest. Ask your chair and faculty for suggestions and tips, even personal anecdotes. Most faculty members will be happy to assist your initiative; they have an interest in your success because it makes the department look good, and in any case they do want to help. Write to potential contacts with a few insightful questions, and let a dialogue develop. While there are some who are simply too self-important to answer student queries, many anthropologists you contact will be surprisingly collegial. Attend as many annual meetings as you can afford, and introduce yourself after sessions or in the halls, at the socials, or in the bars. Have a business card of some type to hand out. The book exhibition hall is usually a good place to find people in an informal setting.

Former faculty members and alumni from your program should not be overlooked: they may even be your best advocates. My first two free lunches when I relocated were provided by former faculty members of my department. Go outside of anthropology circles to network, of course, and attend other local or national gatherings and meetings. Many M.A. anthropologists attend American Evaluation Association or American Public Health Association annual meetings, for example.

Interpersonal contact may reveal leads not only for open job positions but also about upcoming funding, grants, and contracts. Also, networking is not only for sorting out the job market but for getting to know your colleagues and potential collaborators, finding a possible mentor, or even making new friends. If appropriate, make sure to send a quick e-mail afterward letting the person know you enjoyed meeting them and look forward to keeping in touch. It sounds pedantic, but many of your peers neglect that little courtesy.

A crucial component in moving from graduate school into the workforce may be selling your skill set to an employer who does not know what an applied or practicing anthropologist does. You may have already had a taste of this via an internship. Perhaps it would be useful for graduate programs to offer a workshop for departing students in order to brainstorm ideas and discuss strategies for and successes in getting interviews and job offers.

If your program required an internship, its benefits will be reinforced when you arrive in the workplace to begin a career. You will have already had a chance to compare how your classroom knowledge relates to what you are getting paid to do, and have a sense of how best to apply your skills and knowledge. Many graduate students already spent time in the workforce, and have a sense of the politics and social realities of an office setting. Whether through an internship or prior work experience, the importance of fostering relationships, learning that your priorities may not mesh with your supervisor's, and knowing how to bring your skills to bear on a particular problem will already be known to you. We will return to networking and internships shortly.

There are many strategies for finding a job. U.S. Department of Labor statistics show that for jobseekers in 2005, 61 percent contacted potential employers directly, 55 percent sent out resumes or filled out applications, and only 15 percent responded to an advertisement. The data do not show a "networking" type category, although it does mention that 18 percent contacted family or friends (U.S. Department of Labor 2005). Let us address some job search methods.

Searching through job postings: The national associations and some LPOs have relevant job postings on their websites (SfAA: www.sfaa.net/sfaajobs.html; NAPA: www.practicinganthropology.org/employment; WAPA: www.wapadc.org/jobs.html), and most large associations, organizations, and private sector firms have a "positions available" page on their websites.

Specialty job sites: There are some specialty job sites such as the Communication Initiative (aka the "Drumbeat"), which posts international development positions (www.comminit.com/vacancies.html), the American Public Health Association International Health Section, which posts positions in international health (www.apha-ih.org/jobopportunities.htm), and the Environment Directory, a list of links to job postings in the environmental sector (www.webdirectory.com/employment/).

If you begin scanning these postings a year or so before you graduate, you should have a good idea of what types of jobs will be available and if any trends are underway when you are ready to enter the job market.

Cold calling: Many of us found our internships by contacting organizations we thought would be of value to work with. Once again, it is relevant grounding for a job search. The traditional approach is to contact the human resources director, submit a resume, and then follow up with a request for an informational interview, although there are other permutations. The business sector often advises going around the human resources department and directly contacting a manager or director for whom you wish to work, although I am uncertain whether this aggressive approach works as well for anthropologists. It may also ruffle the feathers of the person you need to impress if you do not follow the organization's protocols.

An enhancement to this strategy is to monitor the funding granted by large providers (e.g., U.S. Agency for International Development, NIH, NSF, Bill and Melinda Gates Foundation, Ford Foundation). If you see that a funder has provided a significant amount of money to an organization, you may wish to contact them about being included in a project.

Placement services: Employment services, executive search firms, college placement offices: there are a range of services available, both public and private, often requiring some type of fee. Be very careful if you go this route because private service fees can vary wildly, and may often involve quite a big chunk of your first year's annual salary.

Networking/referrals: We have already discussed networking-as-job-search. We have not yet discussed regional realities. If you wish to work in the United States, only a few areas have a critical mass of applied and practicing anthropologists and the types of jobs most are seeking. Washington, D.C., New York City, Boston, Chicago, California, and Arizona are among the best bets. If you wish to be in another area you will have to network well outside the anthropological community.

Not that this is a bad thing for a discipline that embraces a multidisciplinary approach. It may, however, affect the way you present yourself. Many practicing anthropologists will refer to themselves as social scientists or social researchers to those not keyed in to what applied anthropologists do. Many M.As. will find themselves filling roles at various health and human services type organizations and agencies, both public and nonprofit: child welfare, juvenile justice, aging services, adult literacy, and community health are just a few. Colleagues and team members may represent other social and biological sciences, law enforcement and legal services, medical and clinical services, and education.

If you wish to work abroad, most skills (interviewing, observation, organization) are applicable, but a few additional factors are involved. First is proficiency in a second language (currently, Spanish and Arabic are in high demand). Any specific cultural skills will be a plus (e.g., Peace Corps work with a specific group) and in most cases you will have to already have served in an international setting before being hired for international work. You may also have to get used to working with an interpreter, and be amenable to traveling and living in uncomfortable conditions. Record keeping also demands extra attention because you often will not be able to go back and reinterview someone, or find lost notes.

The range of international jobs is more limited in general than domestic options (the bulk of jobs will be in development, such as health, agriculture, water, forestry, or economics) but have the added bonus of keeping you well within the cross-cultural milieu. Perform extra research on the organization and job position before you go, because it may be hard to leave once you are there. Common job positions are research analyst, program associate, project manager, evaluator, and technical specialist.

I contacted a few working M.A.s around the country and asked what helped most in making the transition into the workforce and finding a job. Not surprisingly, all cited the experience gained in their internships as a key factor.

Sean Ryan offers a relevant case study. As a student from the University of California, Long Beach, searching for an internship, a fellow student mentioned that his employer might have some leads of interest. However, after a talk with the employer, Ken Erickson, Sean was offered a research opportunity doing corporate ethnographic research. This was a change in direction, but Sean was flexible enough to move from his original intent of doing tourism research to a business anthropology internship.

During the internship, Erickson and some colleagues formed their own company and invited Sean to work part time. As more projects came in the door, Sean was brought up to full-time work. Erickson helped Sean make contact with several practitioner anthropologists for his thesis, and the experience gained from the consumer ethnographic work led to a job at the corporate level with the office supply firm Staples. After working with Staples' Usability Group for a year, one of the contacts from Sean's thesis research told him of an ideal job opportunity at Bose (the audio technology company), across the street from his office at Staples. Sean was working for Bose as this *NAPA Bulletin* went to press.

"Ultimately what led to all of these opportunities were the connections I had established both in grad school and through professional organizations like NAPA," Sean noted. "Networking is a key skill, for business anthropology in particular. I believe many practitioners are finding jobs through user groups such as Anthrodesign, a Yahoo Group comprised of designers and practicing anthropologists. There are also conferences such as Ethnographic Praxis in Industry Conference (EPIC) that should provide even more networking and job opportunities in this growing field of business anthropology." Sean demonstrates those attributes that, quite literally, pay off: networking, flexibility, persistence, and applying class and internship experiences to workplace responsibilities (e-mails from Sean Ryan, December 4 and 11, 2006).

It is instructive to turn to a survey of applied anthropology M.A. program graduates conducted by Robert Harman, Jim Hess, and Amir Shafe in 2000. A one-page questionnaire with four open-ended questions was completed by 113 respondents, primarily from four of the largest applied programs (South Florida, Northern Arizona, Memphis, and Maryland). Not surprisingly, 19 primary job categories (not mutually exclusive) emerged, with twice as many of these being in the government as in either private or education sectors. It should be noted that respondents included archaeologists, and were skewed toward recent graduates. The average age was 40 (mean and median), and 50 percent more females than males responded (Harman et al. 2004).

The top ten occupations or occupational realms listed by respondents were, in descending order of frequency: researcher, manager, government, archaeologist, planner, administrator, medical, private sector, education, and program services. Obviously the open nature of the responses elicited rather vague categories, with some overlap. For example, the remaining categories were teaching, information specialist, student, entrepreneur, development, consultant, writer, and environment.

The authors note that "Many, although by no means all, of the researchers are in entry-level positions. As many practicing anthropology careers evolve, many individuals move into planning, managerial, and administrative positions, in which research skills become a backdrop rather than the focus of their work" (Harman et al. 2001). An interesting table compared skills that respondents used in their workplaces with skills taught in their programs. While most reported that their programs had prepared them well, the skills most used in the workplace that had not been addressed in their applied programs were supervision/personnel (by far the most cited skill), project planning, organizing, unspec-ified interaction, budget/finances, coordinating activities, other data analysis, evaluation, unspecified management, other personal strategies, and training. Those skills that most closely matched graduate program educations were critical thinking, qualitative analysis, quantitative analysis, grant writing, archaeological field methods, and archival research.

It is also of interest that only one quarter of respondents noted overtly that their anthropological perspective and knowledge was applied in their workplaces, although the authors interpret this to mean "that the anthropological perspective and knowledge are internalized and contribute implicitly to the practitioners' effectiveness at work" (Harman et al. 2001). Thirteen respondents volunteered that they were not actually "working in anthropology," some of whom appear to feel disenfranchised (Harman et al. 2004). If you find yourself feeling isolated because you are employed outside of an overtly anthropological context, stay involved through the associations. The ANTHAP listserv, while quiet, is available, and many of the LPOs have e-mail groups.

The survey highlights the need of the M.A. to be adaptable. Particularly because you may not likely have been hired as an "applied anthropologist," as a new professional you will learn by doing a variety of assignments, many of which may not relate to your job title or training. Your adaptability in learning new skills will determine whether you take on greater responsibilities. Flexibility will be critical as you and your employer sort through your strengths and weaknesses. While some roles, especially those designed for Ph.D. holders, are often clearly defined in job postings or position descriptions (e.g., lead scientist, principal investigator), you may be called on to perform or attempt a variety of tasks and to try on new roles and positions.

My own story is a bit atypical, or perhaps not. As I mentioned, I began dabbling in the World Wide Web soon after entering my program. A colleague showed me the basics of HTML coding and I picked up the rest by trial and error. I hoped to intern in Washington and was chosen for a new project at the Smithsonian because of my combination of anthropology, Internet, and communications experience. While there, I also obtained a brief internship with the AAA because of my journalism background.

When I moved away after finishing my thesis, I was hired in the private sector by the region's largest woman-owned business, a national travel agency that managed large federal accounts, among others. I had responded to an interesting newspaper advertise-ment on a lark, and they liked the combination of communication and anthropology. Not long after I began work, an article appeared in *USA Today* discussing the benefits to the corporate sector of having an anthropologist on staff (Jones 1999).

You may recall that I contacted Niel Tashima about turning my thesis into a *NAPA Bulletin*. His company, LTG Associates, Inc., was sometime later awarded a large project from USAID, and he called me to assess my interest in joining their project staff. My first title was assistant editor. By the end of the project, my title and duties morphed into Information Resources Specialist, but you can see where all this is heading: it was usually the combination of skills that helped get the job. Given that, it is not much of a surprise that my current title (although I am on something of a sabbatical) is Communications Director, with a small, Florida-based nonprofit called Beta Social Research.

In fact, I have not yet worked in "typical" applied anthropology contexts, although I do use my training in subtle or unconscious ways. I learned to never assume anything, to never be satisfied that the way things appear are the way they are, and to watch people's actions rather than their words. As I write this, however, I am embarking on a more typical project of researching disadvantaged youth's access to and interest in the Internet.

Back to the multidisciplinary approach, communications is a natural fit with anthropology. Currently, another great combination is public health and anthropology. There are jobs and funding to be had, as well as natural synergies between the two. Something a little under the radar is a combination of anthropology and various computer technology skills. These would seem mutually exclusive, but there are some with both skill sets. My guess is that environmental studies will also prove a valuable combination in years to come. Naturally, along with those mentioned throughout this chapter, there are many other skills that are a perfect fit with anthropology when it comes to finding a job. Statistics, demography, psychology, counseling, and criminal justice are a few within the social sciences.

Colleagues have combined past social service experience, Peace Corps service, entrepreneurship, language abilities, and technical prowess as part of their overall skills and experience package. It is all a part of the M.A. reality, and it is rare that you will offer the same version of your resume twice to potential employers. Looking for a job with an M.A. provides many challenges but also many options; in most cases it depends on how you prefer to package yourself. While occasionally difficult to find, the employment opportunities are there.

Some respondents to my queries stated that an M.A. was as far as they were going to go academically, even though they had the option of pursuing a Ph.D. It should be noted, however, that a Ph.D. may offer more flexibility over time if you change your mind about careers and directions. Many upper level government jobs require a Ph.D., and you will usually need Ph.D. status to be the principal investigator (PI) on a grant proposal. You can more easily dabble in academia, and publishers of all stripes may prefer seeing a Ph.D. after an author's name. Nonetheless, your ongoing work experience will be the most significant determinant of your access to future jobs and career paths.

I wish that a brilliant postulation existed for making a successful transition from graduate school into the workforce, but it is actually quite pedestrian in simplicity: analyze the market, network with key players, and present yourself appropriately to potential employers. Then work hard at what you enjoy most, keep learning, live long, and share your talents and experiences.

NOTES

1. Several website URLs are listed in this article. Over time their accuracy will diminish, so readers will need to turn to search engines more frequently to find the resources noted.

2. Many thanks to American University, University of Maryland, University of Memphis, UNT, Northern Arizona University, Oregon State University, and University of South Florida.

REFERENCES CITED

Harman, Robert C., James Hess, and Amir Shafe
  2001 Master's of Applied Anthropology Survey. Anthropology News, May.

  2004 Report on Survey of Alumni of Master's Level Applied Anthropology Training Programs. Arlington, VA: American Anthropological Association. NAPA. Electronic document, http://www.practicinganthropology.org/departments/, accessed November 28, 2006.

Jones, Del
  1999 Hot Asset in Corporate: Anthropology Degrees. USA Today, February 18:1B.

Redding, Terry, ed.
  1999 Applied Anthropology on the Internet: Communication and Innovation. NAPA Bulletin 19. Arlington, VA:American Anthropological Association. Electronic document, http://www.aaanet.org/napa/publications/napa19/, accessed December 12, 2006.

U.S. Department of Labor
  2005 Household Data Annual Averages. Current Population Survey Table 33. Washington, DC: U.S. Department of Labor. Bureau of Labor Statistics website. Electronic document, http://www.bls.gov/cps/cpsaat33.pdf, accessed November 29, 2006.

SMALL FISH IN A BIG POND: AN APPLIED ANTHROPOLOGIST IN NATURAL RESOURCE MANAGEMENT

Jennifer Gilden
Pacific Fishery Management Council

This chapter relates the experiences of an applied anthropologist working in fisheries management. Although anthropology and other social sciences have much to contribute to fisheries management, fisheries managers focus mainly on biology and economics, and many are unaware of the contributions that social science can make. Motivation and effort are necessary to counteract the isolation that social scientists in biological fields can experience. Armed with an interdisciplinary background, a supportive community, a strong will, and an open mind, applied anthropologists working in fisheries management can bring new perspectives and solutions to this complex and challenging arena. Keywords: Careers, fisheries, anthropology, social science, fishery management

For the last six years, I have worked for the Pacific Fishery Management Council (hereafter, "Council"), one of eight regional councils that develop fishery management recommendations for the U.S. Secretary of Commerce. As an applied anthropologist working in fisheries management—a field dominated by biologists—my job has involved many types of education: educating myself about fisheries biology, educating managers about the contributions of social science, educating the public about the fisheries management process, and, perhaps most importantly, educating myself about the role and limitations of social science in this particular field. Below, I provide a brief, and candid, account of my experience as an applied anthropologist in fisheries management. I will discuss my career, my experience working with biologists and managers, and what it is like to work with an M.A. in applied anthropology in this field.

ANTHROPOLOGY IN FISHERIES

Anthropologists and other social scientists have a long history of contributing valuable insights into fisheries management. This history is closely tied to National Marine Fisheries Service (NMFS), the agency charged with conserving, protecting, and managing living marine resources in the United States. NMFS was founded in 1970 and hired its first anthropologist, James Acheson, in 1974. Subsequently, the use of anthropology at NMFS has slowly increased. In 1996, the reauthorization of the Magnuson-Stevens

NAPA BULLETIN 29, pp. 41–55. ISBN 9781405190152. © 2008 by the American Anthropological Association. DOI:10.1111/j.1556-4797.2008.00004.x

Fishery Conservation and Management Act (MSA), which directs U.S. fishery management activities, included a National Standard that called for conservation and management measures to "take into account the importance of fishery resources to fishing communities." National Standard 8 drew attention to social and economic analyses and increased the level of funding available for the social sciences in fisheries management. Although the number of anthropologists working in fisheries management is still relatively small, important steps are being taken to increase the use of social data in fisheries management. For example, a "Sociocultural Practitioners Manual" in the works will clarify and guide analysis under National Standard 8, and anthropologists are developing a methodology to identify fishing communities (Abbott-Jamieson and Clay 2006). At the same time, NMFS anthropologists are developing a systematically compiled set of community profiles for use in fishery management, and others are working toward a model for fisheries social impact assessment (Pollnac et al. 2006).

In addition to these efforts at NMFS, there is a long history of academic study into fishing communities, practices, and management. *NAPA Bulletin* 28, in fact, was devoted entirely to articles focusing on the intersection of anthropology and fisheries management in the United States. As well, a brief survey of such work includes general publications on the human dimensions of fisheries (Acheson 1981; Fricke 1985; Hanna and Jentoft 1996; Hillborn 2007; Jentoft 2000; McCay 1978; Pollnac and Littlefield 1983; Sepez et al. 2006; Wilson 2006); on traditional fishing communities worldwide (Cordell 1990; Dyer and McGoodwin 1994; Ruddle 1994); on specific fishing communities (Dalton 2001; Garrity-Blake 1996; Gatewood and McCay 1988; Gilmore 1986; Miller and van Maasen 1979); on fishing families (Danowski 1980; Davis 1986; Dixon et al. 1984; Gersuny and Poggie 1973; Smith 1995); on various aspects of fisheries management (Browman and Stergiou 2005; Davis and Bailey 1996; Hanna and Smith 1993; Jentoft 1989; Jentoft and McCay 1995; Jentoft et al. 1998; McCay et al. 1998; Scholz et al. 2004; Smith 1986; St. Martin 2001; Pinkerton 1989, 1995; Young and McCay 1995); and on theoretical approaches to the "commons" model of fisheries (Berkes 2006; Feeny et al. 1996; Hanna 1990; McCay and Acheson 1990). In addition, literature on other natural resource issues can inform fisheries management (e.g., timber; see Carroll and Lee 1990; Lee 1989).

Despite this body of literature and this history of anthropological effort, however, many fishery managers are unaware of anthropology's past and potential contributions. This is a common challenge for applied anthropologists working with on-the-ground policymakers. Below, I discuss my circuitous route into the world of fisheries management, and ways to reduce isolation and increase the effectiveness of anthropology in this and other natural resource fields.

MY ROUTE FROM GENERALIST TO ANTHROPOLOGIST

Like many who pursue careers in anthropology, I am a generalist—one who is interested in many fields and disciplines, but finds it hard to narrow down these interests and commit to becoming an expert in a single field. This can be both a blessing and a curse:

a blessing because, over time, one develops skills in multiple fields, and enjoys life in its grand variety; a curse, because most job descriptions are not written with the generalist in mind. Generalists benefit from their interest in a wide variety of subjects, but society encourages them to specialize in one particular area. Anthropology is an ideal field for generalists because its flexibility allows them to specialize in a discipline that can be used to explore a wide variety of topics: Siberian shamans, cocktail waitresses, corporate practices, fisheries management.

As a generalist, it took me a while to choose a career. As an undergraduate at Vassar College, I studied political science and focused on issues in developing countries. I took one physical anthropology class, but no more. After graduating from college, I traveled and explored several different careers and fields. Five years later, I discovered the small applied environmental anthropology program at Oregon State University. This program allowed me to combine my interests in environmental and cultural issues, and offered a variety of interesting career paths. There, I met Dr. Courtland Smith, a fisheries anthropologist, who in time became an invaluable mentor and guide.

It was at Oregon State that my career as an applied anthropologist began. For my master's thesis, I focused on women, families, and gender symbolism in timber communities. It wasn't exactly what I had in mind when I began studying anthropology, but to my surprise I found that studying "domestic" cultures was fascinating. I lived in a small timber community for a summer, working with at-risk middle-school kids in a 4-H program while I conducted interviews in the community. The research reshaped my views about environmental issues. For example, I grew up in an environmentally active community where the timber industry and timber workers were seen as "the bad guys." These views went unquestioned until I entered the homes of timber families and began to talk to them face to face. It became clear that the black-and-white perceptions I had grown up with were overly simplistic, and that this particular issue (like most environmental issues) was made up of complex and shifting shades of grey. Although I retain my environmental values, I realized that pushing for change when you lack understanding of an issue's complexities can do much more harm than good.

After completing my thesis in 1996, my focus gradually shifted from timber communities to fishing communities. I worked with Oregon Sea Grant on several projects, studying salmon trollers' and gillnetters' attitudes toward salmon disaster relief programs, the lives of fishermen's wives, the culture of a multidisciplinary research team, and fishermen's attitudes about fisheries management. With Dr. Smith, I also worked with watershed councils, studying their social networks, decision-making processes, and values.

Although I enjoyed conducting research, I was not particularly interested in working in academia. Attending a meeting of the Society for Applied Anthropology (SfAA), I met other researchers who were looking for careers outside academia. We discussed our ideas over email and decided to found a "think tank" that became the Institute for Culture and Ecology (IFCAE), an independent research group that focuses on the human dimensions of natural resources. I worked with IFCAE part-time for several years and served on its board. Although I am no longer directly involved, researchers for IFCAE continue to study natural resource issues, particularly those related to nontimber forest products.

When my last research project with Oregon Sea Grant ended, I contacted the Council about career opportunities. Because I had spent time studying communications in fisheries management, I was familiar with their work, and they with mine. They hired me for a one-year appointment. Six years later, I am still in a position that I have tailored around my skills and interests.

AN EDUCATION IN FISHERIES

Beginning work at the Council was an education in itself. The Council is one of eight regional councils created by Congress and designed to allow regional management of fisheries. The Council recommends harvest levels and management measures for fish in federal waters off the Washington, Oregon, and California coasts. We are a quasigovernmental organization, in that we are funded by Congress but are technically a nonprofit. The Council staff (of which I am a member) supports the Council itself, a body of about 15 members who forward management recommendations to the Secretary of Commerce through NMFS. The Council staff does not conduct research; research used in fisheries management is usually conducted by NMFS, the states, or academics.

Because I had just completed a study of communications in fisheries management, my role on the Council staff was to focus on social science, outreach and communication, media relations, and staffing the Council's habitat committee. Given my background, I naturally saw anthropologist as the most important of these roles.

On starting, two things immediately became clear: I would need to learn a lot about fisheries, and I would need to revise my ideas about my anthropological role. My knowledge of fisheries management was based on readings I had done, interviews I had conducted with managers and commercial fishermen, and discussions I had had with other academics. I was well-informed about fishermen's perceptions of management, but I did not understand how environmental laws influence management, or, for that matter, why the size of a trawl footrope matters. And my focus was mainly on commercial fishermen, to the exclusion of other fisheries stakeholders. Still, I brimmed with good ideas about how to improve management and outreach. I had formed an idea about what needed to be done, and I was eager to apply my knowledge. But first I needed to become a student again.

One of the first tasks I undertook was to revise the existing guide to the Council process. This was a good choice, because it meant educating myself about the role of the Council and the fisheries that it manages. I quickly learned about the politics, funding, scientific challenges, and workload pressures involved in actually managing fisheries. I learned about the different types of groundfish, and the implications of their life histories; about the difference between the National Environmental Policy Act (NEPA) and the Magnuson-Stevens Fishery Conservation and Management Act (MSA), and many other things that I had not covered during my ethnographic research. Because part of my role was to answer questions from the public and the media, I needed to learn these things rather quickly.

I also learned (and am still learning) about where anthropology fits into fisheries management. Six years later, my goals, focus, and roles have changed considerably, and sometimes I am not sure whether I still qualify as an applied anthropologist. Do positions that do not involve research count as applied anthropology? There are many definitions, some of which imply that research or inquiry must be involved, and some that suggest applying an anthropological perspective to problems is sufficient. John van Willigen (2002:8) defines applied anthropology as "anthropology put to use ... It is viewed as encompassing the tremendous variety of activities anthropologists do now and have done in the past, when engaged in solving practical problems." In this case, a position that does not involve research can still be considered "applied anthropology."

Still, I do not always describe myself as an anthropologist. Instead, I consider myself someone with a "background in anthropology." I do a small amount of direct "social science work," but all of my work is colored by my background. Because much of what I do for outreach communications is based on the research I conducted before I began working here, I am clearly applying information gained using anthropological methods. However, I am not currently using anthropological research methods in this position.

A LONE ANTHROPOLOGIST IN A BIOLOGICAL FIELD

There are many challenges to applying anthropology in a natural resource field. These range from the biological focus of most management staff to the biological focus of natural resource management itself.

Fields like fisheries management, forestry, and other natural resource fields tend to attract biologists, which is natural given their subject matter. (That said, the Forest Service has a very active social science component.) Although fisheries management is more about managing people than managing fish, social science receives very little funding and attention. Currently, for example, the NMFS Northwest Fisheries Science Center, which employs approximately 300 people (adding up to 180 FTE), has five economists and two noneconomic social scientists on staff. One of those is an anthropologist. There has been discussion about increasing the number of anthropologists working for NMFS, but so far the numbers haven't changed significantly.

Regional fishery management councils have a similar record. During my tenure here, I have always been the only staff member with an anthropological background. At this point I believe I am the only such staff member on any of the fishery management councils. (The South Atlantic Fishery Management Council used to employ a full-time anthropologist, but that position is currently open). This means that there was little support for my anthropological imagination, and nobody who could relate to my anthropological perspective and ideas. It wasn't that my supervisors discouraged me; it was just that they were biologists and administrators who were concerned with other things, and social research was not a part of the Council's mission.

I needed a support network, and I didn't have one. Anthropologists working at NMFS had group meetings that I occasionally attended, but their focus was usually on issues that didn't relate directly to my work. In addition, most had Ph.D.s, and were involved in research activities that I could not pursue in my position. On the other hand, when I met anthropologists outside the Council arena, they were also primarily involved in conducting research, rather than applying the knowledge gained from research in an administrative setting. Although it felt good to be around other anthropologists, discussing theories and methods and philosophies, I still found myself alone among biologists when I returned to work.

This brings me to the difference between those with Ph.D.s in anthropology and those with M.As.—a potentially sensitive subject. When surrounded by anthropologists with Ph.D.s (particularly those who were actively conducting research), I admit to feeling some insecurity about my status. This may be owing to my own neuroses, or may be a common issue with anthropologists with a master's degree; either way, I hope my experience will be instructional. Without diminishing M.A. programs, it is fair to say that Ph.D. programs are generally more intense, demanding, and rigorous. This, and the length of time it takes to earn a Ph.D., can lead to a more solid sense of identification as an "anthropologist" than I attained in my M.A. program. In addition, because my position does not "use" me consistently as an anthropologist, I am less familiar with current theories and research methods. This emphasizes the need to network with other anthropologists with M.A.s; to keep up with current anthropological theories and ideas; to consider how important the role of anthropologist is to one's identity; to understand and value the unique role that an applied anthropologist fills in a nonresearch organization. I will discuss these recommendations in a later section of this chapter.

SOCIAL SCIENCE AND THE STRUCTURE OF FISHERIES MANAGEMENT

Despite the wealth of fisheries social science literature, few fishery managers truly understand how social science can contribute. During interviews for a paper on social science needs in the Council process (Gilden 2005), Council members freely admitted that they did not understand exactly what social science was, how to apply it, or how it could help management. They didn't understand the difference between sociology, anthropology, and economics, and were unaware of the large body of literature available. Many did not seem to consider anthropology a "real" science (like biology). To them, social science is the public testimony given by fishermen at management meetings: it tells them that communities are either suffering or benefiting from management decisions (usually the former), but because of the structure of the management process, how to actually *use* this information is unclear.

This brings me to the biggest challenge, which is that the fisheries management system is focused on managing *fisheries,* not communities. Despite mandates to consider community impacts, community concerns are secondary to the councils' function. There are times when community issues become a high priority, like when dealing with allocation or when developing individual fishing quota programs, as we are now. Usually, however, councils focus on harvest limits, the status of fish stocks, management measures (such as closed areas or gear restrictions), and to a much lesser extent, community impacts. When they do focus on communities, they usually look at effects on a large geographic scale, such as a region or state, rather than individual communities.

The Council is required by law to collect and use social science data. (The data are usually collected by NMFS or other agencies.) This information is mainly used in the "affected environment" sections of environmental impact statements required by NEPA, as well as socioeconomic sections of fishery management plans and other management documents. Most of these data are economic in nature, listing the value of harvests and processing, although community profiles are also included. Social science methods are also used to analyze scoping comments (public comments taken as part of the NEPA process) and to improve communication and involvement in the Council process. During my time here I have contributed to these efforts, and I am currently working on the communities section of an environmental impact statement related to individual fishing quotas.

The social science requirements in NEPA and the Magnuson-Stevens Act are broad and unspecific, and social scientists have spent a lot of time trying to figure out what they mean and how to go about meeting them. For example, discussions about the definition of "community" seem to come up at every meeting of fisheries anthropologists; the problem is that "community" as defined in federal law is not necessarily the best way to define community when it comes to managing fisheries. Other terms, such as "flexibility" and "dependence," also cause disagreements and misunderstanding. These hurdles, which seem relatively minor, have consumed large amounts of time and have slowed the integration of social science into the management process.

An additional obstacle to the use of social science information is that fishermen are not always willing to share socioeconomic information with researchers, especially researchers who work at management agencies. When researchers collect information from the fishing community, there can be no guarantee that the data will not eventually be used in decisions that may reduce harvest levels. This leads to substantial distrust on the part of respondents. Flaxen Conway and I conducted a study (2001) for Oregon Sea Grant that concluded that reducing distrust was the best long-term solution to the problem of data collection in fisheries management. Educating the public about management and more effectively involving the fishing community in data collection and decision making would help them understand the relevance and need for both biological and socioeconomic data.

Finally, money is an obstacle. Although funding for social science has increased in recent years, social science funding remains at a very low level, especially given the federal mandates for socioeconomic data collection. This is a reflection of both congressional and agency priorities.

Although social science has not been used to its fullest extent in fisheries management, it does have much to offer, and future generations of applied anthropologists and other social scientists may eventually contribute to a shift in perspective in the field.

Fishery managers need information about who fishes, why they fish, and where, how, and when they fish; about the values, goals, and resilience of commercial and recreational fishing communities; how they interact with management; and how management can use social information. Anthropology and other social sciences broaden the management information base beyond the biological resource, providing a greater array of information managers can use to make decisions. Social science recognizes that communities and fishery participants are multifaceted, and that they are affected by management actions in ways that are not solely economic.

Apart from studying community impacts, anthropology can be used in other ways that benefit management. Understanding human motivations, values, and strategies can help managers develop relevant, effective, and enforceable management practices; reduce conflict among user groups; and increase stakeholder involvement in decision making. Social science methods can also capture local knowledge about biology, resource stewardship, harvest methods, and environmental factors.

Collaborative research—the involvement of stakeholders in research—is an evolving field that combines social science with biological or environmental science. Such research is being used effectively on both coasts, and can involve anthropologists both in the research itself and in developing networks between stakeholders, researchers, and managers. (The websites fishresearch.org and fishresearchwest.org are devoted to collaborative research.) Collaborative research offers an opportunity to increase the public's involvement and investment in fishery management while improving data collection. Like any research, collaborative projects must meet high standards for research design and data collection.

Social science can also be used to lend stability to fisheries management. When dealing with depleted fish stocks, managers may steeply reduce harvest levels, causing economic hardship to fishing businesses and the communities that depend on them. Managers could take a different approach by focusing on the long-term stability of human communities rather than focusing on a single fish species or complex ecosystems. Such an effort would require a fundamental change in management philosophy and a large investment in social science information.

Finally, social science has been used, and will continue to be used, to learn about communication between fisheries managers and the public, to enhance constituent involvement and representation, and to find better ways to educate the public about the management process.

The responsibility for integrating social science in fisheries management goes both ways. Scientists need to understand managers' objectives in order to provide useful information. Sometimes anthropologists and others get caught up in text-heavy descriptions of communities, history, values, and interesting cultural details that are less than useful for managers making harvest decisions under pressure. Anthropologists need to ask themselves what meaning their research will have to management, and focus on the connection between their data and the managers' current needs.

The way the information is presented is also important. Qualitative data are often presented in a narrative form, while quantitative results are usually presented as tables or graphs. Unlike narrative data, numbers can be easily summarized and compared, and tables and graphs are often easier for managers to digest. In addition, managers are typically better at digesting quantitative information than qualitative information. Developing quantitative indicators of community impacts, while educating managers about qualitative data collection, analysis, and use, would increase the effectiveness of social science in the fisheries management process.

To summarize, there is room for many types of social science in fisheries management—including pure research on communities, impacts, motivations and values, and applied efforts such as developing collaborative projects, improving communications and outreach, and improving stakeholder involvement.

ACADEMIC PREPARATION

As noted above, applied anthropology is unique in its flexibility. My M.A. focused on environmental anthropology, but an M.A. in applied anthropology could focus on virtually any meaningful topic. My comments here are directed toward students interested in natural resource management, but many points apply to any graduate student in applied anthropology.

To prepare academically, I recommend a program that provides practical experience and the opportunity to explore multiple disciplines. For those interested in natural resource management, a joint major in anthropology and natural resource studies would provide a useful overview and would be valuable in the job market.

Natural resource management is inherently multidisciplinary. Management work requires skill in relating to people from a wide variety of backgrounds, so experience in meeting facilitation, conflict management, and diplomacy are all helpful. Communication skills such as writing, listening, speaking, and the ability to absorb large amounts of information are vital. In addition, a general knowledge of biology is useful (in my case, fish biology; but this could also apply to wildlife biology, forestry, or other areas). Find a program that isn't too narrowly focused, and that allows you to take classes in other disciplines. For example, I was a liberal arts major, but went to a land-grant, Sea Grant university that had a very practical, applied focus. This was very useful for me in gaining practical experience. When looking for a school, remember that you are interviewing them about what they can offer you. Visit the school, talk to professors, and talk to students.

Many graduate programs require some sort of internship. Choose carefully. As I described above, my internship was with a 4-H program in a small timber community. I worked with at-risk youth and conducted interviews with timber family members in my off hours. The work was often active and challenging, giving me a useful entrée into the community, but there were also days of preparing art supplies and name tags for youth groups. Although some "grunt work" is normal in an internship, beware of those that relegate you to a back office to collate binders and stuff envelopes. An internship should not merely be unpaid temporary labor for the sponsoring organization. In the best positions, the intern has responsibility for a discrete project, or works closely with staff on a joint project. I recommend that potential interns interview their prospective "employers" about how much latitude they will have to develop their own projects, and make sure the employers have clear ideas about how they will be used. For fisheries, look for internships at state fish and wildlife departments, the National Marine Fisheries Service, environmental organizations, or fishing community organizations. Other natural resource management agencies and nongovernmental organizations offer potential in other resource areas.

Once you're in graduate school, there will probably be a core curriculum that you need to follow, including statistics, theory, and research design. Each of these is important for students planning to apply their knowledge. If possible, find courses in the psychology and culture of natural resources, and take classes in natural resource management. Strive to understand the everyday, real world issues and needs of resource managers.

GETTING A FOOT IN THE DOOR

Apart from internships, there are several other ways to learn about fisheries management. First, spend time researching a specific management decision that interests you and, if possible, attend a fishery management council meeting in your area. Because the Council meetings themselves can be extremely formal and, dare I say, boring to an outsider, try attending an advisory body meeting (e.g., the Pacific Council's Groundfish Advisory Subpanel). These are conducted jointly with Council meetings and tend to be more lively and informal. All meetings, apart from some that deal with personnel issues, are open to the public. Second, learn as much as possible about how the management system works. There are educational resources on the Pacific Council website (www.pcouncil.org) and on other agencies' sites. Third, talk to fishermen (and women) and members of environmental groups about their views and concerns. Go to the docks and strike up a conversation with a fisherman; tell them you want to hear their side of the story. Most are happy to talk, although there will probably be some venting as well. Fourth, if you're interested in terrestrial (as opposed to marine) fisheries, attend a watershed council meeting in your area. Fifth, volunteer to work on a field project, such as a watershed restoration project or a fisheries survey, to gain on-the-ground experience. And finally, call people at NMFS or the Councils to ask questions and learn about opportunities.

FINDING AN ANTHROPOLOGICAL POSITION IN FISHERIES

As I have described, applied anthropology jobs at regional fishery management councils are rare, and do not involve much research. (Because there are only eight councils and most of them are quite small, any type of job with councils is hard to come by). Other management agencies such as NMFS, state fish and wildlife departments, and the three interstate fisheries commissions (Pacific States, Atlantic States, and Gulf States) are the primary sources for management positions. However, other organizations peripherally involved in management may also offer interesting positions to applied anthropologists. These include other federal agencies such as the National Marine Sanctuary Program; advocacy and conservation groups like the Natural Resources Defense Council, Environmental Defense, Oceana, and the Ocean Conservancy; fishing associations and community groups (both recreational and commercial); Sea Grant institutions; and private consulting firms specializing in fisheries.

Because most positions with management agencies rely on federal funding, the number of available positions fluctuates with the political tide. However, fisheries will always need to be managed, and the tide is gradually changing in favor of hiring more social scientists. New initiatives, such as ecosystem-based management, rights-based management, collaborative research, and community-based management may offer interesting opportunities for applied anthropologists in the future.

REDUCING AND ADAPTING TO ISOLATION

It can be a challenge for lone anthropologists in biological fields to remain connected to the field of anthropology. Awareness, motivation, and effort are all necessary.

First, it is important to clearly understand your own needs, goals, and motivations. Consider how important it is for you to practice anthropology. Are you content with having a background in anthropology and implicitly applying that knowledge in your everyday, nonanthropological work, or do you need to do more explicitly anthropological work, like conducting ethnographic interviews or spending time in the field? Your satisfaction as an applied anthropologist will depend on how your needs and interests match up with those of your employers. If there is absolutely no support for any anthropological approach, yet you identify closely with the anthropological label and will not feel fulfilled unless you are out conducting interviews every day, then you are probably in for some frustration. If, on the other hand, you are content to apply knowledge that you gained during graduate school, but do not feel driven to conduct much research, or if your supervisors are open and able to facilitate anthropological research, then you may be satisfied. Carefully consider your expectations, goals, and needs in relation to what the position actually allows you to do—and what you can make it do. Learn about the historical role of social science in the field, and whether there is funding for, or interest in, anthropological methods; explore how your organization and your own work can benefit from anthropology. Will your supervisors and coworkers support your efforts?

Once you do find a position—particularly a federal or state position in a management agency—do not be surprised if you are the sole liberal arts major in the office. Your coworkers may not understand the value of social science methods and perspectives, so you may need to do some gentle education. Do not assume that because you're excited about anthropology, everyone else will be too. Managers have specific information needs, are often under pressure, and need to absorb information quickly. Specificity, relevance, clarity, and simplicity in presentation are key. It may be sadly disillusioning at first when they do not get excited about your beautifully detailed ethnographic descriptions; the fact is that their values lie elsewhere, and to be useful you must recognize and respect these values.

Once in a position, network as much as possible with others in your field. The support you need to maintain your anthropological perspective may have to come from outside your organization. Maintain contact with other anthropology students who have gone on to nonacademic careers, and, if possible, keep in touch with a favorite academic advisor. Talk to them regularly about experiences and challenges. (Consider setting up a regular meeting time so other work responsibilities do not distract you). Subscribe to *NAPA Bulletin* and *Practicing Anthropology* (published by SfAA), and actually read them when they arrive in your mailbox. Join an online forum like the SfAA Social Network, which provides a forum for members of the SfAA and other applied social scientists "who are interested in sharing information about their interests, work, expertise, and research" (www.sfaa.net). Offer yourself as a resource for students who are entering the field; this will remind you of your own expectations and goals on graduation. Consider starting your own discussion group for applied anthropologists, either in person or online. If possible, attend professional meetings, even if you do not plan to present a paper; just being around other anthropologists will be good for your soul. Most importantly, remember that when you are surrounded by people who do not share this particular perspective or interest, it will take time and effort and even some fighting spirit to maintain your connection to anthropology. Other responsibilities and interests will intrude, and will distract you.

Once you are firmly ensconced in your position, take advantage of opportunities to learn about the biological aspects of natural resources. A few years ago I went out on a chartered trawler for a week to participate in research conducted by NMFS. For a week, I was a biologist—measuring and weighing fish, cutting them open, and learning firsthand about the fish we manage, how trawl vessels work, and how fishing crew survive those months at sea (hard work and lots of junk food). Learn about biology and other aspects of the business from staff members who are willing to share. This will increase both your understanding of your role in the organization and your value as an employee.

Being an anthropologist in a field dominated by biologists can be difficult. However, anthropology and other social sciences have a great deal to contribute. Maintaining and restoring a healthy environment in the face of growing populations, evolving technologies, shifting societal values, and growing demand for natural resources is a challenge. Fisheries management and other natural resource management fields are just beginning to understand the contributions that social science can make. Armed with a strong interdisciplinary background, a supportive community, a strong will, and an open mind, a new generation of applied anthropologists may bring new perspectives and solutions to these complex and challenging fields.

NOTE

1. Several website URLs are listed in this article. Over time their accuracy will diminish, so readers will need to turn to search engines more frequently to find the resources noted.

REFERENCES CITED

Abbott-Jamieson, Susan, and Patricia M. Clay
   2006 Comparative Analysis in Federal Fisheries Management: Synchronic Community Assessments and Diachronic Predictions. Paper presented at the Annual Meeting of the Society for Anthropological Sciences, Savannah, February 22–26.
Acheson, James M.
   1981 Anthropology of Fishing. Annual Review of Anthropology 10:275–316.
Berkes, Fikret
   2006 From Community-Based Resource Management to Complex Systems: The Scale Issue and Marine Commons. Ecology and Society 11(1):45.
Browman, Howard I., and Konstantinos I. Stergiou, eds.
   2005 Politics and Socioeconomics of Ecosystem-Based Management of Marine Resources. Marine Ecology Progress Series 300:241–296.
Carroll, Matthew S., and Robert G. Lee.
   1990 Occupational Community and Identity Among Pacific Northwestern Loggers: Implications for Adapting to Economic Changes. *In* Community and Forestry: Continuities in the Sociology of Natural Resources. Robert G. Lee, Donald R. Field, and William R. Burch Jr., eds. Pp. 141–155. Boulder, CO: Westview Press.
Cordell, John, ed.
   1990 A Sea of Small Boats. Cambridge, MA: Cultural Survival.
Dalton, Michael
   2001 El Nino, Expectations, and Fishing Effort in Monterey Bay, California. Journal of Environmental Economics and Management 42:336–359.
Danowski, Fran
   1980 Fishermen's Wives: Coping with an Extraordinary Occupation. NOAA/Sea Grant Marine Bulletin 37. Kingston, RI: University of Rhode Island, Department of Sociology and Anthropology.
Davis, Anthony, and Conner Bailey
   1996 Common in Custom, Uncommon in Advantage: Common Property, Local Elites, and Alternative Approaches to Fisheries Management. Society and Natural Resources 9:251–265.
Davis, Dona L.
   1986 Occupational Community and Fishermen's Wives in a Newfoundland Fishing Village. Anthropology Quarterly 59(3):129–142.
Dixon, Richard D., Roger C. Lowery, James Sabella, and Marcus J. Hepburn
   1984 Fishermen's Wives: A Case Study of a Middle Atlantic Coastal Fishing Community. Sex Roles 10(1–2):33–52.
Dyer, Christopher L., and James R. McGoodwin, eds.
   1994 Folk Management in the World's Fisheries: Lessons for Modern Fisheries Management. Niwot, CO: University Press of Colorado.
Feeny, David, Susan Hanna, and A. F. McEvoy
   1996 Questioning the Assumptions of the "Tragedy of the Commons" Model of Fisheries. Land Economics 72(2):187–205.

Fricke, Peter

1985 Use of Sociological Data in the Allocation of Common Property Resources: A Comparison of Practices. Marine Policy 9(1):39–52.

Garrity-Blake, Barbara J.

1996 To Fish or Not to Fish: Occupational Transitions within the Commercial Fishing Community of Carteret County, NC. UNC-SG 96-06. Raleigh: North Carolina Sea Grant.

Gatewood, John B., and Bonnie J. McCay

1988 Job Satisfaction and the Culture of Fishing: A Comparison of Six New Jersey Fisheries. MAST/Maritime Anthropological Studies 1(2):103–128.

Gersuny, Carl, and John J. Poggie, Jr.

1973 The Uncertain Future of Fishing Families. The Family Coordinator 22(2):241–244.

Gilden, Jennifer D.

2005 Social Science in the Pacific Fishery Management Council Process. Portland, Oregon: Pacific Fishery Management Council. Electronic document, http://www.pcouncil.org/research/resdocs/sswp_final.pdf, accessed November 10, 2007.

Gilden, Jennifer D., and Flaxen D. L. Conway

2001 An Investment in Trust: Communication in the Commercial Fishing and Fisheries Management Communities. ORESU-G-01-004. Corvallis: Oregon Sea Grant.

Gilmore, Janet C.

1986 The World of the Oregon Fishboat: A Study in Maritime Folklife. Ann Arbor: UMI Research Press.

Hanna, Susan

1990 The Eighteenth Century English Commons: A Model for Ocean Management. Journal of Ocean and Shoreline Management 14:155–172.

Hanna, Susan, and Svein Jentoft

1996 Human Use of the Natural Environment: An Overview of Social and Economic Dimensions. In Rights to Nature: Ecological, Economic, Cultural and Political Principles of Institutions for the Environment. Susan Hanna, Carl Folke, and Karl-Goran Maler, eds. Pp. 35–56. Washington, DC: Island Press.

Hanna, Susan, and Courtland L. Smith

1993 Resolving Allocation Conflicts in Fishery Management. Society and Natural Resources 6(1):55–69.

Hillborn, Ray

2007 Moving to Sustainability by Learning from Successful Fisheries. Ambio 36(4):296–303.

Jentoft, Svein

1989 Fisheries Co-Management: Delegating Government Responsibility to Fishermen's Organizations. Marine Policy 13(2):137–154.

2000 The Community: A Missing Link of Fisheries Management. Marine Policy 24:53–60.

Jentoft, Svein, and Bonnie J. McCay

1995 User Participation in Fisheries Management: Lessons Drawn From International Experiences. Marine Policy 19(3):227–246.

Jentoft, Svein, Bonnie J. McCay, and Douglas C. Wilson

1998 Social Theory and Fisheries Co-Management. Marine Policy 22(4–5):423–436.

Lee, Robert G.

1989 Community Stability: Symbol or Social Reality? In Community Stability in Forest-Based Economies. Dennis C. LeMaster and John H. Beuter, eds. Pp. 36–48. Portland, OR: Timber Press.

McCay, Bonnie J.

1978 Systems Ecology, People Ecology and the Anthropology of Fishing Communities. Human Ecology 6:397–422.

McCay, Bonnie J., and James Acheson, eds.

1990 The Question of the Commons: The Culture and Ecology of Community Resources. Tucson: University of Arizona Press.

McCay, Bonnie J., Richard Apostle, and Carolyn F. Creed

1998 Individual Transferable Quotas, Co-Management, and Community. Fisheries 23(4):20–23.

Miller, Marc L., and John van Maasen
  1979 Boats Don't Fish, People Do: Some Ethnographic Notes on the Federal Management of Fisheries in Gloucester. Human Organization 38(4):377–385.

Pinkerton, Evelyn W.
  1995 Fisheries that Work: Sustainability Through Community-Based Management: A Report to the David Suzuki Foundation. Vancouver: David Suzuki Foundation.

Pinkerton, Evelyn W., ed.
  1989 Cooperative Management of Local Fisheries: New Directions for Improved Management and Community Development. Vancouver: University of British Columbia Press.

Pollnac, Richard B., Susan Abbott-Jamieson, Courtland Smith, Marc L. Miller, Patricia M. Clay, and Bryan Oles
  2006 Toward a Model for Fisheries Social Impact Assessment. Marine Fisheries Review 68(1–4):1–18.

Pollnac, Richard B., and Susan J. Littlefield
  1983 Sociocultural Aspects of Fisheries Management. Ocean Development and International Law Journal 12(3–4):209–246.

Ruddle, Kenneth
  1994 A Guide to the Literature on Traditional Community-Based Fishery Management in the Asia-Pacific Tropics. Fisheries Circular Number 869, FIPP/C869. Rome: Food and Agriculture Organization.

Scholz, Astrid, Kate Bonzon, Rod Fujita, Natasha Benjamin, Nicole Woodling, Peter Black, and Charles Steinback
  2004 Participatory Socioeconomic Analysis: Drawing on Fishermen's Knowledge for Marine Protected Area Planning in California. Marine Policy 28(4):335–349.

Sepez, Jennifer, Karma Norman, Amanda Poole, and Bryan Tilt
  2006 Fish Scales: Scale, and Method in Social Science Research for North Pacific and West Coast Fishing Communities. Human Organization 65:280–293.

Smith, Courtland L.
  1986 The Life Cycle of Fisheries. Fisheries 11(4):20–25.

Smith, S.
  1995 Social Implications of Changes in Fisheries Regulations for Commercial Fishing Families. Fisheries 20(7):24–26.

St. Martin, Kevin
  2001 Making Space for Community Resource Management in Fisheries. Annals of the Association of American Geographers 91(1):122–142.

van Willigen, John
  2002 Applied Anthropology: An Introduction. Westport, CT: Bergin and Garvey.

Wilson, James A.
  2006 Matching Social and Ecological Systems in Complex Ocean Fisheries. Ecology and Society 11(1):9.

Young, Michael D., and Bonnie J. McCay.
  1995 Building Equity, Stewardship, and Resilience into Market-Based Property Rights Systems. *In* Property Rights and the Environment: Social and Ecological Issues. Susan Hanna and Mohan Munasinghe, eds. Pp. 87–102. Washington, DC: World Bank.

PRACTICING ANTHROPOLOGY FROM WITHIN THE ACADEMY: COMBINING CAREERS

PHILIP D. YOUNG
University of Oregon

In this article, I use my own career as a lens through which to view the challenges of combining an academic career with that of a (part-time) practitioner of applied anthropology. My main focus is on the particular variety of practice known as international development. Based mostly on my own experiences both in and outside of academia, but with occasional references to what I know of the experiences of academic colleagues who have also done applied work, I offer advice to students who want an academic job and would also like to do applied anthropology of one sort or another. Lessons and advice are derived from three long-term projects in which I participated as a practitioner: Plan Guaymí (Panama), the Southern Manpower Development Project (SMDP—Sudan), and Development Strategies for Fragile Lands in Latin America and the Caribbean (DESFIL). I examine the challenges and rewards of combining an academic career in anthropology with work in the nonacademic world of the practitioner. I highlight contrasts between what is valued in academe and in the world of practice. Finally, I suggest a series of strategies for promotion and tenure. Keywords: international development, career advice, ethics, training

I see my task in this article as twofold: (1) to provide some insight, based mostly on my own experience, into the challenges and rewards of combining an academic career in anthropology with some forays into the nonacademic world of the practitioner of anthropology, in my case specifically, the world of international development;[1] and (2) to provide advice to students who are considering an academic career but wish to be part-time practitioners as well. Others who have combined careers may have had different experiences and thus would provide different advice. I can only tell what I know. When I began to do applied anthropology from an academic base in the mid-1970s, the road was still very bumpy, much more so than I realized at the time. Hopefully, the road is smoother now and will be more so in the future but, as Riall Nolan (2003) has observed, the disjuncture between academic and applied anthropology has lessened little in the past 30 years.

Is it possible to combine a career as an academic anthropologist with that of a practitioner? The short answer is yes, but some types of applied anthropology are easier to combine than others and you need to carefully consider this in making your choices. What you can do depends on many variables, among the most important of which are how your department and your college define "research" and where you publish your

NAPA BULLETIN 29, pp. 56–69. ISBN 9781405190152. © 2008 by the American Anthropological Association. DOI:10.1111/j.1556-4797.2008.00005.x

results. Most highly valued in the Academy are peer-reviewed publications; most highly valued in the practice of anthropology in the big wide world are positive results. You will likely find yourself living in two parallel worlds that only touch tentatively here and there. So perhaps your first decision needs to be whether you want to be a full-time practitioner or a part-time practitioner with an academic base. There is no better advice to be found that I know of than Riall Nolan's book *Anthropology in Practice* (2003) if you are considering a career as a full-time practitioner. It is well worth reading even if you only aspire to being a part-time practitioner because, in many ways, it is an insightful ethnography of the world of practice. If you are serious about being an academically based applied anthropologist of the type that also engages in practice, then I hope that some of what I have to tell you will help you to combine these careers.

MY BACKGROUND AS A PRACTITIONER IN BRIEF

None of the courses I took as an anthropology graduate student really prepared me for the practitioner part of my career. I learned by doing, and by making lots of mistakes along the way. Some were almost immediately self-evident; some were pointed out by others, usually by means of constructive criticism with the intention of being helpful; and there were probably still other errors of judgment of which I remained unaware and about which others remained silent. Hopefully there were not too many of the latter.

I did not start out to be an applied anthropologist. You might say I entered through the back door, and that was after I had been a tenured associate professor for five years. For the first ten years of my professional career my research was strictly that of an academic ethnologist, although some of my interests were those shared by applied anthropologists. But once inside the door, I found the particular variety of applied anthropology that I had stumbled into, international development, both challenging and rewarding. On returning from my first long-term venture into the world of practice, I added courses in applied anthropology to my teaching repertoire. With each of the next two long-term ventures—there have been only three in all, plus a few short-term consultancies—I honed my skills at teaching applied anthropology and something about the application of anthropological knowledge to the solution of contemporary human problems (that's how I define applied anthropology) became a part of every course I taught.

In all three of my long-term assignments as a practicing anthropologist, I took over positions in ongoing projects formerly occupied by nonanthropologists. I mention this because I think it may be unusual. In the first instance I replaced a former USAID employee (I never met him nor learned what his specialty was; only that he was not an anthropologist). In the second instance, I replaced an agronomist; and in the third, an economist. Anthropologists are versatile! The first and third positions were managerial; the second was a long-term consultancy (one year). The first and third were also in or focused on Latin America, my geographic area of specialization; the second was in sub-Saharan Africa, an area where my knowledge was based mainly on a single course I had taken as a graduate student.

For each of my long-term assignments, I had to request a leave of absence from the university. Such leaves must be approved by both the department head and the dean of the college. Leaves of absence are often approved for one year, two years is unusual, three years virtually unheard of in academe. My first leave was for two years, my second for the customary one year. For my third leave, I needed three years. I was granted two years, near the end of which my request for a third year was initially denied. That decision was subsequently (and in the nick of time) reversed, because of budgetary considerations (there was not enough money in the departmental budget to pay my salary if I returned that year). That first leave cost me a promotion to full professor, but I did get the promotion the following year because of a sympathetic department chair who believed I had deserved the promotion in the first place. It also cost me two years of retirement benefits because in my enthusiasm and naïveté I failed to negotiate any substitute for the retirement benefits that the university would not be paying into my account during my absence. None of my extended periods of practicing anthropology really counted for much in terms of my academic career in the eyes of some of my colleagues.

Plan Guaymí

My first experience in international development was that of director for a project whose short name was Plan Guaymí. I joined the project in October 1976 after it had been functioning for about 18 months and remained as project director through its scheduled termination date at the end of June 1978. It was labeled a nonformal education project and was intended to prepare the Ngöbe (formerly called Guaymí) indigenous people of western Panama for the rapid socioeconomic changes that would occur with the expected opening of a very large open pit copper mine in the middle of their territory. This was to be done by training Ngöbe as *promotores sociales* (social change agents) to work in their communities. (See Gjording 1991 for an account of the mining venture up to 1981; see Young and Bort 1999 for a recent update. As of late 2006, exploratory activities were in abeyance and the mine had not opened.) The project was carried out jointly between the Interamerican Development Institute ([IDI]; formerly Inter-American Literacy Foundation—IALF), a nonprofit NGO, and the Panamanian Ministry of Education (MOE, now MEDUCA).

The project was in trouble. The former project director had somehow made himself persona non grata with both the Panamanian government and the Ngöbe people, an almost impossible feat because the government and the Ngöbe were at odds with each other. After a ten-day consultancy in Panama, I was offered the job as project director. I asked for a couple of weeks to consider, for two reasons.[2] First, I needed to find out if I could get a leave from the university on very short notice. The fall term would begin in three weeks and I was scheduled to teach two classes. Second, I had ethical qualms about accepting the job (see below).

I was fortunate to have a sympathetic department chair, an archaeologist who saw value in applied work and agreed that this was a career opportunity for me. He approved my request for a two year leave of absence (without pay) and forwarded my request to the dean, a sociologist who also considered applied work a legitimate academic activity. My request was granted. I packed my bags and was off to IDI headquarters in Washington, DC for a week's briefing. By October of 1976 I was in Panama as the new project director of Plan Guaymí.

I quickly discovered three things. First, despite my reasonably fluent Spanish, I could not understand much of what was being discussed in the meetings of the Intra-Ministerial Committee that was charged with oversight and activity planning for the project. I found myself on the unfamiliar terrain of Spanish Acronymlandia. In self-defense, I wrote down as best I could the acronyms as I heard them and later asked others what they stood for. In most cases I got a translation, but in a few instances no one seemed to know exactly what the acronym stood for so I had to settle for an explanation of what the organization or unit labeled by the acronym did.

Second, I realized that the minutes of the meetings were not taken; thus there was no way to check discussions or decisions made at earlier meetings during the 18 months the project had been running before my arrival. I had to rely on someone's word, and when I asked more than one someone, I found that there was sometimes disagreement.

Third, and most problematic from the standpoint of efficient project management, I was informed that the Intra-Ministerial Committee, which consisted of the department heads of every department in the MOE, had to unanimously approve any decisions regarding activities or policies of the project. This explained why progress on project activities was often at a standstill, and I knew that somehow I had to get this changed (see below).

Among the lessons I learned from this project were the following:

- Fluency in the national language does not automatically convey understanding of organizational and interpersonal relationships.
- It is important to take careful notes in meetings, just as you would in the field. Meetings *are* an important part of the field context in an applied project.
- Managing a project is difficult and there is at least one crisis to be resolved every day.
- Something always goes wrong and, as project manager, you are responsible for fixing it.
- Starry-eyed idealists cannot successfully manage an international development project, or even be a successful team member; negotiation and compromise is the name of the game.
- In collaborating with a host country agency, it is imperative to recognize that the agency, too, and not just the intended beneficiary population, is a stakeholder in the process.
- Achieving project goals is dependent on amicable relations with key agency personnel, which in turn is dependent on an understanding of the political dynamics of the agency.

SMDP

My second adventure in international development was as a long-term consultant from July 1981 to August 1982 (one year or more is considered a long-term consultancy) on the Southern Manpower Development Project (SMDP), in the southern Sudan. This was a USAID project contracted to Development Alternatives, Inc. (DAI). My task was to provide guidance and recommendations for curriculum development and revision, and educational administration at the Yambio Institute of Agriculture (YIA), a two year training facility for agricultural extension agents in Yambio, a town in the southwesternmost corner of the southern Sudan. The overall project goal was to assess the current trained manpower resources in the southern Sudan, assess future needs, and provide training to meet those needs. This project was implemented during the interregnum between civil strife in the southern region. After what proved to be a difficult year, educational administration was improved and the entire first year curriculum was restructured to include a heavy in-the-field practicum component. The overall project did achieve results, as did projects of the UNDP and the GTZ in the area, all of which were quickly wiped out with the resumption of hostilities in 1983.

Among the lessons this experience taught me were the following:

- Reasonable fluency in the local lingua franca makes life easier. I know Spanish and was comfortable working in Latin America. Although English was one lingua franca in the southern Sudan, I spoke no Arabic, which was the other, and this was definitely a handicap.
- Anthropological training *does* make a difference (a lesson that my wife pointed out to me when I was feeling really frustrated and believed that I was accomplishing little or nothing).
- In the words of Chinua Achebe, "things fall apart" (1959). Shortly before my departure, the YIA closed for lack of funds and substantial indebtedness. Although the closure was supposed to be temporary, civil war in the southern Sudan resumed about a year and a half later and, to my knowledge, the YIA never reopened.

DESFIL

My third international development experience was as Senior Program Manager for Development Strategies for Fragile Lands in Latin America and the Caribbean (DESFIL), another USAID project contracted to DAI, with Tropical Research and Development (TRD), based in Gainesville, Florida, as a major subcontractor. I was based at DAI in the Washington, D.C., area, but made several trips to Latin America. The overall goal of the program was to work with USAID missions in selected LAC (Latin America and the Caribbean) countries to develop technologies and management strategies (e.g., agricultural, forestry, agroforestry, and agro–silvo–pastoral systems) for achieving sustainable use of fragile lands, which included steep slopes and tropical forests. Fragile lands make up about 80 percent of the land area of LAC. Many of the individual DESFIL projects managed by DAI had subcontractors in addition to TRD. This was a five year project and I took over as the manager in July 1989 and saw the project through to completion at the end of November 1991 and then stayed on as a DAI employee through June 1992.

In addition to reinforcing earlier lessons, this project taught me some things I had not learned on the previous two projects:

- Managing a program consisting of several separate (albeit related) projects is a much more complex and difficult task than managing a project.
- Making oral presentations to a room full of USAID personnel is an art that I did not master (and maybe never will) because where I saw complexities and talked about them, they wanted simplification and straightforward recommendations.
- USAID's view of how a conference or workshop should be organized and structured is different from that of the usual organization and structure of a scientific conference, and when USAID "observers" are present they do intrude and try to have you run things their way.

Much more could be said about each of these projects, so I hope that this brief background provides sufficient context for my advice, suggestions, and recommendations for those of you who are seriously contemplating the possibility of combining an academic career with a career as a practitioner.

TEACHING APPLIED ANTHROPOLOGY

In order to be really effective in teaching applied anthropology, you need some applied experience. But, as noted above, when you hold an academic position, except for short-term consulting, arranging for a long-term applied experience may not be easy and may not be viewed by your colleagues as the kind of anthropology that contributes to your professional advancement. There are ways to gain some experience as a graduate student (or even as an undergraduate). The most common way is the internship, which can be with any organization where you apply your anthropological knowledge and skills to further the projects and goals of the organization. Interns are sometimes paid, but most often this is voluntary work for nonprofit or other organizations with small budgets that provide social services. If your intent is to do your applied work in the field of international development, then you should try to serve an internship in an overseas location.

Most government agencies and international development organizations such as the World Bank or the Inter-American Development Bank (or other regional development banks), and for-profit firms whose contracts are mainly with these organizations, require considerable overseas experience and an overseas internship will help you to meet this requirement. To get even a short-term overseas consultancy you may need to show several years of overseas experience, and, of course, you will usually need to speak, with reasonable fluency, the language of the country. In countries where many languages are spoken, it is usually sufficient to speak the official lingua franca, but in some instances some knowledge of a minority language may be necessary. You can put together your total months or years of overseas experience from military service, field research, internships, field schools, Peace Corps service, and even short vacation visits. When I was hired by the IDI, a nonprofit NGO, I was told that the project I was to manage for them required five years of overseas experience, and I was three months shy of this, but they accepted this as close enough because I had a set of unique qualifications for the job. I had done my doctoral research with the indigenous people in Panama who were the recipients of this project's development activities, I had some understanding of the Panamanian bureaucracy, and I spoke reasonably fluent Spanish. But this was a managerial position; I was to be the project director, and at the time my only managerial experience had been that of supervising students in anthropological field schools. This helped, but more useful would have been a basic course in business management, and I had never taken one. By the time I finished this assignment I had spent another 20 months overseas. This made me well qualified for future overseas assignments.

ON ETHICS IN PRACTICE AND IN THE ACADEMY

Academically based anthropologists, when conducting conventional ethnographic research, certainly face ethical dilemmas. Much has been written about this. Practitioners are likely to face ethical dilemmas that are different from those faced in conventional research, that are more frequent, more complex, and consequently more difficult to resolve. Little has been written about this. (See Nolan 2003:158–166 for a discussion of some types of ethical dilemmas faced by practitioners and some contrasts with those faced by academic researchers; see, e.g., Appell 1978, Caplan 2003, Cassell and Jacobs 1987, Fluehr-Lobban 1991, Meskell and Pels 2005, and Rynkiewich and Spradley 1976, for cases of ethical dilemmas faced by academic anthropologists doing ethnographic research.)

Be prepared to confront ethical dilemmas on a daily basis in the world of practice. Most of these will be small, but some will be of great magnitude and import. In either case, you will have to quickly decide on a course of action. This will invariably involve weighing costs and benefits to intended beneficiaries, other stakeholders, and the future of the project itself against the standards established by your profession and your own standards. It will involve wrestling with your conscience and your own principles and deciding whether to take a rigid moral stance (which may cost you your job) or to engage in negotiation and compromise in order to achieve the best possible outcome for all concerned. And keep in mind that this will always be a judgment call; there is no right answer. The world of international development is no place for uncompromising idealists but it can be rewarding for realistic, dedicated practitioners.

To illustrate, I faced two large ethical dilemmas (and many small ones, not recounted here) with Plan Guaymí. The first was whether to accept the job as project director in the first place. I knew, after a ten-day consulting trip to Panama, that the project was in trouble and that some things about the organization, management, and implementation activities of the project could not be changed. I knew that the Ngöbe (Guaymí) had not been adequately consulted before implementation and that their views were not being adequately considered, especially by the MEDUCA, as the project progressed; this despite the fact that two young Ngöbe men were working in the project office in Panama City as part of the IDI staff. I did not have a lot of time to decide. I reasoned that (at the time) I knew more about the Ngöbe and their culture—about their beliefs, practices, and their experiences of the outside world that had shaped their attitudes—than anyone else except the Ngöbe themselves. I reasoned that if I did not accept the position, someone with lesser understanding of the Ngöbe condition would occupy it. (At the time there were no Ngöbe qualified for this position. There are now.) I reasoned that I could serve better than anyone else as a communication link, an intermediary, between the Ngöbe and the various agencies involved in the project: IDI as grant holder, MEDUCA as counterpart cooperative agency, and USAID Panama, through its Special Projects Office, as U.S. government agency to whom quarterly progress reports and accounts of expenditures had to be submitted by IDI. Based on these considerations, I accepted the job, with the hope, in the end only partially realized, that I could turn the project in a direction more responsive to Ngöbe concerns and needs.

The second large ethical dilemma presented itself a few months after I began my task as project director. Project activities were not proceeding on schedule and I reported this to the Director of IDI. I was then asked to submit a detailed report to the Chairman of the IDI Board of Directors on the status of the project, the problems I saw, and my recommendations for remedial action to speed up implementation activities. I submitted a long list of problems and my proposed solutions. The IDI Board Chairman, a former U.S. ambassador to Panama, and an old friend of the minister of education, flew down from Washington, D.C., and arranged a meeting with the minister, which he and I would attend, along with the heads of all departments in MEDUCA, all of whom were members of the Intra-Ministerial Committee charged with oversight of the project.

During a premeeting discussion he made it plain that it would not be possible to make all of my recommended changes. For example, I had recommended that ties with MEDUCA be severed and that the Department of Indian Affairs within the Ministry of Government and Justice become the national cooperating agency. I was told this would not be possible, for political reasons. As we talked, it became clear that several of my recommendations were unlikely to be accepted by MEDUCA and, although nothing was said explicitly, it was clear that if I was to continue as project director I would have to accept many compromises. The alternative would be to resign. The board chair agreed with my assessment that a key problem was the unwieldy Intra-Ministerial Committee, each member of which had veto power over project decisions. I suggested that an individual ministry employee be appointed as my true counterpart to be jointly responsible with me for project decisions, and I named my candidate. He agreed that this would likely solve many of the project's problems, especially those of timely implementation of project activities and that he would see what he could do in this regard.

The board chair had a private talk with the minister before the meeting. No one at the meeting knew that it had been scripted, not even me. Exact words cannot be recalled after 30 years, but here is what happened. The minister and the IDI Board Chair exchanged formal greetings. At the minister's request, I provided a brief project report, emphasizing the positive, as I had been coached by the board chair. The minister then called on the department heads of Curriculum Development, and of Non-Formal Education, the two units that had been working most closely with the project (and that had been responsible for most of the delays in implementation activities), to say a few words. He then asked

Ms. X, who had been working closely with us but was not a department head, to speak.

A certain amount of puzzlement appeared on the faces of some of the department heads. She spoke briefly about how hard we had all been working to make the project a success. The board chair was then asked for his thoughts. He was very diplomatic in his choice of words but he said, among other things, that we all know that a large committee was not a particularly effective way to run a project. He spoke in generalities. He did not mention the appointment of an individual counterpart or the abolishment of the Intra-Ministerial Committee. This time it was I who had the puzzled look on my face. When he finished, the minister let there be silence for a few moments while he appeared to be thinking about all that had been said. Then he spoke, and his words I do remember vividly, although the following is probably not an exact translation from the Spanish. "The Intra-Ministerial Committee is hereby abolished. Ms. X is hereby appointed to serve as Dr. Young's ministerial counterpart and will be jointly responsible with Dr. Young for project decisions. This meeting is ended." I was astounded, but pleased. The ministerial department heads were shocked and angered, but powerless to do anything directly. A minister in Panama has absolute authority to make decisions and these may not be challenged by anyone in his ministry. Usually much of this decision-making authority is delegated to others. But when the minister pronounces, everyone, like it or not, must obey. (In the months ahead there were some unsuccessful attempts to sabotage the project.) I did not resign. My ethical dilemma had been resolved.

SKILLS AND GUIDANCE FOR A COMBINED CAREER

A solid foundation in ethnographic methods of data collection and analysis, methods of cross-cultural comparison, cultural sensitivity, standard ethnographic area courses, theory courses, in effect, just about all the courses that one takes in an anthropology graduate program in the normal course of preparing for a career as an academic anthropologist will be useful and important, some more important than others, in preparing for your parallel career as a practitioner. But more diverse knowledge and skills will be needed, only some of which are likely to be found in university course work. Often, experience is the best teacher in applied work.

Computer skills are essential these days in academe as well as in the world of practice. But of course everyone these days already has at least basic skills in the use of computer software by the time they get to college, or at least by the time they finish undergraduate work.

You should have at a minimum a course in statistics for social scientists, and a working knowledge of a statistical software program like SPSS. This is a requirement in most graduate anthropology programs these days. Now you may say that a major strength of anthropology is qualitative research and analysis, and you would be right. But even if you never have to do any quantitative analysis yourself, you need to be able to understand the work of others who do use quantitative analysis. International development work is always done by a team. You may not have to crunch any numbers yourself, but you do need to have some understanding of what other members of the team, particularly economists, are doing.

As an academic, you may not have many opportunities to work on long-term projects as a practitioner. Short-term consulting is easier to fit into an academic schedule. This being the case, it would be wise to learn the techniques of what is called Rapid Rural Appraisal (RRA) and Participatory Rural Appraisal (PRA). This is not likely to be included in a standard course on ethnographic field methods (unless it is being taught by someone who has done international development work, which is unlikely). A good source to begin with is R. Chambers (1992). Sources that can be found online are Chapter 8 of the FAO *Marketing Research and Information Systems* (Crawford 1997) at http://www.fao.org/docrep/W3241E/w3241e09.htm. Although oriented toward marketing research for agriculture, it provides a good summary. A good source on the limitations of rapid appraisal methods can be found at http://www.iisd.org/casl/CASLGuide/Guide-Purpose.htm.

I would also recommend a course in economics—introductory, micro, or development economics—if available on your campus. A basic business management or accounting course will also be useful, anything that teaches you basic budgeting and accounting practices. All such introductory courses these days are likely to contain materials on how to use spreadsheet software.

International development projects are always done by teams. Even the evaluations of such projects are done by teams. It is important to understand the jargon of the other disciplines represented on the team in order to minimize miscommunication. Economics, for example, has its own jargon just like anthropology. This was emphatically brought home to me when I was working on the DESFIL program and I proposed an *optimal* sustainability model that required the conjuncture of three variables: ecology, economics, and cultural practices. A DAI economist told me I could not do this. When I asked why, he replied that in economics, optimality refers specifically to the best balance or fit between two and only two variables.

Language training is essential if you intend to do your practicing in overseas locations. Two years of a language other than English is mandatory anyway for a B.A. degree. But you should choose your world region early on and take enough courses in the most useful language of the region to become reasonably fluent in reading, writing, speaking, and comprehension. Two years just does not do it unless you have a genius facility for language learning.

Negotiate a program with your advisor, and your doctoral committee if you are post-M.A., that will be tailored to meet your future needs in your combined careers. And of course a step prior to this is to choose a graduate program where you can do this. There are now several anthropology departments in the United States that offer at least an M.A. in applied anthropology and these are your best bets. You can find a list of current applied and practice oriented programs in the United States and Canada on the Society for Applied Anthropology's web site at http://www.sfaa.net/sfaaorgs.html.

Choose the research topic for your Ph.D. with your future applied work in mind. Realize that while it is true that a Ph.D. provides little advantage over an M.A. for full-time practitioners outside the academy (Nolan 2003), you must have a Ph.D. to get an academic position.

STRATEGIES FOR PROMOTION AND TENURE

In seeking an academic position, the job interview stage is when you should inquire about the institution's and the department's standards for promotion and tenure. Some departments have written standards. Others do not, and in these cases answers from different potential colleagues may vary. Be aware that academe is a conservative closed society with its own definition of what constitutes professional accomplishments. The definition varies from one university to the next and from one university personnel committee to the next, but within a narrow range, which usually does not place a high value on applied work, or at least not on certain types of applied work. If the department places little or no value on applied activities and you are offered the job, attempt to negotiate the terms for promotion and tenure as a part of your written contract. If the terms are not negotiable and you have no reasonable alternative to accepting the position (i.e., you have no other firm offers), then at the outset you should formulate a strategy for meeting the promotion and tenure standards of the department that may still permit some practitioner activities. And before you request a leave of absence to work as a practicing anthropologist, be sure to check again to determine whether the specific applied work away from the university is going to count for anything in the eyes of your academic colleagues, especially if you are as yet untenured.

As the number of anthropology Ph.D.s has continued to grow faster than the number of available academic jobs, more publications are expected than ever before when you are being considered for tenure. And while securing an academic position has become more competitive, as has promotion and tenure, the attitude in academe toward applied anthropology has not changed very much in the past 35 years. Unless you choose an applied specialty that is considered legitimate research in your department and at your university, the rewards of doing applied work from an academic base are likely to be more personal than professional. Some types of applied anthropology are much easier to combine with an academic career than is international development. Medical anthropology and nutritional anthropology are two examples. This is because the work you do in these specialties is considered legitimate research within the academy, and much or all of this kind of applied anthropology can be done without the need to temporarily leave your academic position. Some tracts within the rapidly expanding subfields of environmental anthropology and the anthropology of tourism are two more applied specialties that usually fit more or less comfortably within an academic career setting. As long as you do these kinds of applied work from within the academy it will certainly be counted as research, but if you take a leave for an extended period to work for an NGO or a for-profit consulting firm, your work may not be seen in the same light. When it comes tenure time, some of your colleagues may not see your work as a practitioner as real research, even though you may have done essentially the same kind of work that was grant funded.

Applied work in international development, on the other hand, which essentially means working on projects of directed culture change that will hopefully have results for the stakeholders that are beneficial and sustainable, is somehow not seen as falling within the normal parameters of what the academy considers research. It is also the kind of applied anthropology that academic granting agencies are not interested in funding, so if you want to do it you will have to periodically take leaves of absence from your academic job, as I did. And while this may not place your academic position completely in jeopardy, be prepared to have it slow down the long journey to a full professorship. I did not begin my international development work until several years after I became a tenured associate professor. This was not a case of prior planning on my part, but it would be wise to consider that maybe it should be on your part. Even short-term consulting trips may be difficult to fit into an academic schedule.

You have a chance for promotion and tenure only if you are also a publishing scholar. An important way to further your academic career is to do what it takes to turn as much as possible of the "gray" literature—all those reports that you produce as a practitioner outside the academy—into papers that can be presented at professional meetings, and published in peer-reviewed professional journals or as book chapters. I did not do much of this, but hindsight, as we all know, generates really good advice.

As Nolan (2003) points out, the writing styles of academe and the world of practice are quite different. This is because the audience and the expectations are different. Most academic writing begins with the sacred abstract. An academic audience expects considerable detail and a theoretical discussion, and is familiar with the jargon of the discipline. Academic writing often lacks any explicit focus on real world problems and recommendations for solving them. These characteristics of academic writing Nolan calls a "ceremonial style" that is widespread in academe (2003:154).

Most writing in the world of practice begins with the equally sacred executive summary, which concisely states the problem or issue, the major findings, and recommendations. A practitioner's audience is most often made up of intelligent professionals and policy makers from a variety of disciplines, who appreciate—indeed demand—succinct, clear writing. They expect a clear presentation of the problem or issue, the inclusion of only those details that are directly relevant to the problem, a highly focused analysis, and clear, persuasive recommendations.

Realize that the worst case scenario may be that you must postpone applied work until after you have been promoted and tenured, that is, if you wish to continue in your academic position. But on the bright side, realize also that in carrying out academic research at your research site(s) you have the opportunity to lay the groundwork for future applied projects based on what you learn about community needs and desires and the extent to which collaborative effort on the part of community members is likely.

CONCLUSION

With some notable exceptions, combining an academic career in an anthropology department with a parallel career as a practitioner, even if part time, is no easy task. It involves mastering two writing styles, often the mastery of a second or even a third language, developing skills often not taught in anthropology departments, and survival in institutional settings with radically different expectations and criteria for judging success. Being a part-time practitioner can be personally rewarding, but may slow down professional advancement in your academic career. Caution is in order if you attempt to combine careers, except perhaps in a minor way, before you have passed that big hurdle in academe, promotion to associate professor with tenure, which takes six years in a normal academic career trajectory. But, again, much depends on what specialty in applied anthropology you are pursuing, and also whether your appointment is in an anthropology department or some other university department or school. Medical anthropology, nutritional anthropology, and some types of environmental anthropology are currently more amenable to a combined career in an anthropology department than is practice in the field of international development, and these specialties also fit well in practice-oriented academic units such as a School of Public Health or an Environmental Studies program. An International Affairs or International Studies program may be a better base for a combined career and smooth the road to promotion and tenure if your applied work is in international development.

NOTES

1. Throughout this article, when I use *anthropology* or *anthropologist(s)*, I am referring only to cultural anthropology and cultural anthropologists. There are academically based biological anthropologists, archaeologists, and anthropological linguists who combine academic careers with practice, but some of the problems of making their career combinations successful are different and often less difficult. Space does not permit elaboration here. I would note that the distinction between some varieties of biological anthropology and cultural anthropology can become quite fuzzy at times, especially in the applied arena.

2. I was not married at the time, so I did not have to consult with a spouse before making a decision.

REFERENCES CITED

Achebe, Chinua
   1959 Things Fall Apart. New York: Astor-Honor.
Appell, George N.
   1978 Ethical Dilemmas in Anthropological Inquiry: A Case Book. Waltham, MA: Crossroads Press.
Caplan, Pat, ed.
   2003 The Ethics of Anthropology: Debates and Dilemmas. London: Routledge.
Cassell, Joan, and Sue-Ellen Jacobs, eds.
   1987 Handbook on Ethical Issues in Anthropology. Washington, DC: American Anthropological Association.
Chambers, Robert
   1992 Rural Appraisal: Rapid, Relaxed, and Participatory. IDS Discussion Paper 311. Sussex: Institute of Development Studies.

Crawford, I. M.

  1997 Marketing Research and Information Systems, Chapter 8. FAO Rome: Food and Agriculture Organization.

Fluehr-Lobban, Carolyn, ed.

  1991 Ethics and the Profession of Anthropology: Dialogue for a New Era. Philadelphia: University of Pennsylvania Press.

Gjording, Chris N.

  1991 Conditions Not of Their Choosing: The Guaymí Indians and Mining Multinationals in Panama. Washington, DC: Smithsonian Institution Press.

Meskell, Lynn, and Peter Pels, eds.

  2005 Embedding Ethics. Wenner-Gren Foundation for Anthropological Research. Oxford: Berg.

Nolan, Riall W.

  2003 Anthropology in Practice: Building a Career Outside the Academy. Boulder, CO: Lynne Rienner.

Rynkiewich, Michael A., and James P. Spradley

  1976 Ethics and Anthropology: Dilemmas in Fieldwork. New York: Wiley.

Young, Philip D., and John R. Bort

  1999 Ngöbe adaptive responses to globalization in Panama. *In* Globalization and the Rural Poor in Latin America. William M. Loker, ed. Pp. 111–136. Boulder: Lynne Rienner.

MOVING PAST PUBLIC ANTHROPOLOGY AND DOING COLLABORATIVE RESEARCH

LUKE ERIC LASSITER

Marshall University Graduate College

This article is about moving past the debates and arguments concerning public anthropology and how students can realize public engagement via collaborative research (i.e., between and among researchers and local communities of collaborators). I suggest that students should be aware of at least the basics of the current debates surrounding public anthropology; that they should appreciate, as many have argued before, that these debates represent only a point of departure in a much larger anthropological project; and finally, that although students can engage in applied, publicly oriented work (regardless of what you may call it) in many different ways, collaborative research practice presents a special opportunity to do so. I thus begin with a very brief statement about moving past public anthropology, follow this with some of my own ideas about collaborative ethnography and public engagement, and suggest some general advice for doing collaborative research. Keywords: public anthropology, collaborative research, collaborative ethnography, applied anthropology

This article is about moving past the debates and arguments concerning public anthropology and how students can realize public engagement via collaborative research (i.e., between and among researchers and local communities of collaborators). I should admit right up front, though, that as I was originally asked to write about public anthropology for this volume, I struggled for quite some time about exactly what advice I would offer within the context of this larger NAPA Bulletin, crafted to help students navigate careers in applied anthropology. My dilemma had less to do with the sometimes rocky relationship between public and applied anthropology (see Stull 2006)—although that was certainly a factor—and more to do with my own struggle to place myself and my work under the subject heading about which I had been asked to write. While I have indeed argued in previous writings for a more publicly engaged anthropology (see, e.g., Lassiter 2005b), and have been a participant in discussions about public/engaged anthropology (see, e.g., Lassiter 2005c), I find that most of my ideas do not fit all that well within the now dominant discourse on public anthropology (see, e.g., Borofsky 2006). Moreover, my focus on the local (see, e.g., Lassiter 2003), expressive culture (see, e.g., Lassiter 2004b), collaborative ethnography (Lassiter 2005a), and pedagogy (see, e.g., Lassiter 2006)—as well as my "academic applied research" (Erwin 2000:2–4), which includes practice such as consulting for archives and museums, working for and administering local nonprofits, and conducting evaluation research (see, e.g., Lassiter 1998a, 1999a; Lassiter and Heaton 2006; respectively)—often seems distant from these prevailing conversations.

NAPA BULLETIN 29, pp. 70–86. ISBN 9781405190152. © 2008 by the American Anthropological Association. DOI:10.1111/j.1556-4797.2008.00006.x

Of course, I could have easily settled my dilemma by abandoning this writing project altogether (which I considered several times) or writing on something completely different from public anthropology and submitting that (which I considered many times over). But after much thought, I decided that perhaps the ambiguity of my position vis-à-vis public anthropology might resonate with those coming of age during this time, and that I might have something to offer: namely, I think that students should be aware of at least the basics of the current debates surrounding public anthropology; that they should appreciate, as many have argued before, that these debates represent only a point of departure in a much larger anthropological project; and finally, that although students can engage in applied, publicly oriented work (regardless of what you may call it) in many different ways, collaborative research practice presents a special opportunity to do so. I thus begin with a very brief statement about moving past public anthropology, follow this with some of my own ideas about collaborative ethnography and public engagement, and suggest some general advice for doing collaborative research.

MOVING PAST PUBLIC ANTHROPOLOGY

In recent years, "public anthropology" has become one of the many labels used to describe a growing and ever-more ubiquitous concern with anthropological relevance, public engagement, and action. While there is little agreement about just what exactly "public anthropology" is (Purcell 2000), it nevertheless has come to have many different and overlapping meanings. In its most commonly cited sense, public anthropology can be a kind of public scholarship, one that more universally enlists anthropology and anthropologists in a larger stream of public issues, concerns, and debates; cultivates a more aggressive public presence through print and other media; and enlarges public outreach, which may or may not be meant to influence public policy (see, e.g., Borofsky 1999, 2006; Eriksen 2006; Lamphere 2003). This kind of public engagement is similar to "public ethnography," which more directly engages ethnographic research and writing "with the critical social issues of our time" (Tedlock 2005:473; cf. MacClancy 2002; Sanjek 2004); and "public archaeology," which mobilizes the public benefits of archaeological research in museums, schools, governmental and other public institutions (see, e.g., Little 2002; Merriman 2002). In another but closely related sense, public anthropology may also imply an amplification of action or activist anthropology, a "public interest anthropology" that challenges the theory/practice divide; reconfigures an anthropological praxis established on equity and social justice; and augments moral, ethical, and political action, which, again, may or may not be meant to influence public policy (see, e.g., Sanday 1976, 1998; cf. Basch et al. 1999; Hill and Baba 1999). In this same vein, this practice may employ a kind of participatory action research that plants roots in locality, and assembles cooperative cocitizenships and coactivisms built on the counderstandings emergent in the collaborative research partnerships between and among anthropologists and local publics (see, e.g., Lassiter 2001a, 2003, 2005b; cf. Checker and Fishman 2004).

Obviously, the issues revolving around public anthropology—whether called "public interest anthropology," "public archaeology," "public ethnography," or just "engaged anthropology"—are very closely aligned with applied and practicing anthropology (see Lamphere 2004).[1] After all, they all draw from the same sources of inspiration: Franz Boas, Ruth Benedict, and Margaret Mead are a few oft-cited examples. Given this, though, many applied and practicing anthropologists argue that many of those who espouse a public anthropology are ignoring and usurping the important role that applied anthropology has long played in our field (see, e.g., Singer 2000). Past SfAA president Donald D. Stull, for example, points out that

> anthropology newsletters, listservs, and letters to editors are rife with hand wringing about how, despite the growing public fascination with things anthropological, no one pays any attention to anthropologists. Invariably, there are reports that Margaret Mead has left the building. . . . I disagree profoundly with the very premise of such arguments. None here [i.e., SfAA members] need to be told that anthropologists and kindred social scientists are actively engaged in public policies and actions. [Stull 2005:2]

Barbara Rylko-Bauer and colleagues (2006) echo this sentiment, noting that while "recent movements toward a more public anthropology have done a useful service for the general discipline" (186), "critiques grounded in labeling and othering or those based on dismissal of large portions of anthropologically informed work and erasure of disciplinary history are counterproductive, because they overlook significant areas of creative accomplishment" (187). They suggest that instead of worrying about the differences between applied/practicing and public anthropology—as some anthropologists apparently have (see, e.g., Wickens and Grant 2005),

> a meaningful convergence of methodologically sound, critical, reflexive, and engaged anthropology—a convergence that builds on and learns from the extensive past experiences of putting anthropology to use—will free us up to focus on differences that actually do matter in the real world: the compelling divides that separate those who have from those who do not, those who are honored from those who are stigmatized, those wielding disproportionate power from those with limited agency and voice, and those who are central from those who are marginalized. [Rylko-Bauer et al. 2006:187]

I think this is particularly useful advice for moving past public anthropology—especially because such divisions between public and applied or practicing anthropology are increasingly becoming less pronounced (if they ever were that relevant; see Lassiter 2001a). For contemporary students of anthropology, this seems truer now than ever before (cf. Nader 2001).

Les Field and Richard Fox argue in *Anthropology Put to Work* (2007) that such divisions and the recent calls for a public anthropology are out of touch with contemporary practice. Field and Fox point out that the disintegration of such divisions—such as that between "pure" and "applied" research—has already happened, mainly because the contemporary work conditions of anthropology require an ever-expanding range of conceptual and practical expertise. Discussions about singling out this or that anthropology are increasingly irrelevant to the latest generation of anthropologists, especially as the dichotomies between theory and practice—long prevalent in the United States but less so in other parts of the world (see Nader 2000)—now invoke less meaning than they have in the past (see Bennett 1996). Students today, then, must be prepared to be expert theoretical, applied, public, and practicing anthropologists all at the same time, no matter where their career trajectories take them, in or out of academia.

Simply put, rather than worrying about which side of the argument on which you fall, or more precisely, rigidly demarcating what you do as applied, public, practicing or academic anthropology, students should be charting, as *anthropologists*, how best to connect with the central questions and problems of a larger anthropological project (Lamphere 2004:432)—questions such as, to borrow from Rylko-Bauer and colleagues (2006:186) again, "How do we operationalize the goals of addressing and ameliorating social problems? How do we translate knowledge successfully into pragmatic action? Which strategies work?"

One of the ways we can engage such questions is through collaborative research, to which I now turn.

COLLABORATIVE RESEARCH

While many of the prevailing arguments about public anthropology have envisioned theorizing, problematizing, and engaging multivariate "publics" on a grand scale, my own vision for public engagement is more modest. Only a very few of us will ever have the opportunity to write widely read books or engage in activisms that have far-ranging effects on the public at large. But most of us, faculty, students, and practitioners alike, will have the opportunity to more systematically involve the various publics with whom we work in collaborative research partnerships, many of which will transpire on a local level.

Applied anthropologists have written a great deal about collaborative partnerships between researchers and local communities, and offer many exemplary models for doing this kind of work (see, e.g., Austin 2004; LeCompte et al. 1999; Stull and Schensul 1987). Collaborative research can have a variety of names, including "community-based research," "action research," "participatory action research," or "participatory community research" (Wali 2006:6). Although the various labels for collaborative research may denote a wide and diverse range of applications, and implement collaboration to varying degrees, the "underlying spirit is that of working, learning, and moving toward positive social change together" (Wali 2006:6).

My own interests along these lines have focused on doing and writing *collaborative ethnography*—a very specific kind of ethnography that builds on the cooperative relationships already present in the ethnographic research process (i.e., between ethnographers and informants/consultants) and endeavors to engender texts that are more readable, relevant, and applicable to local communities of ethnographic collaborators (i.e., local publics). While I have in previous works outlined the relationships between collaborative ethnography and discussions of public and applied anthropology (see, e.g., Lassiter 2005b), in this article, I briefly introduce what I see as some of the key attributes of collaborative ethnography, with particular emphasis on how students can engage in collaborative ethnography as applied and public practice. In this section I will build on my most recent work, *The Chicago Guide to Collaborative Ethnography* (Lassiter 2005a), and briefly describe some of the potentials and problems of collaborative ethnography.

To start, a definition. In *The Chicago Guide to Collaborative Ethnography*, I define collaborative ethnography as

> an approach to ethnography that *deliberately* and *explicitly* emphasizes collaboration at every point in the ethnographic process, without veiling it—from project conceptualization, to fieldwork, and, especially, through the writing process. Collaborative ethnography invites commentary from our consultants and seeks to make that commentary overtly part of the ethnographic text as it develops. In turn, this negotiation is reintegrated back into the fieldwork process itself. Importantly, the process yields texts that are co-conceived or cowritten with local communities of collaborators and consider multiple audiences outside the confines of academic discourse, including local constituencies. [Lassiter 2005a:16]

Collaborative ethnography implies more than what this brief definition might at first glance suggest. In the *Chicago Guide*, I argue that collaborative ethnography rests on an understanding of the historical and theoretical trajectories of collaborative research (see Lassiter 2005a:1–75); and importantly, is founded on four main commitments:

1. ethical and moral responsibility to ethnographic consultants—whereby moral and ethical commitments between researcher(s) and research participant(s) frame the contours of many ethnographic projects;
2. honesty about the fieldwork process—whereby the ethnographic fieldwork experience (including that of both the ethnographer[s] and interlocutor[s]) is honestly discussed, explored, and evaluated within the context of collaborative research partnerships;
3. accessible and dialogic writing—whereby the ethnographic account not only represents diverse experiences and voices, but is clearly written, free from the highly specialized discourse of the academy, so that ethnographic consultants can actually read, engage, and respond to ethnographic texts; and subsequently,
4. collaborative reading, writing, and co-interpretation of ethnographic texts with consultants—whereby ethnographer(s) and research participant(s) work together (via, for example, focus groups, community forums, editorial boards, ethnographer/consultant research and writing teams) to co-interpret ethnographic representations as they develop and evolve. [see Lassiter 2005a:77–154]

Such collaboratively based commitments are not the final step in practicing collaborative research and practice, however. These cocommitments have the potential to establish a foundation for community-based collaborative action as well, where ethnographers and consultants choose to work together to make a difference in their local communities via the coproduction of ethnography. As a kind of participatory action research, I thus believe that collaborative ethnography has something to offer "the many kinds of public and activist efforts that have long abounded in our field" (Lassiter 2005a:154). (I return to this point below.)

As I stress in the *Chicago Guide,* this particular vision for collaborative ethnography "may be appropriate for neither all researchers nor all types of ethnographic projects" (Lassiter 2005a:xi). In reality, our moral and ethical commitments to our ethnographic collaborators may take us in very different directions, where the coproduction of texts is secondary to other more pressing community-based issues and concerns (see Lassiter 2004a:8). Collaborative ethnography, though, is often most appropriate when dealing with issues of voice and representation—such as, in my own research, when documenting American Indian song traditions (see, e.g., Lassiter 1998b; Lassiter et al. 2002; Kotay et al. 2004; Horse and Lassiter 1998, 1999) or redressing the representation of African Americans in the famous Middletown studies literature (see, e.g., Lassiter 2004c; Lassiter et al. 2004; Papa and Lassiter 2003). Other recent examples include Robin Ridington and Dennis Hastings's *Blessing for a Long Time* (1997), in which an anthropologist and a tribal historian chronicle for the Omaha people, using Omaha conventions of storytelling, the history, meaning, and contemporary significance of the venerable Sacred Pole; Alison K. Brown and Laura Peers's *Pictures Bring Us Messages* (2006), in which Brown and Peers cointerpret with members of the Kainai Nation the repatriation of Kainai images from the University of Oxford's Pitt Rivers Museum; Cedric N. Chatterley and colleagues *"I Was Content and Not Content"* (2000), in which researchers document along with consultant Linda Lord the closing of the poultry plant in which Lord worked; and Laurie Thorp's *Pull of the Earth* (2006), in which Thorp and the teachers and students of a local elementary school together recount the story of a school garden and its transformative effects on their school and everyday lives.

Such projects, and others like them that also struggle within collaborative research frameworks, illustrate that there are many and diverse visions for constructing a collaborative ethnography—which actually may fall under a host of other labels, including, to name a few, dialogic editing (see, e.g., Feld 1987), reciprocal ethnography (see, e.g., Lawless 1992), collaborative biography or life history (see, e.g., Rios and Sands 2000), collaborative oral history (see, e.g., Rouverol 2003), and action, participatory, or cooperative inquiry (see, e.g., Heron 1996; Heron and Reason 1997).

Regardless of what you call it, though, collaborative ethnography can be extremely challenging (cf. Lawless 2000). For students who might want to do this kind of collaborative research as part of their larger applied or publicly engaged anthropological practice or both, it is important to recognize that any such venture requires constant negotiation—moral, ethical, political and otherwise (see Brettell 1996). As a matter of course, "our key consultants have visions, agendas, and expectations, and so do we" (Lassiter 2005a:141). Negotiating these diverse visions, agendas, and expectations is the real challenge of collaborative ethnography. I offer several negotiations from my own collaborative research in the *Chicago Guide* (see, e.g., Lassiter 2005a:88–97), but different ethnographers deal with these dialogic processes differently, incorporating (and experimenting with) collaborative research and writing to varying degrees (cf. Lavie with Hajj and Rouse 1993; Marcus and Mascarenhas 2005; Rappaport 2005). Ethnographer and oral historian Alicia Rouverol, for example, describes a point of disagreement with consultant Linda Lord in researching and writing "*I Was Content and Not Content*": *The Story of Linda Lord and the Closing of Penobscot Poultry* (Chatterley et al. 2000) thus:

> Our key area of disagreement . . . was in the question of what businesses owe communities when they shut down. I believe that some sort of restitution is in order when long-time businesses close and leave a community that is significantly dependent on that industry for its livelihood. Linda believes that businesses do not necessarily owe a community anything when they leave. We chose to include in the book's edited interviews our exchange on this point, to draw attention to our differing perspectives. [Rouverol 2003:66–67]

Rouverol included these exchanges, she writes, "to show the dynamic of our collaborative exchange, to make plain our respective interpretations, and to suggest that meaning forged through dialogue is not necessarily arrived at through agreement and shared perspectives" (Rouverol 2000:72–73). Other ethnographers have chosen to deal similarly with the divergent visions, agendas, and expectations inherent to collaborative research and writing, such as including consultant responses to the manuscript in a final chapter or epilogue (see, e.g., Stacey 1991), soliciting consultant-written contributions (see, e.g., Field 2008), inviting community-wide reviews (see, e.g., Foley 1995, 2002), or working consultant commentary back into the text as it develops (see, e.g., Hinson 2000). Collaborative ethnography, then, does not require that we flatten, homogenize, or even "whitewash" differences (cf. Foley and Valenzuela 2005). As in any collaboration, both ethnographer(s) and consultant(s) must be willing to make concessions so they can work together in the first place; but they must also be willing to open themselves up to a dynamic knowledge exchange, to stick it out, and to discover in their work together emergent counderstandings, cointerpretations, and coinscriptions (which will always include points of disagreement). As Rouverol (2003:84) contends, "dialogue—and social change, if that's what we are after—simply cannot happen unless we are open to hearing perspectives other than our own." But more than this, collaborative ethnographers must also be willing, as Glenn Hinson (2000:324) writes, to "surrender the interpretive authority they have historically assumed, seeking instead a collaboration that draws consultants into the analysis as equal partners and then creates textual space for the ensuing conversation."

Some might suggest that collaborative ethnography is a kind of collusion; but as I have stated before, "there is never a time when we are *not* colluding—with our institutions, our colleagues, our disciplines, our presses, or with other centers of power" (*Anthropology News* 2006). In actuality, collaborative research struggles within and against a multitude of simultaneous and often conflicting motives. It is often, for instance, an academically based project, one that requires, on the part of the ethnographer(s), balancing the demands of producing relevant knowledge (and, for academic practitioners, all that goes with it, including the demands to "publish or perish") with the desire to do applied research, to "make a difference" in local communities. Such a balancing act is not necessarily a bad thing; like all anthropological practice, especially today (to recall Field and Fox 2007), collaborative research is neither purely academic nor purely applied. When, for instance, as an undergraduate I sought to understand the experience of drug addiction and recovery via my first real ethnographic project, utilizing a collaborative ethnographic approach opened up the possibility for discussing with my collaborators the applied dimensions of my student project: my consultants fancied the idea of coproducing a text that they could give to the still-suffering addict, and we together produced a manuscript that served both an academic and community purpose (albeit, I will admit, very tentatively; see Lassiter 1999b).

This, I believe, is the whole point of doing collaborative ethnography: to realize along with our consultants both collaborative meanings *and* collaborative actions (see Lassiter 2005a:151–54). In the *Other Side of Middletown* project (see Lassiter et al. 2004), to offer a more recent example from my own research experience, faculty, students, and community members worked to coproduce a text that addressed a community-based concern, in this case, about the exclusion of black experience from both classic and ongoing studies of Middletown (which had largely ignored the contributions of African Americans to the city of Muncie, Indiana). We were charged, as a group, to write a text to rectify this problem. And as its completion was so important to many in the community—in fact, some had already begun the work years before we started—its very collaborative inscription was a powerful way to engage in collaborative action from the very beginning (see Miles 2004). This initial collaborative process yielded still other collaborative actions, though, as members of the community guided faculty and students into the realm of larger community-centered issues, concerns, and activisms. Several of the students, for example, became closely involved in community debates, forums, and protests that surrounded a contentious community conflict to rename a local city street to Martin Luther King, Jr., Boulevard (see Williams 2003).

Does such an approach have limitations? Of course it does (see, e.g., Lassiter 2004a:8–9). Again, collaborative ethnography is neither an end-all method that we can use to study everything nor a one-size-fits-all public–applied–action anthropology. I do think, however, that collaborative ethnography—with all of its complexities, conflicting motives, limitations, as well as possibilities—is, to recall the advice of Rylko-Bauer and colleagues (2006) cited above, a strategy that can work. In addition to having the potential to narrow the gap between academic and applied anthropologies (see Lassiter 2005b), I believe that collaborative ethnography has something to offer to a larger engaged anthropological project that, along with our consultants, endeavors to "operationalize the goals of addressing and ameliorating social problems" and to "translate knowledge successfully into pragmatic action" (Rylko-Bauer et al. 2006:186).

With this in mind, I now turn to some brief advice for students who might want to engage local publics in collaborative research as part of their anthropological practice, now or in the future.

Collaborative ethnography is just one small part of a larger commitment to community-based, collaborative research. Not all students of anthropology will choose to do collaborative research as part of their applied or publicly engaged anthropological practice, but for those who do, and for the purposes of this volume, I offer the following brief notes of advice (not meant in any way to be complete, of course).

Familiarize yourself with the history and broad range of collaborative and community-based research. Many will be happy to know that practitioners across several disciplines, not just in anthropology, are doing collaborative research, too, and have been, in some cases, for quite some time—including in fields such as sociology (see, e.g., Nyden and Wiewel 1992), psychology (Jason et al. 2003), folklore (see, e.g., Evers and Toelken 2001), oral history (see, e.g., Thomson 2003), public health (see, e.g., Wallerstein 2006), and education (see, e.g., Staikidis 2006). Be especially aware, however, that different disciplines and their various scholar–activists have a diversity of visions for what this collaborative research practice should look like. These different visions, of course, are often based in the history and traditions of any given discipline. In anthropology, for example, calls for a more collaborative ethnography materialized, as is well-known, in the vibrant discussions of ethnographic authority emanating from critical theory, feminist, and postmodern anthropology in the 1960s, 70s, and 80s; but the roots of collaborative research go much deeper than this (see Lassiter 2005a:25–47). Paul Radin (1923, 1927, 1933), for example, did much to push our field in this direction (see Darnell 2001:137–70). In the end, though, we cannot presume to know everything about every historical moment or every collaborative research model. But we can push ourselves to appreciate—and this is the point—that doing collaborative research is part of a much larger project in the social sciences, past and present. And that when we choose to do this kind of research, we are, first, not alone in our efforts, and second, in the company of many fellow travelers who have much to offer each other in our common efforts to realize a more equitable social science. If you can, get to know these "fellow travelers" and their collaborative researches. There is much for all of us to learn.

Choose your methods with care. Being familiar with the history and broad range of collaborative research, of course, provides the foundation for choosing collaborative research methods that best suit the goals of you and your collaborators in any given project or partnership. For me, collaborative ethnography has often worked extremely well for apprehending the common goals that emerge in collaborative inquiry: whether researching drug addiction and recovery, Kiowa song, or black Muncie, collaborative ethnography seemed the best approach for articulating multicultural understanding and, my collaborators and I have hoped, social change. In other cases, however, my consultants and I have sought out other methods and procedures that were best suited to the context of the collaborative partnership in which we worked. I have mentioned this elsewhere—for example, doing more traditional ethnographic surveys for Muncie's African American community in the wake of *The Other Side of Middletown* collaboration (see Lassiter 2004a:8–9). Most recently, in my job as the director of a program closely associated with a school of education, I am now working to varying degrees with a diversity of local teachers and administrators, school districts, service agencies, state officials, higher education faculty and students in the context of a wide range of collaborative research projects meant to improve teacher training and student learning (see Lassiter 2007). In these partnerships, we have pulled together several different research approaches, from quantitative and qualitative methods to collaborative ethnography and action research. While these combined research approaches deploy collaboration in very different ways, they share a commitment to community-based collaborations that are responsive to the needs and goals of the parties involved. What this requires, of course, is openness to and the careful selection and utilization of multiple approaches that allow for diverse collaborative research partnerships and projects.

Acknowledge that collaborative research is challenging and that it requires time. Of all the research approaches available to anthropologists and other social scientists, collaborative research is perhaps the most time consuming. Collaboration rests, first and foremost, on trust, and building trust does not happen overnight; it grows—often, over the course of years—as any given project or partnership develops and evolves. For example, in a recent publication of the Field Museum's Center for Cultural Understanding and Change, *Collaborative Research* (Wali 2006), the authors line out for both scholars and community-based organizations seven steps for doing participatory action research: finding a partner, forming a research question, planning, conducting research, analyzing the data, sharing the findings, and taking action. As each of these steps is built on cooperation and mutual respect for varying viewpoints, each of these steps accordingly requires time and the ongoing nurturing of relationships: "Planning meetings, hosting social events in each other's neighborhood and homes," the authors point out, "and openness to constructive criticism all help to create bonds during the research process" (Wali 2006:33). Such commitments to collaboration, of course, require that we learn to work effectively with many different people, to listen, and to take others seriously. I have already mentioned, above, that the negotiation of diverse visions, agendas, and expectations can be challenging intellectually. But collaborative research can also be challenging on a personal level. It often requires us to surrender authority and control, shifting the role of the researcher(s) from one of "expert" to one of "facilitator." This can be hard for some, especially as collaborative research may necessitate that we put aside our own egos in order to bring about more multidimensional, dialogic understandings.

Look for and take opportunities to collaborate. While not all research will fit well within the contours of collaborative research, plenty does. And once you start looking for opportunities to collaborate, the opportunities tend to only multiply—in my experience, at least, collaborative research projects seem to beget more collaborative research projects. My work with Kiowa hymn singer Ralph Kotay, for example, grew out of earlier collaborative research on Kiowa song. After the completion of *The Power of Kiowa Song* (Lassiter 1998b), Kotay, one of many consultants who worked on the initial ethnography, wanted to continue our work together, focusing specifically on Kiowa hymns—an oral song tradition that combines elements of traditional Kiowa song with Christian hymnody.

In particular, Kotay wanted to augment the impact of his Kiowa hymn class, which he taught each week as a way to preserve and maintain the Kiowa song, language, and larger community and spiritual relationships associated with Kiowa hymns (see Lassiter 2001b). Our work together, and with historian Clyde Ellis, and later, graduate student Chris Wendt, produced two major collaborative projects—the book *The Jesus Road* (Lassiter et al. 2002) and the audio recording *Kiowa Hymns* (Kotay et al. 2004)—as well as several other smaller projects.

Similar processes have transpired in other collaborative partnerships. A collaborative museum exhibit on African American pioneers originated the partnership that would eventually establish *The Other Side of Middletown* project (see Lassiter et al. 2004:4–5), which, in turn, produced—in addition to the already mentioned collaborative actions— collaboratively based undergraduate and graduate theses, a video documentary, a photo exhibit, a library digitization project, public school programs, a range of community events, and another state museum exhibit (see, e.g., Indiana State Museum 2007). The possibilities for collaboration can thus be endless. Indeed, one could spend a lifetime doing collaborative research: if we are open to the collaborative process, then we need only look for and take opportunities when they arise.

But when to get started? This raises another set of issues, and summons some advice that may be unpleasant to bear in mind; but important nonetheless for any student considering collaborative research now or in the future.

Start early, but proceed cautiously. Doing collaborative research is not just for the seasoned practitioner. In my mind, students who are interested in doing collaborative research should start as early as possible. It may not always be feasible, though: academic environments, especially, are not at all times as open as we think they might (or should) be. I now realize that I was extremely fortunate to "come of age" as both an undergraduate and graduate student in departments of anthropology that supported and encouraged collaborative research practice (see Lassiter 2004a:5–8). When I wrote my dissertation on Kiowa song, for example, my Kiowa consultants—particularly Billy Evans Horse, tribal chairman and key consultant—insisted that Kiowas be able to read the dissertation and comment on its evolution. My dissertation committee was open to this idea and allowed the student training inherent to the dissertation process to unfold accordingly as we negotiated a middle ground.[2] But after leaving graduate school and working in other academic environments, I discovered that this kind of openness to student collaborative research—and for that matter, open-ended cooperation with one's professors—does not always proceed this smoothly (see, e.g., Lassiter 2005b:102). Many academics, including anthropologists, still seem suspicious of collaborative research approaches: while it can be theoretically appealing to many, in practice collaborative research still seems to pose, for some, a threat to academic privilege, authority, and control. Given this, though, the validity and value of collaborative research seems to be growing, and I suspect that students will have less trouble doing collaborative research earlier in their career as our field, as many predict, steadily turns once again toward more public and applied emphases. In the interim, students should be especially cognizant that while many academic environments support and nurture collaborative research, others may not, and in fact, may actively discourage it.

Be aware of the larger risks. A closely related issue is how collaborative research situates your overall work as an anthropologist. Put another way, the work you do as a student, especially as a graduate student, will define your career trajectory (at least in its earliest stages). On the one hand, doing collaborative research as a student may enhance your future job prospects if you envision doing applied anthropology outside academia. On the other hand, doing collaborative research as a student *may* pose a risk to future job prospects (and future job security) if you envision yourself doing this kind of applied anthropology within the context of academia. Right now, and perhaps for some time to come, multisited, theoretically couched, and academically situated research is king in anthropology. As anthropologist and educator Douglas Foley writes about critical ethnography, for example, "the technical, theory-driven academic ethnography remains the standard through which young scholars must aspire. The senior scholars who control the machinery of academic production and promotion maintain a tight grip on the conventions of social scientific writing. This surely will be the last bastion to fall, if it ever does. In the meantime, the social sciences remain a rather elitist, 'high culture' form of social commentary" (Foley and Valenzuela 2005:224).

What this means, of course, is that these same senior scholars—who may view collaborative research as compromising, to paraphrase Foley, the "high culture" of social commentary—may also have considerable sway over the machinery of hiring new faculty. Although, again, collaborative research may be more common and acceptable in some academic circles (perhaps especially so in programs that comprise a strong applied curriculum), students who are doing (or imagine themselves doing) collaborative research should at least bear all of this in mind as they consider jobs in academe. Ultimately, however, I suspect that many of us who do collaborative research do not choose this practice first and foremost because of our career trajectories; we choose it because we believe in and value its approach, results, and outcomes (see Lassiter 2005a:147–51).

CONCLUSION

The discussions about public anthropology will no doubt continue for some time, especially as many anthropologists maintain—in some cases, convincingly—that "public anthropology is not just old wine in new bottles" (McGranahan 2006:256). These dialogues will no doubt, too, continue providing "a useful service for the general discipline" (Rylko-Bauer et al. 2006:86). But if we are to get beyond public anthropology (particularly those arguments and debates that separate out this anthropology from that anthropology), and chart the central questions and problems of the larger anthropological project, then we—students included—must resist the temptation of academic solipsism and together build more deliberate opportunities for public engagement. A powerful way in which we can do so is through collaborative research. Such research— and the partnerships on which it is based—can press theory and practice into service in ways more direct and immediate in our common search to make a difference in our world, however small or large.

NOTES

1. Although the critique of academic anthropology's sequestration within the academy—which had its roots in early Americanist anthropology (see, e.g., Boas 1928; Mead 1928; Radin 1933), surfaced in various forms in the 1960s and 70s (see, e.g., Hymes 1969; Sanday 1976), gained traction in the 1980s (Marcus and Fischer 1986), and peaked in the late 1990s (see, e.g., Peacock 1997)—arguably gave rise to current discussions of public anthropology, such critiques were not limited to anthropology. Various forms of these critiques cut across several other disciplines in the social sciences and humanities as well (see, e.g., Jacoby 1987). Indeed, anthropologists' latest discussions about public engagement share common ground with other discussions and movements such as public folklore, public history, and public humanities (see, e.g., Baron and Spitzer 1992; Grele 1981; and American Council of Learned Societies 1990, respectively)—discussions and movements that also materialized in the context of similar critiques, and subsequently, sought to more systematically situate "the public" closer to the center of knowledge production and dissemination.

2. My dissertation committee, of course, had expectations for the work, which influenced the dissertation's evolution as they, too, made comments and shaped its outcome. Negotiating these variant outlooks, agendas, and expectations became a major factor in crafting the collaborative ethnography I wrote (see Lassiter 2005a:92–93; cf. Lassiter 1998b).

REFERENCES CITED

American Council of Learned Societies, ed.
    1990 National Task Force on Scholarship and the Public Humanities. New York: American Council of Learned Societies.
Anthropology News
    2006 Collaborative Ethnography Matters. Anthropology News 47(5):20–21.
Austin, Diane E.
    2004 Partnerships, Not Projects! Improving the Environment through Collaborative Research and Action. Human Organization 63(4):419–430.
Baron, Robert, and Nicholas R. Spitzer, eds.
    1992 Public Folklore. Washington, DC: Smithsonian Institution Press.
Basch, Linda G., Lucie Wood Saunders, Jagna Wojcicka Sharff, and James Peacock, eds.
    1999 Transforming Academia: Challenges and Opportunities for an Engaged Anthropology. Washington, DC: American Anthropological Association.
Bennett, John W.
    1996 Applied and Action Anthropology: Ideological and Conceptual Aspects. Current Anthropology 36(suppl.):S23–S58.
Boas, Franz
    1928 Anthropology and Modern Life. New York: W. W. Norton.
Borofsky, Robert
    1999 Public anthropology. Anthropology News 40(1):6–7.
    2006 Conceptualizing Public Anthropology (A Personal Perspective). Electronic Document, http://www.publicanthropology.org/Defining/publicanth-07Oct10.htm, accessed December 20, 2006.
Brettell, Caroline B.
    1996 When They Read What We Write: The Politics of Ethnography. Westport: Bergin and Garvey.
Brown, Alison K., and Laura Peers
    2006 "Pictures Bring Us Messages" / Sinaakssiiksi aohtsimaahpihkookiyaawa: Photographs and Histories from the Kainai Nation. Alison K. Brown and Laura Peers with members of the Kainai Nation. Toronto: University of Toronto Press.

Chatterley, Cedric N., Alicia J. Rouverol, and Stephen A. Cole

    2000 "I Was Content and Not Content": The Story of Linda Lord and the Closing of Penobscot Poultry. Carbondale: Southern Illinois University Press.

Checker, Melissa, and Maggie Fishman, eds.

    2004 Local Actions: Cultural Activism, Power, and Public Life in America. New York: Columbia University Press.

Darnell, Regna

    2001 Invisible Genealogies: A History of Americanist Anthropology. Lincoln: University of Nebraska Press.

Eriksen, Thomas Hylland

    2006 Engaging Anthropology: The Case for a Public Presence. Oxford: Berg.

Erwin, Alexander M.

    2000 Applied Anthropology: Tools and Perspectives for Contemporary Practice. Boston: Allyn and Bacon.

Evers, Larry, and Barre Toelken, eds.

    2001 Native American Oral Traditions: Collaboration and Interpretation. Logan: Utah State University Press.

Feld, Steven

    1987 Dialogic Editing: Interpreting How Kaluli Read *Sound and Sentiment*. Cultural Anthropology 2(2):190–210.

Field, Les

    2008 Abalone Tales: Collaborative Explorations of California Indian Sovereignty and Identity. Durham, NC: Duke University Press.

Field, Les, and Richard G. Fox, eds.

    2007 Anthropology Put to Work. Oxford: Berg.

Foley, Douglas E.

    1995 The Heartland Chronicles. Philadelphia: University of Pennsylvania Press.

    2002 Critical Ethnography: The Reflexive Turn. Qualitative Studies in Education 15(4):469–490.

Foley, Douglas, and Angela Valenzuela

    2005 Critical Ethnography: The Politics of Collaboration. In The Sage Handbook of Qualitative Research, 3rd ed. Norman K. Denzin and Yvonna S. Lincoln, eds. Pp. 217–234. London: Sage.

Grele, Ronald J.

    1981 Whose Public? Whose History? What is the Goal of the Public Historian? The Public Historian 3:40–48.

Heron, John

    1996 Co-Operative Inquiry: Research into the Human Condition. London: Sage.

Heron, John, and Peter Reason

    1997 A Participatory Inquiry Paradigm. Qualitative Inquiry 3(3):274–294.

Hill, Carole E., and Marietta L. Baba, eds.

    1999 The Unity of Theory and Practice in Anthropology: Rebuilding a Fractured Synthesis. Washington, DC: American Anthropological Association.

Hinson, Glenn

    2000 Fire in My Bones: Transcendence and the Holy Spirit in African American Gospel. Philadelphia: University of Pennsylvania Press.

Horse, Billy Evans, and Luke Eric Lassiter

    1998 Billy Evans Horse Sings Kiowa Gourd Dance Songs. Audiocassette with Notes. Muncie: Ball State University.

    1999 Kiowa Powwow Songs. Audiocassette with Notes. Muncie: Ball State University.

Hymes, Dell, ed.

    1969 Reinventing Anthropology. New York: Pantheon.

Indiana State Museum

    2007 The Other Side of Middletown. Electronic document, http://www.in.gov/ism/Middletown/index.asp, accessed October 26, 2007.

Jacoby, Russell

    1987 The Last Intellectuals: American Culture in the Age of Academe. New York: Basic Books.

Jason, Leonard A., Christopher B. Keys, Yolanda Suarez-Balcazar, Renee R. Taylor, and Margaret I. Davis, eds.

    2003 Participatory Community Research: Theories and Methods in Action. Washington, DC: American Psychological Association.

Kotay, Ralph, Luke Eric Lassiter, and Chris Wendt

    2004 Kiowa Hymns, Sung by Ralph Kotay. Audio Recording with Notes. Lincoln: University of Nebraska Press.

Lamphere, Louise

    2003 The Perils and Prospects for an Engaged Anthropology: A View From the United States. Social Anthropology 11(2):153–168.

    2004 The Convergence of Applied, Practicing, and Public Anthropology in the 21st Century. Human Organization 63(4):431–443.

Lassiter, Luke Eric

    1998a American Indian Musical Collection: Impressions, Problems and Recommendations. Oklahoma City: Consultation Report for the Oklahoma Historical Society.

    1998b The Power of Kiowa Song. Tucson: University of Arizona Press.

    1999a Director's Report: Mission Statement for the Kiowa Education Fund. Anadarko, OK: Annual Report prepared for Satethieday Khatgomebaugh.

    1999b We Keep What We Have by Giving it Away. Anthropology News 40(1):3, 7.

    2001a Engaging a Localized Public Anthropology. Anthropology News 42(2):7–8.

    2001b "From Here On, I Will Be Praying to You": Indian Churches, Kiowa Hymns, and Native American Christianity in Southwestern Oklahoma. Ethnomusicology 45(2):338–352.

    2003 Theorizing the Local. Anthropology News 44(5):13.

    2004a Collaborative Ethnography. AnthroNotes 25(1):1–9.

    2004b Music. In A Companion to the Anthropology of American Indians. Thomas Biolsi, ed. Pp. 196–211. Oxford: Blackwell.

    2004c Teachers' Corner: Doing Collaborative Ethnography. AnthroNotes 25(1):10–14.

    2005a The Chicago Guide to Collaborative Ethnography. Chicago: University of Chicago Press.

    2005b Collaborative Ethnography and Public Anthropology. Current Anthropology 46(1):83–106.

    2005c Collaborative Ethnography, Collaborative Engagement. Paper presented at the 104th Annual Meeting of the American Anthropological Association, Washington, DC, November 30–December 4.

    2006 Invitation to Anthropology. 2nd edition. Lanham, MD: AltaMira Press.

    2007 On the Job: Applied Anthropology in a Graduate Humanities Program. Society for Applied Anthropology Newsletter 18(3):8–10.

Lassiter, Luke Eric, Clyde Ellis, and Ralph Kotay

    2002 The Jesus Road: Kiowas, Christianity, and Indian Hymns. Lincoln: University of Nebraska Press.

Lassiter, Luke Eric, Hurley Goodall, Elizabeth Campbell, and Michelle Natasya Johnson

    2004 The Other Side of Middletown: Exploring Muncie's African American Community. Walnut Creek, CA: AltaMira Press.

Lassiter, Luke Eric, and Lisa A. Heaton

    2006 Evaluation Report of the Principals' Leadership Academy. Charleston, WV: Center for Professional Development.

Lavie, Smadar, with A. Hajj and Forest Rouse

    1993 Notes on the Fantastic Journey of the Hajj, His Anthropologist, and Her American Passport. American Ethnologist 20(2):363–84.

Lawless, Elaine

    1992 "I Was Afraid Someone Like You . . . An Outsider . . . Would Misunderstand": Negotiating Interpretative Differences between Ethnographers and Subjects. Journal of American Folklore 105:302–314.

    2000 "Reciprocal" Ethnography: No One Said It Was Easy. Journal of Folklore Research 37(2–3):197–205.

LeCompte, Margaret D., Jean J. Schensul, Margaret Weeks, and Merrill Singer

    1999 Researcher Roles and Research Partnerships. Walnut Creek, CA: AltaMira Press.

Little, Barbara J., ed.

  2002 The Public Benefits of Archaeology. Gainesville: University Press of Florida.

MacClancy, Jeremy, ed.

  2002 Exotic No More: Anthropology on the Front Lines. Chicago: University of Chicago Press.

Marcus, George E., and Michael M.J. Fischer

  1986 Anthropology as Cultural Critique: An Experimental Moment in the Human Sciences. Chicago: University of Chicago Press.

Marcus, George E., and Fernando Mascarenhas

  2005 Ocasião: The Marquis and the Anthropologist, a Collaboration. Walnut Creek, CA: AltaMira Press.

McGranahan, Carole

  2006 Introduction: Public Anthropology. India Review 5(3–4):255–267.

Mead, Margaret

  1928 Coming of Age in Samoa. New York: Morrow.

Merriman, Nick, ed.

  2002 Public Archaeology. London: Routledge.

Miles, James, dir.

  2004 Middletown Redux. DVD documentary. Walnut Creek, CA: AltaMira Press.

Nader, Laura

  2000 Preface. *In* The Unity of Theory and Practice in Anthropology: Rebuilding a Fractured Synthesis. Carole E. Hill and Marietta L. Baba, eds. Pp. v–vii. Washington, DC: American Anthropological Association.

  2001 Anthropology! Distinguished Lecture—2000. American Anthropologist 103(3):609–620.

Nyden, Philip, and Wim Wiewel

  1992 Collaborative Research: Harnessing the Tensions between Researcher and Practitioner. American Sociologist 23(4):43–55.

Papa, Lee, and Luke Eric Lassiter

  2003 The Muncie Race Riots of 1967, Representing Community Memory through Public Performance, and Collaborative Ethnography between Faculty, Students and the Local Community. Journal of Contemporary Ethnography 32(2):147–166.

Peacock, James L.

  1997 The Future of Anthropology. American Anthropologist 99(1):9–17.

Purcell, Trevor W.

  2000 Public Anthropology: An Idea Searching for a Reality. Transforming Anthropology 9(2):30–33.

Radin, Paul

  1923 The Winnebago Tribe. Twenty-Seventh Annual Report of the Bureau of American Ethnology. Washington, DC: Government Printing Office.

  1927 Primitive Man as Philosopher. New York: Appleton and Company.

  1933 The Method and Theory of Ethnology: An Essay in Criticism. New York: McGraw-Hill.

Rappaport, Joanne

  2005 Intercultural Utopias: Public Intellectuals, Cultural Experimentation, and Ethnic Pluralism in Columbia. Durham, NC: Duke University Press.

Ridington, Robin, and Dennis Hastings

  1997 Blessing for a Long Time: The Sacred Pole of the Omaha Tribe. Lincoln: University of Nebraska Press.

Rios, Theodore, and Kathleen Mullen Sands

  2000 Telling a Good One: The Process of a Native American Collaborative Biography. Lincoln: University of Nebraska Press.

Rouverol, Alicia J.

  2000 "I Was Content and Not Content": Oral History and the Collaborative Process. Oral History 28(2):66–78.

  2003 Collaborative Oral History in a Correctional Setting: Promise and Pitfalls. The Oral History Review 30(1):61–85.

Rylko-Bauer, Barbara, Merrill Singer, and John vanWilligen
  2006 Reclaiming Applied Anthropology: Its Past, Present, and Future. American Anthropologist 108(1):178–190.
Sanday, Peggy Reeves
  1976 Anthropology and the Public Interest. New York: Academic Press.
  1998 Opening Statement: Defining Public Interest Anthropology. Paper presented at the 97th Annual Meeting of the American Anthropological Association, Philadelphia, December 2–6.
Sanjek, Roger
  2004 Going Public: Responsibilities and Strategies in the Aftermath of Ethnography. Human Organization 63(4):444–456.
Singer, Merrill
  2000 Why I Am Not a Public Anthropologist. Anthropology News 41(6):6–7.
Stacey, Judith
  1991 Brave New Families: Stories of Domestic Upheaval in Late Twentieth Century America. New York: Basic Books.
Staikidis, Kryssi
  2006 Personal and Cultural Narrative as Inspiration: A Painting and Pedagogical Collaboration with Mayan Artists. Studies in Art Education 47(2):118–138.
Stull, Donald D.
  2005 President's Letter. Society for Applied Anthropology Newsletter 16(2):1–4.
  2006 President's Letter. Society for Applied Anthropology Newsletter 17(2):1–3.
Stull, Donald D., and Jean J. Schensul, eds.
  1987 Collaborative Research and Social Change: Applied Anthropology in Action. Boulder, CO: Westview Press.
Tedlock, Barbara
  2005 The Observation of Participation and the Emergence of Public Ethnography. In The Sage Handbook of Qualitative Research. 3rd edition. Norman K. Denzin and Yvonna S. Lincoln, eds. Pp. 467–481. London: Sage.
Thomson, Alistair
  2003 Sharing Authority: Oral History and the Collaborative Process. Oral History Review 30(1):23–26.
Thorp, Laurie
  2006 The Pull of the Earth: Participatory Ethnography in the School Garden. Walnut Creek, CA: AltaMira Press.
Wali, Alaka, ed.
  2006 Collaborative Research: A Practical Introduction to Participatory Action Research (PAR) for Communities and Scholars. Chicago: Field Museum.
Wallerstein. Nina B.
  2006 Using Community-Based Participatory Research to Address Health Disparities. Health Promotion Practice 7(3):312–323.
Wickens, Matthew, and Kathleen Grant
  2005 Public Anthropology. Anthropology News 46(1):50–51.
Williams, Marco, dir.
  2003 MLK Boulevard: The Concrete Dream. New York: Discovery-Times Channel.

COLLABORATION, COOPERATION, AND WORKING TOGETHER: ANTHROPOLOGISTS CREATING A SPACE FOR RESEARCH AND ACADEMIC PARTNERSHIPS

GERALDINE MORENO-BLACK
University of Oregon

PISSAMAI HOMCHAMPA
Burapha University

In this chapter, we discuss the nature and growing reliance on collaborative work. We specifically focus on the current literature on collaboration and the use and relevance of collaborative work for anthropologists. We also note differences in perceptions about collaboration, as well as the acceptability of collaborative research and coauthorship across disciplines. We use instances from our careers as a way to illustrate examples of collaborative work in Anthropology. Our main focus is to highlight the productive and sometimes transformative nature of this type of work. We also discuss the barriers that collaborators may face as well as some of the problems they can encounter. Although each collaborative situation is different we identify several areas and issues that can be addressed at the early stages and that can be helpful for developing a successful collaboration. We also offer suggestions for successful collaborative research and writing and provide some guidelines and advice to those who may be considering or embarking on collaborative work. Finally, because collaborative work between professors and students can present unique issues, we highlight several important aspects of the professor–student relationship that need to be addressed in order for this type of collaboration to be successful. Keywords: applied anthropology, research collaboration, research cooperation, academic partnerships, mentorship

As anthropologists who conduct research and field work in a multiplicity of sites (e.g., local, regional, national and international), we are aware of the potentially contested nature of our work. Our field work usually brings us in contact with groups of interacting and positioned individuals who eventually develop a relationship with us. Working with people is the mainstay of anthropological research. However, in the academic arena we are not encouraged to engage in collaborative research, and our academic worth is carefully evaluated and gauged by the number of individually authored articles and books. Indeed, as Gottlieb (1995:21) indicated more than a decade ago, most anthropologists and social scientists in general tend to see the "author," in particular, as a singular creation standing alone in her or his academic achievement. This situation, however, is not the gold standard in many other disciplines where collaborative situations are considered

NAPA BULLETIN 29, pp. 87–98. ISBN 9781405190152. © 2008 by the American Anthropological Association. DOI:10.1111/j.1556-4797.2008.00007.x

common and often essential (e.g., health science [Hanawalt 2006], communication science [Thompson 2001], and engineering [Pawlowski 2002]).

In this chapter we (1) discuss the current literature on collaboration by researchers; (2) provide some insight, based mainly on our own experiences, into the rewards and challenges of collaborative work; and (3) provide some guidelines and advice to those who may be considering or embarking on collaborative work. We come to this work through our relationship, which has moved from professor–student to professional colleagues. We are both trained as biological anthropologists with a biocultural theoretical orientation. Geraldine Moreno-Black (GMB) is a biological anthropologist and a certified nutrition specialist (CNS), and Pissamai Homchampa (PH) has a degree in nursing, an M.P. H. and a Ph.D. in Anthropology.

ON COLLABORATION

Although there is burgeoning literature in anthropology about collaborative relationships and the position between the researcher and the researched individuals, little has been written or discussed about the relationship among researchers who work together. According to Kennedy (1995), three major intellectual developments have led to the changing climate regarding collaborative work in anthropology: feminist scholarship, anticolonialist scholarship, and interpretative anthropology. Feminist and interpretive scholarship have been especially important in reinforcing collaborative research by critiquing gender hierarchies and highlighting issues concerning the researcher's position and relationship with the research participants, while anticolonialist scholarship has provided important discussions about ownership and intellectual property rights.

One of the distinguishing features of collaborative work is that the relationship among the collaborators is often as important as the project. The interaction among individuals facilitates learning and achieving the goals of the project. A collaborative research project goes beyond work in which researchers cooperate with each other; it involves working with and through others (Hanawalt 2006; Saltiel 1998; Wildavsky 1986). Some researchers indicate that collaboration can truly bring about a multiplier effect. However, they also found that there are effects that can interfere with the collaborative process. Views about authority and ownership of the research among team members affect personal and professional satisfaction levels, and thus different views of authority or "co-optation" can potentially hinder the participation (Thompson 2001:166). However, most collaborative researchers discuss the facts that their research results are enhanced by collaboration and that the networks the researchers create help them decrease a sense of isolation, acquire new knowledge, develop lasting relationships, and grow personally. Some even refer to the process as being transformative (Clark and Watson 1998; Cottrell and Parpart 2006; Hiemstra and Brockett 1998; Kennedy 1995; Laband and Tollison 2000; Quandt et al. 2001).

From an academic perspective, a number of researchers have written about the effectiveness of collaborative work for facilitating and enhancing learning. Sharing responsibility for defining and addressing research questions promotes learning from peers, and in some professions, such as the health sciences models, also promotes organizational structure and clinical activities (Caulkins 1999; Madariaga et al. 2006; Taylor 2006). In these settings, the collaborative process also provides an avenue for sharing challenging problems and facilitating students' development through enabling them to progress from descriptive level to the deeper levels of synthesis. Furthermore, there is increasing support from university administrators and government organizations for collaboration among researchers both nationally and internationally, as well as across disciplines and working spaces (Galiana 2006).

There also has been some work on defining and isolating different models of collaboration. Thompson reviewed 55 journal articles from between 1990 and 1999 that focused on collaboration and, using a content analysis, summarized four different models. Thompson's models, based on lines of authority and the division of labor within the research team members, were labeled (1) hierarchical or formal process model, where individuals perform the tasks assigned to them in isolation with an emphasis on singular rather than consensual authority; (2) swap meet or division of labor model, where individuals perform tasks in isolation but come back together to review or revise; (3) asymmetrical model, where collaborators cannot be viewed as equals, such as teacher–student collaboration; and (4) dialogic or integrated team or symphony model, where tasks are performed together by all members of the group (2001:166).

Additionally, a number of researchers have discussed the differences that appear to exist in perceptions about collaboration, as well as the incidence and acceptability of collaborative research and subsequent coauthorship, when they are compared across disciplines. Some researchers feel that, in general, the results of collaborative research are of higher quality and have more professional significance. Collaborative research has also been found to be cited more highly than single-authored work and thus appears to have greater epistemic authority (Beaver 2004). Endersby (1996) surveyed 13 journals from a variety of fields in the social sciences and found that nearly half of the articles had joint authorship and that different fields had different styles of collaboration. Laband and Tollison (2000) found that the incidence and extent of formal coauthorship was greater in biology than in economics; however, the extent of intellectual collaboration was greater in economics. These types of comparisons have begun to highlight the need for refining the concept of collaboration.

OUR EXPERIENCES AS COLLABORATIVE RESEARCHERS

Collaboration, for both of us, is a learning experience. It is not only promoting the transmission of information, but it is also a reflective and critical active learning experience that leads to professional competency, creativity, intellectual growth, and maturation. In applied anthropology, a large part of our learning experience derives from "mentorship" wherein the advisor is a mentor and the student is a learner. The two are engaged in working collaboratively either in the classroom setting or in the research study. We see efforts to develop a collaborative learning relationship between mentor and learner in anthropology, like in any other field of study, as a way to share information and experiences, receive support, and provide feedback. This process eventually facilitates changes and further influences educational and professional development for all members of the collaborative group. We also believe that collaboration works toward making anthropology a more holistic science. In this section, each using our own voice, we discuss our experiences as collaborators.

Case Study: From Research Assistant to Graduate Student–Professor Relationship and Ultimately Colleague Collaborators (GMB and PH)

The projects we describe span more than two decades and involve relationships that varied from PI–assistant roles, professor–graduate student roles, and colleague roles. The breadth and depth of our collaboration shifted over time as we each grew professionally and personally. Although the case study we describe has some unique features, we believe it has much in common with other collegial collaborations that grow out of professor–student relationships.

The Collaboration: GMB's Perspective

My (GMB) work in Thailand began with what I call "The Wild Food in Isan Culture Project," which spanned more than a 12-year period. I wrote and received numerous grant proposals from both internal (CSWS, University of Oregon Faculty Summer Awards, among others) and external (NSF, Wenner-Gren, Fulbright, among others) agencies and foundations. With a multiple data collection method and a stratified research design, I monitored 15 local morning markets and conducted research in two villages in the heart of Northeastern Thailand. The Wild Food Project involved collaborations with a number of Thai professionals, including PH, who originally joined the project as a research assistant. PH worked with me on the project for several years. In the early years of this project, we worked with a Thai colleague, Dr. Somnasang, who also participated as a research assistant. We traveled throughout the region visiting markets that often began at 3:00 in the morning. The first step involved an initial "sweep" through the market, with the assistance of hired assistants, to record all of the items sold at all of the fresh food stalls. In the second step, we interviewed vendors; this was sometimes a process that took several days. Finally, some vendors from each market were interviewed at a later time in their home village.

An important outgrowth of the Wild Food Project was that PH and I developed a long term relationship with each other. At the end of the Wild Food Project, PH moved to join the Faculty of Public Health at Burapha University, and she invited me to speak at the program there. At that time, we began to think about future collaborations and possible projects. Soon afterward, PH was accepted into the doctoral program at the University of Oregon, and I became her doctoral advisor. This move heralded a change in our professional relationship. However, as PH successfully moved through the program, we began to think about future collaborations, focusing on our mutual interest in the health and well-being of a population of Thai industrial workers and their families.

For her doctoral dissertation, PH decided to focus her research on how industrial workers took care of their health and on how such practices contributed to their and their family members' health and well-being. Through our discussions, I developed an interest in researching how the health and nutritional status of the children of the industrial workers, particularly preschool children, were being impacted by industrial development in Thailand.

Our projects evolved into overlapping studies that led to considerable collaboration. PH focused primarily on the health and self-care practices of factory workers, while I focused on the children of factory workers, some of who were in PH's sample. PH conducted the survey interviews and completed nutritional status assessments of the industrial workers at two study factories. She also conducted home visits with a sample of the survey participants and specifically asked those who had 0–5-year-old children for permission to include them in my project. We both visited the industrial workers and their families for the in-depth interviews at their places of residence on their vacation. I included the 24-hour dietary interviews and anthropometric measurement of the preschool children in the appropriate households. We also visited and interviewed key persons, such as community leaders, public health personnel at two community health centers, village health volunteers, principals of two primary schools and related teachers, as well as owners of food shops.

Later, after PH had received her doctorate and returned to Thailand and her position at Burapha University, I expanded the nutritional aspect of the study by focusing on two schools in the Industrial Park. The focus of this phase of the project was on nutritional status (anthropometric measurements) of preschool children and household food security. Together, we interviewed teachers at the schools, monitored the school lunch program, and observed lunch activities. We also interviewed a sample of the children's mothers or caretakers (grandmother, aunt). I took primary responsibility for this part of the project and employed assistants to help with recording measurements. PH facilitated many of the arrangements and assisted with the home interviews.

Throughout our years of collaboration we did not formalize agreements concerning ownership of the data. However, we each identified material that was the main focus of our work as well as information that was easily shared by both of us. PH used her data for her doctoral dissertation, and, after receiving her doctoral degree, she returned to the faculty of Public Health at Burapha University in Thailand. We continue to have an excellent relationship. There were moments when my role as a dissertation advisor made our power relationship unequal and made open communication difficult and more delicate. In looking back at the process, there were times when I found it difficult to negotiate my different roles: my advisor role was compromised by my collaborator role and vice versa. Ultimately, however, I believe we successfully bridged cultural barriers around discussing some of the difficulties that came from this unequal positionality. We continue to collaborate on coauthored articles.

The Collaboration: PH's Perspective

My collaborative work as a graduate student in the doctoral degree program in anthropology at the University of Oregon during the year 1996–2001 with a professor (GMB) was a valuable learning experience. In the research part, our collaborative work stemmed from mutual interest on health and well-being of the industrial working population and their families, including those who migrated from multiregions to the industrializing communities. As has been mentioned, we collaborated both on the data collection and analysis phases while still maintaining our individual foci: health and self-care practices of the industrial workers for me, and nutritional status of the 0–5-year-old children of the industrial workers and their coping strategies for GMB.

Our data collection was both individual and collaborative. For example, my work included survey interviews, anthropometric measurement, and some in-depth interviews while our collaborative work involved home visits and diet-related interviews. Some of the difficulties involved in our collaboration included making sure that there were enough individuals to meet the sample size needed for both projects and including key people who were appropriate for both projects (i.e., factory managers, community leaders, health workers, caretakers, and school teachers).

We also found ourselves in the position of having to negotiate shifting status positions between ourselves and between each of us and the interviewees. For example, one or both of us had to sit lower than or on the same level with the senior informants and address ourselves (in Thai) as *Pii* if we were older than the interviewee or *Nong* if younger. This was instead of the more formal word of *chan,* which means "I" for a woman. These varying positions sometimes conflicted with our personal relationship, which, although primarily defined as professor–student, were sometimes reversed or changed to the more equal collaborator level. The tension that occasionally resulted from the shifts in these roles was usually overcome by our ability to discuss issues and our mutual respect for each other.

Through our collaboration, I had the opportunity to observe and echo GMB's methods of organizing data, keeping and labeling records and field notes, validating research tools, and modifying the in-depth interview. We also discussed issues of cultural relativism and of being aware of emic and etic points of views while gathering data.

Our collaboration allowed both of us to share our data while conducting fieldwork. For example, our review of data from the field notes, interview sheets, and other related sources periodically allowed us to gain more accurate data from the test and retest of research hypotheses or assumptions. This led to the conclusion or emergence of new inquiries while still at the study site. We were also able to share relevant information while writing the research results. For example, I was able to provide relevant information from my interviews regarding the low consumption of dairy products among the Thai industrial workers. I was also able to contribute information about how higher priced dairy products limited consumption and how many industrial workers considered dairy and some other food products as "extraordinary" items.

We were also able to work together to develop mutually beneficial data analysis techniques, especially the use of statistical analysis programs and thematic reading for content analysis. In addition, I have to reiterate that the large part of my successful collaborative work in this last phase derived from receiving constructive comments in a timely fashion as well as encouragement from GMB. However, points to be considered on my part as a learner and a research collaborator include working toward keeping a two-way communication open, particularly when differences arose concerning ideas about addressing issues relevant to writing the research results. It was also important for me to be sensitive to the issue of not letting our personal relationships influence my requests for extension of deadlines or my preparedness for meetings and classes.

SUGGESTIONS FOR SUCCESSFUL COLLABORATIONS

In the preceding section, we outlined and discussed our experiences in our collaborative research. We both have gone on to have collaborations with other colleagues, which we do not discuss in this article. Our experiences as collaborators on all of our different projects, under diverse conditions and working with various researchers, have not always been completely unproblematic; however, they always have led to an enriching and productive experience. Each collaboration is different, and thus it is difficult to provide a solid set of guidelines that will be appropriate for everyone. Nonetheless, our experiences have enabled us to identify several issues that can be addressed at the early stages and that can be helpful for developing a successful collaboration.

Work Styles

It is important to recognize that the individuals on a collaborative team may have very different work styles. Each of us has a personal style and different ways of relating to others. Some individuals may prefer, or even need, to be very formal in their interactions. Others may be more informal and relaxed. Consequently, some individuals may prefer formal agreements with documentation and precise description of responsibilities; others may be comfortable allowing the process to evolve over time without strict guidelines. However, even if all of the researchers work easily with each other, it may still be valuable to work on formulating formal written agreements. This will be especially important for projects that involve shared grants, data, and other material. Although these documents may seem difficult to develop at the onset of a project and may seem rigid, it is usually possible and often necessary, to revisit and revise them as the work progresses. Additionally, if the project involves grant funds it may be necessary to involve university grants and contract offices to facilitate the management and dispersal of monies.

Communication

In all cases, regardless of the type of agreements that are made, communication among the group members is vital. It is essential to remember that no one should take anything for granted. The success of the project is dependent on keeping lines of communication open among everyone. Researchers need to discuss ways to communicate regardless of whether they work at the same locale or if they are separated by great distances. Currently, communication is made easy by the availability of telephones, fax machines, and e-mail. Despite the easy access to means of communication it is essential to recognize that each person is responsible for keeping the lines of communication open. Everyone should be involved in establishing, maintaining, and even terminating communication.

Communicating with each other, especially at the beginning of the collaboration, will enable everyone to express their expectations and facilitate the process of defining and setting goals. It is important for everyone to be willing to express their goals and their expectations in terms of outcomes. This process will allow for the development of guidelines and clarification of the roles each person will have in the project. These can include such activities as who will manage the data collection, who will oversee the project, and who will take responsibility for keeping track of expenditures and managing the budget. Although discussing these types of issues in advance is invaluable, it is also important to recognize that they may change as the project evolves. For example, it will be important to be able to discuss how individuals may be impacted when a research project changes direction. It will also be important for individuals to discuss and develop a process for adding new members with particular expertise or how to go about ending the collaboration. The latter issue is one of the most important because termination of a relationship without open discussion and agreement can lead to misunderstandings, the intrusion of bad feelings into evaluations and unethical behavior in peer review.

Authorship and Ownership

Maintaining open lines of communication will enable researchers to discuss different issues as they arise and potentially ward off feelings of resentment or behaviors that may hinder the successful completion of the project. One of the most important issues centers on authorship and data ownership. It is good practice to initiate a discussion clarifying the way authorship of papers will occur. Disciplines may vary in terms of the standards for determining authorship; consequently, it is important to discuss expectations and to agree on the process that will be used in the assignment of authorship. In this discussion it will be important to highlight the fact that responsibility and authorship are deeply connected. This type of discussion will also enable everyone to express their ideas about how to deal with the differing expertise levels that may exist among group members. Establishing a process for developing and writing manuscripts will enable the group to ascertain their roles so that input from all participants can be achieved.

Data Management and Transfer

In productive collaborations, such as the one we discussed, we collected information that was directly relevant to our own work and also valuable to the collaborative project. It is important to clarify who has rights to the data and how the data can be used or transferred to the other members. These matters are obviously related to issues of authorship and ownership but may go beyond that because the data collected by one researcher may be vital to the other aspects of the project. Sometimes researchers feel they own the data collected; however, this information may be vital for analysis of other aspects of the project, manuscript preparation, and future grant writing. Consequently it is important to have agreements clarified and plans for how the data can or cannot be used and how it will be transferred from one individual to the other at the outset of the project.

Notes on Faculty–Student Collaboration from the Perspective of GMB

Throughout my professional career, I have attempted to position myself in a collaborative research atmosphere. I realize that the model for collaborative research that I use, which is nonhierarchical, is not very common in my field. However, it is common in other disciplines, especially the sciences, for faculty members to collaborate with students and colleagues. Much of my work has been, and continues to be, done in conjunction with colleagues, graduate students, and undergraduates. I believe it is important to work with graduate and undergraduate students in a way that facilitates learning in a collaborative and supportive environment. Consequently, I have conceived my work in such a way that students are integral members of a research team, sharing in the development of research projects, data collection, analysis, and writing. I also believe it is important to acknowledge the colleagues and assistants who have contributed to the success of my projects, and whenever possible I have included them through coauthorship. This, however, has proven to be detrimental in terms of my professional advancement. My coauthored articles were not considered as important in my tenure and advancement to professor-level reviews. In my promotion to Full Professor, I was required to provide a full accounting of all of my coauthored projects with complete description on my involvement as well as a description of the role of the other participants. My statement was 11 single-spaced pages. Despite the difficulties I have experienced receiving recognition from academic colleagues for my collaborative work, I continue to involve students and work collaboratively with colleagues. However, I do not recommend this path to everyone. I believe the price is high and the benefits should be weighed very carefully against the disadvantages. In reflecting on my career and my heavy involvement in collaborative work, I usually advise others to do collaborative work if it fits with their personality and work style.

Collaborative work with students can present unique issues. Several important aspects of the professor–student relationship need to be addressed in order for this type of collaboration to be successful.

It is important for collaborators to be aware of the sensitive nature of asymmetric power. Given the nature of a student–professor status, it is unlikely that they will have the same career track record. In our case, PH came to our graduate program with a degree in nursing, an M.P.H., and a substantial career on the faculty of Medicine at a Thai university. However, she did not have training in anthropology and ultimately chose to obtain both a master's and a doctorate in Anthropology. Despite her strong background and work, we still found ourselves having to negotiate the power differentials that existed between us.

The student–professor relationship led others to perceive status differentials between us that we did not feel ourselves. Even though PH was an experienced professional in her own right, in the collaborative project she was often perceived as "junior." Being aware of power differences and "location" is an important way to address the issues. All participants should be required to explore their positionality in a manner that is relative, relational, contextual, and continuous.

Although members of the research team may appear to be united by the goals of the study, each brings different understandings and reasons for participating. In the case of the professor–student relationship the differences may seem clear; however, from the professor's perspective, it is important to recognize that mentoring is only one layer of the motivation for collaborating. It is important to repeatedly reflect on the motivations that are driving the project and be sensitive to those places where personal gain in terms of professional advancement may impact the tone or plans for the project. Being clear about the goals of the project at the outset is a useful way to decrease the tensions that can result from different motivations and hidden agendas. Additionally, it is valuable to negotiate commitment to goals in detail and discuss them as the project progresses.

My familiarity with the literature on cross-cultural and feminist thinking and research prepared me to be aware of my power and privilege as a researcher, but it did not always provide me with ways to resolve issues. I have found ongoing discussions and agreements to be very important. Keeping written records of these agreements can help refresh our memories, and I try to encourage my collaborators to keep their own notes and written records of our meetings and commitments. I have found it useful to write a contract and to have students develop their own written contract. These contracts provide us a way to discuss our expectations, timeline, and responsibilities. Students have told me this has been a very positive way to reduce the potential for abuse of power and has been invaluable for keeping themselves on track in accomplishing their goals.

Authorship is one of the most important aspects of collaborative research that needs to be discussed and dealt with in a clear manner. Collaborators should agree on criteria for authorship as well as discuss the possibilities for developing several papers. I have found it helpful to include our agreements related to authorship and data sharing in the contracts we develop. I also find it necessary to develop guidelines that are specific to each situation and to recognize that agreements may be different for the primary paper and for subpapers. In my experience, the time and energy spent discussing issues of authorship and coming to agreements can prevent problems, including hurt feelings and animosity. From my experiences, including the writing of this article, I know it is possible to use the guidelines presented above as ways to avoid some of the pitfalls of collaborations and to have enjoyable, rewarding coauthoring experiences.

Notes on Faculty–Student Collaboration from the Perspective of PH

Based on my experience in the research setting, I reiterate that successful collaborative work involving a mentor and a student requires a positive attitude toward collaboration by both individuals. For me, collaboration has always been a learning experience. It allows students, as coresearchers, to discuss, share, and reflect on information and opinions in the context of a shared research experience. It also results in gaining knowledge and skills from both mentors and peers. In order to engage in successful research collaboration, students as coresearchers need to

1. develop a sense of sharing, particularly with the mentor in terms of times, data collection, and data analysis;
2. maintain a two-way communication with the mentor to minimize misunderstandings and to gain better understanding and support;
3. be open to learning new knowledge and skills deriving from collaborative work, comments, and suggestions. In order to do this, one must realize that only a friend will offer suggestions and comments on one's pitfalls;
4. be able to adjust to work with other people who may have a different style and pace of working;
5. view the mentor–learner relationship as the most important part of research collaboration (as such, one must preserve this relationship and not allow small matters to destroy such friendship);
6. be considerate, particularly on the issue of personal relationships with family;
7. be organized and well prepared at all times.

Points to be considered on the part of the mentor to enhance research collaboration with students include

1. having a sense of sharing in terms of time and information in data collection, analysis, and writing up research results;
2. providing constructive advice or comments in a timely fashion;
3. using a two-way communication to develop clear understanding, support, and feedback to the students;
4. considering the mentor–learner relationship as the most important facet for successful research collaboration;
5. offering reasonable suggestions without being judgmental;
6. considering that the mentor is a role model for students.

Consequently, it is important that the mentor develops motivation and encouragement in students' professional advancement in their career as anthropologists. Ultimately, mentors need to demonstrate professional skills and competencies in their teaching, research studies, academic services, coaching, and advising.

REFERENCES CITED

Beaver, Donald
    2004 Does Collaborative Research Have Greater Epistemic Authority? Scientometrics 60:399–408.
Caulkins, D. Douglas
    1999 Student-Faculty Research: Collaboration in a Liberal Arts College. Anthropology of Work Review 19:18–23.

Clark, Carolyn, and Denise Watson
    1998 Women's Experience of Academic Collaboration. New Directions for Adult Continuing Education 79:63–74.
Cottrell, Barbara, and Jane Parpart
    2006 Academic-Community Collaboration, Gender Research, and Development: Pitfalls and Possibilities. Development in Practice 16:15–26.
Endersby, James
    1996 Collaborative Research in the Social Sciences: Multiple Authorship and Publication Credit. Social Science Quarterly 77:375–392.
Galiana, Francisco D.
    2006 Collaboration Among Researchers: Some Thought and Experiences. Presentation at the "International Engineering Collaboration" panel, IEEE/PES, Montreal, Canada, June 18–22, 2006.
Gottlieb, Alma
    1995 Beyond the Lonely Anthropologist: Collaboration in Research and Writing. American Anthropologist 97(1):21–26.
Hanawalt, Philip C.
    2006 Research Collaborations: Trial, Trust and Truth. Cell 126:823–825.
Hiemstra, Roger, and Ralph Brockett
    1998 From Mentor to Partner: Lessons from a Personal Journey. New Directions for Adult and Continuing Education 79:43–51.
Kennedy, Elizabeth
    1995 In Pursuit of Connection: Reflections on Collaborative Work. American Anthropologist 97(1):26–33.
Laband, David, and Robert Tollison
    2000 Intellectual Collaboration. Journal of Political Economy 108:632–662.
Madariaga, Miguel, Authur Evans, Wahab Brobbey, Martin Phillips, Evelyn Lo, Katayoun Rezai, David N. Schwartz, Gordon M. Trenholme, and Robert A. Weinstein
    2006 Learning by Doing: Developing Fellows' Academic Skills Through Collaborative Research. Medical Teacher 28:77–80.
Pawlowski, Diane R.
    2002 Ethnography and Changing Engineering Education Culture. Paper presented at the 32 nd ASEE/IEEE Frontiers in Education Conference, Boston, MA, November 6–9.
Quandt, Sara, Thomas Arcury, and Aaron Pell
    2001 Something for Everyone? A Community and Academic Partnership to Address Farmworker Pesticide Exposure in North Carolina. Environmental Health Perspectives 109:435–441.
Saltiel, Iris
    1998 Defining Collaborative Partnerships. New Directions for Adult and Continuing Education 79:5–11.
Taylor, Cathy
    2006 A Collaborative Approach to Developing "Learning Synergy" in Primary Health Care. Nurse Education in Practice 7(1):18–25.
Thompson, Isabelle
    2001 Collaboration in Technical Communication: A Qualitative Content Analysis of Journal Articles, 1990–1999. IEEE Transactions on Professional Communication 44(3):161–173.
Wildavsky, Aaron
    1986 On collaboration. Political Science and Politics 19:s237–s248.

LEARNING APPLIED ANTHROPOLOGY IN FIELD SCHOOLS: LESSONS FROM BOSNIA AND ROMANIA

Peter W. Van Arsdale
University of Denver

This chapter illustrates how principles of applied anthropology can be learned through ethnographic or "cultural" field schools. Aside from a well-rounded classroom education, aspiring applied anthropologists ideally should have substantial "experience in the field" before graduating, either through individualized experiences (the more common approach), or through group experiences. The chapter focuses on the latter, and discusses how such field experiences can enhance a student's emerging undergraduate or graduate career track. In addition, using two complementary types of field school (Project Bosnia and Project Romania, both at the University of Denver), the author addresses the concept of pragmatic humanitarianism, as well as the benefits of hands-on group experiences of this nature for students and civil society at large. Keywords: ethnographic field schools, service learning, applied anthropology, internships, Europe

The machine gun fire rattled my brain. The gunner was only a few feet away, and the sound was deafening. Our convoy ground to a halt. The walls of the narrow mountain valley seemed suddenly too close. The drivers jumped out and ran into the forest. A burly, ominous-looking man with a bandanna wrapped around his forehead and ammunition belts draped over his shoulders ran into the road and waved his AK-47 in our direction. "I am Dracul. We are taking over!"

"Get out of those trucks, now!" Dracul shouted. He waved his gun in the direction of my students, riding in the cargo bays, and then added: "You'll be sorry if you do not move." Other guerrillas, following their leader's command, converged around the rear doors of the three convoy vehicles and herded the students off. Some stumbled, because they'd been forced to put on blindfolds a moment earlier and couldn't get their bearings.

The guerrillas lined the students up near a small stream. "Put your hands behind your heads, spread your legs, and shut up," one yelled. "Keep those blindfolds on," another screamed. Female guerrillas then began patting down the female students; male guerrillas began patting down the male students. "All clear," one woman stated in a matter-of-fact fashion.

"You do not have authority to enter our territory," Dracul said. "Did you think you could bring these trucks in without our permission? Did you think you could help those refugees without going through us?" He poked his gun at one of my students, a young man who himself had been in the military, and said: "Did you?" "No, sir," my student replied. "Then take off those blindfolds and get out of the way. We are in charge here."

NAPA BULLETIN 29, pp. 99–109. ISBN 9781405190152. © 2008 by the American Anthropological Association. DOI:10.1111/j.1556-4797.2008.00008.x

With that, Dracul and his ten colleagues jumped into the trucks, turned them around, and drove them back down the valley. My students, seemingly dazed, also turned around and began the journey back on foot, trudging the three miles to where they had begun their relief operation hours earlier.

FIELD SCHOOLS AS SITES OF LEARNING

I will return to the above scenario, which unfolded in Romania's Transylvanian mountains during the summer of 2004, later in this chapter. It exemplifies an unusual—perhaps unique—kind of field school and field experience. This chapter illustrates how principles of applied anthropology can be learned through ethnographic (or "cultural") field schools; two complementary types are presented. The chapter also illustrates how such field experiences can enhance a student's emerging career. Skills such as disaster relief planning, personnel deployment, supplies procurement, mass casualty aid, site security, threat assessment, map interpretation, and interethnic communication can be acquired. Writing skills, as exemplified through the production of briefs, issue papers, and after-action reports, can be improved.

A career track can be mapped in a number of ways as one moves through undergraduate and graduate education. In addition to a well-rounded classroom education, aspiring applied anthropologists ideally should have substantial "experience in the field" before graduating. There are two primary ways of doing this: through an individualized experience, where one functions a bit like the Lone Ranger; and a group experience, where one functions as a member of a team. The former is more common, the latter less common. Capture by guerrillas is very uncommon indeed.

Since the late 19th century, substantial numbers of field opportunities have been created for individual students of cultural anthropology and allied subdisciplines (such as medical anthropology and rural sociology). These opportunities usually have emerged through the joint efforts of the student and his or her faculty advisor. A majority have been supported by internal university funding, others by external funders such as the Wenner-Gren Foundation, the National Science Foundation, the National Institutes of Health, and the Pew Charitable Trust. Most students contribute from their own pockets as well. These experiences afford promising M.A. and Ph.D. candidates, as well as the occasional advanced B.A. candidate, the chance to "test the waters" and gather data needed for a thesis or dissertation.

During the post-WWII era, individual internships and field placements also have come to be emphasized. These are geared more to service than applied research. These are featured in Project Bosnia, as described herein.

For many of the faculty members who are supporting students as they seek "experience in the field," a group experience is perceived to be more difficult to arrange, more costly to underwrite, and more complex to administer. These perceptions hold elements of truth. Yet, if properly conceived and efficiently managed, field schools can be the "ultimate group experience" for a budding field researcher. The inclusion of undergraduate students can work well (see, e. g., Miller 2006). For graduate students, while it is more difficult to collect an extensive body of data for a thesis or dissertation through a field school, the opportunity to truly "get the lay of the land" and receive substantive on-site training on a particular topic or field of operations can be maximized.

A comprehensive overview of field schools of various types has been authored by Madelyn ("Micki") Iris (2004). She is a former president of the National Association for the Practice of Anthropology (NAPA), as am I. She notes that, while archaeological field schools have a long tradition within anthropology, those emphasizing cultural issues do not. Archaeology places a team (often composed primarily of students) at a specific site for a specific "season." The camp can be controlled, logistical problems circumscribed, data definitively compiled. Once on site, travel issues usually are minimal because travel usually is minimal. These factors do not apply as stringently to most of the field schools termed "ethnographic" or "cultural."

As Iris (2004) stresses, being "in the field" takes the student away from the familiar, immersing him or her in the challenges of potentially strange lifeways and potentially difficult logistical challenges. All this is deemed essential as the student progresses toward a longer-term goal of truly independent fieldwork, field service, or field operations as a future professional. A field school offers what is often a more supportive psychosocial environment, because one's fellows are around and the field supervisor is (presumably) taking care of most of the more challenging logistical concerns. The stresses and strains of initial field work for students can be extreme (Van Horn and Van Arsdale 1989).

There are several types of ethnographic or cultural field schools. Iris (2004) has identified four: (1) the "problem-focused" field school affords all participants the opportunity to pursue research on the same topic. Single settings, conjoined sites, or multiple independent sites can be used. Topics emerging from the fields of education, health, mental health, and rural agriculture are among those congruent with this type. The central theme is selected in advance by the students themselves; (2) the "instructor-driven" field school represents a complementary type. The same array of settings can be utilized, and the same kinds of topics addressed, as those noted above. The key difference is that all students participate in the instructor's research project, either individually or as a group. For example, over the years several NSF-funded studies have enabled this type to be established in Latin America; (3) the "applied" field school represents a different type, as defined by Iris. Students' research is targeted to needs that have been identified by community members, whether located in domestic or overseas settings. As with that conducted by Iris herself (in Illinois on gerontological issues), this type is highly reliant on long-standing relationships that the faculty leader has cultivated; and (4) what might be called the "hybrid." It combines elements of more traditional study-abroad programs and more recent service-learning programs. The model described in this chapter for Bosnia represents this type (see also Van Arsdale 2004).

Still other types exist. Some emphasize the development of methodological proficiency for students, such as that on tourism sponsored by North Carolina State University (Wallace 2004). Others emphasize the intersection of museum studies and ethnography

(Werner 2004). Most of the remainder represent variants of study abroad programs. That described in this chapter for Romania represents an extreme outlier of this type. Likely the first of its kind, at least as far as the partnering of a Balkan and non-Balkan nation are concerned, our program was built on the notion of "country team operations." While incorporating some of what Iris (2004:11) describes as a "grand tour," with site visits throughout the country, the Romanian field school also was extremely focused. Refugee and internally displaced person (IDP) assistance, couched within the context of civil–military operations, was central.

PROJECT BOSNIA

The University of Denver (DU), where I teach, utilizes variants of the service-learning model in many of its domestic and international student programs. These can be found six miles from campus and 6000 miles from campus. Our program in Bosnia is built on one such variant. This general approach affords students a range of complementary field experiences. It is based, in large part, on the work of our nationally recognized (now retired) colleague David Lisman. His working definition is as follows: "Service learning, or academically based community service, is a form of learning in which students engage in community service as part of academic course work" (Lisman 1998:23). He notes that over 500 universities and colleges within the United States offer one or more variants of it. It is a kind of experiential education, the primary premises being (1) community service experiences connected to the learning outcomes of a course; (2) service experiences planned and implemented to be congruent to the host organization's expressed needs; (3) opportunities for students to obtain "teacher-guided reflections" on their service experiences; (4) the volunteer, that is, the student, being assigned regular organizational tasks by the host organization, rather than focusing on "special assignments;" (5) the use of journaling to record the students' observations and interpretations, these to complement in-class assignments and written reports (Van Arsdale 2004:74).

Service learning builds on the concepts of the apprenticeship, the internship, and cooperative education. DU emphasizes the term *internship,* both to illustrate the experiential emphasis within an agency setting and to market the program more effectively. Four types of stakeholder ultimately benefit from a successful program of this kind: students, faculty, communities, and institutions. Career exploration is presented as a central reason as to why a student should apply. Volunteer work that directly contributes to the ongoing mission of the host agency is presented as a central reason as to why an agency should accept a student.

As Janneli Miller (2006:43) stresses, a "service learning ethnographic design is invaluable." Most service learning programs are designed to be multidisciplinary. In addition to students of cultural anthropology, ours attracts students from international studies, social work, law, political science, psychology, sociology, and art. Although an ethnographic component underlies all of the field assignments, as well as all of the final papers that are submitted on the students' return, this element is presented implicitly rather than explicitly. This allows the emphasis to be on the service learning–career building aspect rather than on the research–analytic aspect (Van Arsdale 2004).

Project Bosnia began in 1996. I joined the program as faculty advisor the following year and served in this role through 2004. Because the Bosnian civil war had just ended in late 1995, and resources still were scarce to support foreign students (or visitors of any kind), the first group of 15 from our university focused on refugee resettlement activities in Bosnia and Croatia. They lived near two refugee/IDP camps and spent a majority of their time with Muslim villagers who themselves were engaged in basic house reconstruction, land reclamation, and livestock herd regeneration. Several students brought back photos of themselves helping farmers transport lambs and piglets, one even stuffing a full-grown and highly agitated sheep into the trunk of a farmer's car.

During the next several years, the project expanded in ways more congruent with the principles espoused by David Lisman. Prospective students filled out formal applications detailing their reasons for wanting to work in Bosnia, the ways in which such placements would complement their studies, and their perceptions of service learning as a means toward these ends. While undergraduate applicants were not grilled as to their career aspirations, graduate student applicants were. The application process came to involve the writing of short essays regarding what the students hoped to accomplish, what strengths they thought they would bring to the program, and what constraints they thought they would encounter "in the field." All applicants were interviewed by a team of faculty and staff members, with as many as four present for each session.

By 1997 an array of prospective NGOs and IGOs had been lined up for those students who had been selected. World Vision International, the American Rescue Committee, the United Methodist Committee on Relief, and the UN High Commission for Refugees were among the dozen organizations stepping forward and offering internships. Following the suggestion of Lisman, as well as that of other faculty at the university experienced in international education, students came to be required to pursue their own placements. That is, for the past ten years, four months before departure each successful applicant has been instructed to begin to e-mail, write, or phone those agencies whose missions appear to match his or her own personal objectives. This rarely proceeds without a hitch. Yet this has become part of the learning process.

Among the most successful of the students have been those studying at the DU College of Law. More than a dozen have participated during the first ten years of Project Bosnia's existence. Three secured placements with the International Commission for Missing Persons, based in Sarajevo. Their assignments included on-site administrative assistance for forensic anthropologists as they exhumed bodies in eastern Bosnia, review of logistical parameters associated with the repatriation of remains, assistance in the writing of legal briefs used outside the court system, and communicating with the families of those who had lost members during the war.

As time and resources have permitted, my colleagues and I have worked for short periods on site with our students. One of the most poignant experiences took place in 2003. It involved a family of Bosnian Muslims who had been living in Scandinavia but had returned temporarily to the Republic of Serbia (i.e., the Serbian portion of Bosnia—

Herzegovina). At first, unbeknownst to our team, it turned out that the reason the family had returned to their home village was to prepare proper graves for two young relatives who had been killed during the war. Their bodies originally had been hastily interred, just before the remaining family members fled, becoming refugees as they crossed the border into Croatia. During the war, Serb and Muslim fighting had been ferocious in this area. It was said that Muslims from this village had killed several Serb leaders, and that revenge by Serb soldiers had been swift. Of the 100 or so families who once had lived here—a small and homogeneous Muslim enclave among thousands of Serbs in dozens of neighboring villages—no one had been left unscathed. Perhaps 15 percent had been killed outright, another 15 percent wounded, and the remainder temporarily or permanently displaced. Eight years after the war, the reconstruction of homes was underway. A number of families had returned to stay. Our student was working, alongside Bosnians of all ethnicities, to assist them. The opportunity to help a family that did not intend to stay, as they once again grieved their loss, came unexpectedly. It proved especially meaningful to all of us. After graduation, the student went on to secure a job assisting refugees.

PROJECT ROMANIA

This chapter comes full circle as we return to the unusual field experience highlighted at the beginning. Dracul and his guerrilla colleagues in fact were Romanian troops in training, members of the elite Romanian Land Forces Academy (similar to the U.S. Army's West Point). They were enacting a scenario or simulation that our staff, in concert with Romanian officers, had concocted days in advance. The 15 students who were "captured" had no idea that this would happen, but had been well versed in country team operations, had been working alongside Romanian soldiers, and had been preparing for unusual and realistic scenarios. As the summer of 2004 went on, they encountered a number of other difficult situations in the Transylvania mountains, some of which are outlined below.

Built in part on service learning principles, the country team operations model incorporates training exercises, scenarios or simulations, and on-site study and guest lectures. It is maximally experiential. While not aimed at community service per se, it is aimed at cross-cultural community integration, manifested through jointly planned and jointly implemented exercises. It employs a type of cooperative learning. A formal, contractual partnering is undertaken. Our version, sponsored jointly by DU and the Romanian Department of Defense, focused on civil–military cooperation.

The initial plan for Project Romania was conceived by Derrin Smith, a former doctoral student of mine, adjunct professor of international studies at our university, and specialist in civil–military operations. (His most recent assignments have taken him to Afghanistan, Iraq, and Israel.) His extensive work in Romania during the previous decade had opened a number of communication channels and a number of transnational training opportunities. His prior service in the U. S. Marine Corps, coupled with his current contractual work with defense agencies, had enabled him to develop expertise in an array of field operations. One of his contacts reached to the office of the Romanian presidency, another to the highest levels of that nation's department of defense. Several senior administrators expressed interest in the possibility of working with a foreign university on joint training operations. This complemented the Romanian president's vision of expanded military cooperation with NATO, which his nation was about to join, as well as expanded educational cooperation with the United States.

On the U.S. side, preparations for a summer of training operations in Romania began with a five-credit, campus-based, graduate-level class entitled "Country Team Operations: Theory and Training." Smith and I offered this during the spring quarter of 2004. "Best practices" associated with materiel deployment, refugee camp operations, recovery operations, and field communications were featured. Also featured were ways to write predeparture reports, field assessments, event-specific briefing papers, and after-action reports. One of my specialties is theory and praxis associated with humanitarian operations and the roles of NGOs, so two three-hour lectures featured this. One of Smith's specialties is field deployment and recovery operations under military supervision, so two of his lectures featured this. Three lectures covered operations of the American Red Cross; these were complemented by all-day certification exercises where our students learned CPR, techniques of basic medical assistance, and ways to construct and use stretchers. Case-based examples of emergency preparedness planning and emergency operations worldwide (incl. some associated with natural disasters) rounded out the classroom lectures.

The class ended with a set of carefully crafted field exercises. These took place near the small mountain town of Creede, Colorado, itself located near the headwaters of the Rio Grande. Activities spanned a three-day period during mid-May, 2004. In addition to Smith and me, our professional field staff consisted of three nonuniversity based professionals. Two had extensive military experience. Students were responsible for planning all basic logistics. Five teams were assembled, each headed by an administrative officer. Supplies were requisitioned in the same manner that they would be in an overseas operation. Convoys were set up, so that students could travel by car from Denver to Creede—a distance of 300 miles—in organized fashion. On arrival in the field, tents were set up and supplies distributed. One student was assigned responsibility for overall site coordination, another for radio communications, still another for field logistics. Each team contributed to cooking, cleaning, and site maintenance.

Field exercises focused on two primary missions: (1) to conduct a search and rescue (SAR) mission for survivors of a 16-seat aircraft accident, and (2) to observe and report the local conditions impacting internally displaced persons (IDPs). Because these in fact were mock operations, built on scenarios the staff had created, a mock nation also was created. The "nation of Anstravia" therefore became the seat of operations. It was deemed to be "under siege" and students cum field operatives–humanitarians were deemed to be operating under a medium-to-high threat level (Fontaine 2004).

As the exercises unfolded, students were able to engage several areas of emergent expertise. In addition to convoy operations, these included the conduct of site surveys, with an emphasis on map interpretation and intelligence. Compass work over rough terrain allowed them to hone their skills. A type of orienteering was employed as they sought clues to the "downed aircraft." Work with threat assessment was complemented by the establishment of security perimeters for our camp, as well as logistical protocols and security practices, which ultimately assisted them as they completed local conditions reports benefiting "Anstravian IDPs."

All of these skills again were utilized when the students arrived in Romania several weeks later. During the first phase of our trip, a kind of "grand tour," we were primarily aided by officers of the Romanian Air Force and were billeted at the equivalent of that nation's Air Force Academy. Several guest lectures were presented. During the second phase of our trip, a targeted "on-site training," we were primarily aided by officers and advanced cadets of the Romanian Land Forces Academy. We were based at one of their primary training camps and shuttled 20 miles west to one of their primary field bases.

The process of entrée to the Transylvanian field camp site was designed in such a way that students were divided into two teams, each charged with mapping out a route, arranging a convoy of military vehicles, loading and transporting supplies, and coordinating radio communications. One team took the "high route," through hills and low mountains. The other took the "low route," through a system of valleys. It was on a follow-up relief operation through the "low route," after both teams had joined, that they were "captured" by Dracul and his band of guerrillas.

A complete relief camp was built, literally from the ground up and centered around large military tents, in a gently rolling field about a mile from the academy's primary field base. Outhouses were constructed and latrines installed. A small communications command post was set up on an adjacent hilltop. A generator-run electrical system was installed. In short, we established a camp that would serve as the center of field operations and as a base to assist "refugees" and "IDPs" whose arrivals were anticipated.

During the next few days, and following scenarios that had been scripted by members of our team in conjunction with the Romanian officers and cadets, a number of difficult situations unfolded. At the ready and working 24/7, our students were variously confronted by "irate peasants" from a "neighboring village," who claimed that our camp's new operations were upsetting the local political situation; the same group, who came again on a subsequent day, claiming that we had inadvertently but thoughtlessly constructed our camp over several community gravesites; "IDPs" who required medical assistance based on a protocol and triage system we previously had practiced (with Red Cross assistance) in Denver; "guerrillas" who attacked our camp at midnight; "refugees" who needed to be evacuated; and a "hostage situation" wherein one of the female students was captured and held at gunpoint in a dilapidated farmhouse until her colleagues could negotiate her release. (She handled the ordeal in remarkably calm fashion.)

These last two incidents illustrate both the realism that our mock operations engendered and the financial costs that our program incurred. The "refugees" were evacuated on Romanian military helicopters. We had access to these for two days, including training in flight operations, the loading of supplies, care of the wounded, and radio communications. The woman's capture was preceded by a battle that included the use of training explosives, dummy mortars and gunfire, and a mock automobile/truck accident. We had six trucks, two ambulances, and ten senior Romanian military officers at our disposal throughout this set of field exercises. We had eight helicopter crewmen at our disposal for two days, including one of the country's senior flight instructors.

Project Romania allowed master's candidates from a wide range of concentrations, all within the DU Graduate School of International Studies, to work together. This included those focusing on homeland security, human rights, international development, and international administration. It afforded students whose political views were more conservative to work alongside those whose views were more liberal. It afforded students who had military experience themselves to work alongside those with no such experience; indeed, some in the latter group had been vocally outspoken against the military prior to joining our program. Of equal importance, it afforded students the opportunity to merge theory with practice, and to hone skills essential to careers involving on-site work in refugee camps, civil–military relief operations, or disaster assistance activities.

LEARNINGS AND OUTCOMES

What students have learned through their participation in Project Bosnia and Project Romania can be measured against the desired, career-oriented outcomes outlined in a recent book by Riall Nolan (2003). In *Anthropology in Practice: Building a Career Outside the Academy,* he stresses that it is essential we build an "anthropology of engagement." This suggests active engagement in human affairs, both civil and military, both profit and nonprofit, in ways that enable us to "be authentic." For students, this suggests participation in field schools that provide definable actions, utilize specific training exercises, and offer workable strategies to aid (often marginalized) target populations. To be able to "go public" with one's skills and to "solve for pattern" with one's analytic abilities is key to a career as a practitioner.

Through the service learning program in Bosnia, the student (previously discussed) who worked on home reconstruction and refugee repatriation involving Muslims within Bosnia's Republic of Serbia, learned about site logistics and construction supply distribution, personnel planning, on-site monitoring of agency operations, and report preparation. More "classically anthropological," he learned a tremendous amount about interethnic relations and interethnic communications. Part of his assignment involved brokering communications among Serb humanitarian workers and the repatriating Muslims whom they were assisting. Other students in Bosnia learned complementary skills (some being more data analytic).

Through country team operations in Romania, students learned disaster relief planning (incl. refugee camp development and maintenance), mass casualty aid (nonmedical), emergency first aid, triage needs assessment (nonmedical), techniques for maintaining site security, the process of threat assessment, the process of personnel deployment and task assignment, map interpretation and intelligence, and radio communication. While not "practicing anthropological skills" per se, these are "field skills of use to practicing anthropologists." A student practicing on- and off-loading of supplies with a helicopter in Romania is authentically preparing for assignment to the most challenging of field situations, anthropological or otherwise.

Both programs have enabled our students to improve their writing skills, specifically in ways that bridge theory and practice. Both require students to maintain daily logs of specific activities, these tied to the administrative and service components of the programs. Both require the writing of briefs, issue papers, and field reports summarizing "key learnings" and "best practices." The journaling by students enrolled in Project Bosnia demands a daily focus on "what works." The after-action briefings and "hot washes" produced by students enrolled in Project Romania—even though derived from simulations—are precisely the kind of briefings they will have to produce should they find themselves working in a refugee camp in Kenya or a hurricane relief encampment in Louisiana.

Both Project Bosnia and Project Romania incorporate elements of what I elsewhere refer to as "pragmatic humanitarianism" (Van Arsdale 2006). Tied to an emerging theory of obligation, this notion of humanitarianism features hands-on training with at-risk populations. It respects rather than castigates humanitarian intervention (i.e., humanitarian operations partnering civil and military personnel in the service of those at risk). It engages the simple liberal premise that what one person does, within one grassroots agency or field site, makes a difference. Through what are termed "obligated actions," the materially possible (e. g., a network of service providers) is linked with the morally possible (e. g., institutional accountability).

I believe that virtually all of the students who participated in Project Bosnia and Project Romania benefited greatly from their experiences. A number used their experiences as "springboards" to other university-based overseas opportunities, many of these also in the Balkans (e. g., Croatia, Albania, Montenegro). A number followed up with undergraduate honors theses and graduate master's theses. Several of these documents dealt with nonprofit organizational issues (e. g., the operations of NGOs in Bosnia), human rights issues (e. g., the repatriation of Bosnian Muslims to their original houses and apartments), and civil–military cooperation issues (e. g., the delivery of humanitarian aid by the Romanian military).

More than 20 of the 100-plus students who have participated in these programs have gone on to secure employment directly linked to their service learning and country team operations experiences. Most recently these have been exemplified by posts with InterAction (as an advocacy specialist), the United Nations (as a gender-abuse specialist), and DU (as a study abroad specialist).

Emergent civil societies also benefit from the participation of students in programs like those in Bosnia and Romania. Stated differently, what goes around comes around. This paraphrases one of David Lisman's central premises regarding service learning (1998). These types of field schools are not targeted exclusively to anthropology students, and indeed, function best when an array of disciplines are represented among participants. I see "cultural" field schools as being those that not only immerse a student in an intriguing overseas, transnational, or cross-ethnic setting but also that engage a student in activities which benefit members of that culture—at times both civilian and military. The field of applied anthropology, broadly defined, also benefits as those who are students of our discipline contribute to ongoing research, community service, and programmatic change.

REFERENCES CITED

Fontaine, Laura, ed.
  2004 Creede Convoy Manual and After-Action Report. Unpublished MS, Graduate School of International Studies, University of Denver.
Iris, Madelyn
  2004 What is a Cultural Anthropology Field School and What is it Good For? *In* Passages: The Ethnographic Field School and First Fieldwork Experiences. NAPA Bulletin 22. Madelyn Iris, ed. Pp. 8–13. Arlington, VA: American Anthropological Association.
Lisman, C. David
  1998 Toward a Civil Society: Civic Literacy and Service Learning. Westport, CT: Bergin and Garvey.
Miller, Janneli F.
  2006 Commentary: Can You Take Undergraduates to the Field? A Field School Example. Practicing Anthropology 28(1):40–43.
Nolan, Riall W.
  2003 Anthropology in Practice: Building a Career Outside the Academy. Boulder, CO: Lynne Rienner.
Van Arsdale, Peter W.
  2004 Rehabilitation, Resistance, and Return: Service Learning and the Quest for Civil Society in Bosnia. *In* Passages: The Ethnographic Field School and First Fieldwork Experiences. NAPA Bulletin 22. Madelyn Iris, ed. Pp. 72–86. Arlington, VA: American Anthropological Association.
  2006 Forced to Flee: Human Rights and Human Wrongs in Refugee Homelands. Lanham, MD: Lexington Books.
Van Horn, Larry, and Peter Van Arsdale
  1989 *Review of* Ethnographers in the Field: The Psychology of Research. High Plains Applied Anthropologist 9:297–302.
Wallace, Tim
  2004 Apprentice Ethnographers and the Anthropology of Tourism in Costa Rica. *In* Passages: The Ethnographic Field School and First Fieldwork Experiences. NAPA Bulletin 22. Madelyn Iris, ed. Pp. 35–54. Arlington, VA: American Anthropological Association.
Werner, Oswald
  2004 Foreword. *In* Passages: The Ethnographic Field School and First Fieldwork Experiences. NAPA Bulletin 22. Madelyn Iris, ed. Pp. 1–7. Arlington, VA: American Anthropological Association.

WORKING FOR THE FEDERAL GOVERNMENT: ANTHROPOLOGY CAREERS

SHIRLEY J. FISKE

Consultant and Adjunct Professor, University of Maryland

The federal government is arguably the largest employer of anthropologists outside of academia. The most comprehensive data on numbers of anthropologists are from the U.S. Office of Personnel Management. These data and their limitations are described. This chapter argues that applied and practicing anthropology are at historic employment levels, with at least five agencies having "institutional presence" of in-house anthropologists. Much of the growth is based on statutes enacted in the 1960s and 1970s, and solidified by anthropologists who codified their use around agency missions. Five agencies with institutional presence are highlighted, as examples of careers in the federal government. In addition the chapter describes careers and career paths in the federal government for a number of specialty areas including international development, both as a consultant and as a full-time permanent government employee, cultural resource management, the legislative branch, forensic and physical anthropology, natural resource management, and defense and security sectors, by using interviews and career cameos of senior anthropologists in those agencies. The chapter concludes with specific information on where to find vacancy announcements and how to respond to them; collective experience of lessons learned in seeking federal careers; and the author's views on the importance of engagement for anthropologists in policies, issues, and program management in the federal sector. Keywords: federal government, applied anthropology, anthropology careers, policy

THE LARGEST MARKET FOR ANTHROPOLOGY CAREERS

The federal government is arguably the largest employer of anthropologists outside of universities if one includes regional and international posts such as foreign service. Not surprisingly, archaeologists account for the great majority of federal hires in anthropology, with cultural anthropologists next, and the number of biological, physical and linguistic anthropologists far fewer.

It is difficult to generalize about anthropological careers in the federal government. Jobs range from work with consulting firms with contracts from the federal government, to employment in the foreign service, to archaeologists in cultural resource management, and social science analysts in the legislative branches. The work varies from managing offices of planners and policy analyst, to leading teams of scientists in reviewing programs,

NAPA BULLETIN 29, pp. 110–130. ISBN 9781405190152. © 2008 by the American Anthropological Association. DOI:10.1111/j.1556-4797.2008.00009.x

assessing public health or social impacts, evaluating federal programs, and directing foreign assistance programs in-country.

The federal governmental sector, along with its allied institutions—consulting firms, contractors, universities—the partners and recipients of contracts, grants, and cooperative agreements—is an economic engine that provides a huge market for anthropologists who seek applied and practicing careers in public issues, management, and policy.

HOW MANY ANTHROPOLOGISTS WORK FOR THE FEDERAL GOVERNMENT?

The Office of Personnel Management (OPM), which tracks the federal government's workforce, identifies 7,500 *social scientists* (job series GS-101) including anthropologists, behavioral scientists, geographers, sociologists, and planners working for the federal government in 2006. In addition, anthropologists are hired under the GS-190 job series, *general anthropologist,* and GS-193s, *archaeologists.* These two job series are specific to anthropologists, meaning that only anthropologists generally qualify. OPM data show 144 general anthropologists and 1,150 archaeologists working for the federal government (see Table 1).

Although OPM data are the most comprehensive data available, they vastly underrepresent the actual number of cultural anthropologists and archaeologists working for the federal government, because many are working in job categories such as social scientist, program analyst, planner, or behavioral scientist. In addition these data do not reflect part-time positions or those who work on contract to the federal government; nor do they include foreign service and U.S. Agency for International Development (USAID) civil service positions and contractors. Still, it is safe to argue that the number of job positions identified for anthropologically trained individuals in the civil and foreign service is far greater than at any time in U.S. history.

WHERE DO ANTHROPOLOGISTS WORK? INSTITUTIONALIZATION OF ANTHROPOLOGY IN FIVE FEDERAL AGENCIES

Anthropologists have developed institutional presence in at least five federal agencies—a historical "first" for professional anthropology. By institutional presence, I mean a critical mass of in-house, permanent expertise from anthropologists working on public issues. To give an idea of anthropology careers in these agencies, I highlight here examples from the U.S. Census Bureau, the National Park Service (NPS), National Marine Fisheries Service (NMFS), Centers for Disease Control and Prevention (CDC), and USAID. These concentrations of anthropological expertise usually result from the hard work and bureaucratic wisdom of dedicated individuals who have devoted their careers to establishing an agency-codified basis for social science research and promoted the hiring of additional social scientists to fill agency needs.

At the U.S. Census Bureau (Department of Commerce), anthropologists have played a critical role in identifying the causes of and recommendations for overcoming the

TABLE 1. Employment of Selected Social Science Job Series As of June 2006

Cabinet Level Agencies

EMPLOYMENT AS VALUES	0101-SOCIAL SCIENCE	0190-GENERAL ANTHROPOLOGY	0193-ARCHEOLOGY	TOTAL 190 AND 193
DEPARTMENT OF DEFENSE	2,358	40	177	217
DEPARTMENT OF AGRICULTURE	202	2	446	448
DEPARTMENT OF COMMERCE	47	1	0	1
DEPARTMENT OF JUSTICE	1,807	0	0	0
DEPARTMENT OF LABOR	8	0	0	0
DEPARTMENT OF ENERGY	2	0	10	10
DEPARTMENT OF EDUCATION	41	0	0	0
DEPARTMENT OF HEALTH AND HUMAN SERVICES	1,088	3	0	0
DEPARTMENT OF HOMELAND SECURITY	210	60	0	60
DEPARTMENT OF HOUSING AND URBAN DEVELOPMENT	23	0	0	0
DEPARTMENT OF INTERIOR	81	38	512	550
DEPARTMENT OF STATE	17	0	0	0
DEPARTMENT OF TRANSPORTATION	25	0	0	0
DEPARTMENT OF TREASURY	33	0	0	0
DEPARTMENT OF VETERANS AFFAIRS	1,585	0	0	0
Cabinet Level Agencies	7,527	144	1,145	1,289

Continued

TABLE 1. *Continue*

EMPLOYMENT AS VALUES	0101-SOCIAL SCIENCE	0190-GENERAL ANTHROPOLOGY	0193-ARCHEOLOGY	TOTAL 190 AND 193
Medium Independent Agencies (100–999 employees)				
U.S. INSTITUTE OF PEACE	2	0	0	0
PRESIDIO TRUST	0	0	2	2
PEACE CORPS	2	0	0	0
Medium Independent Agencies (100–999 employees)	4	0	2	2
Small Independent Agencies (less than 100 employees)				
COMMISSION ON CIVIL RIGHTS	3	0	0	0
VALLES CALDERA TRUST	0	0	2	2
INTER-AMERICAN FOUNDATION	17	0	0	0
OFC OF NAVAJO AND HOPI INDIAN RELOCATION	1	0	0	0
Small Independent Agencies (less than 100 employees)	21	0	2	2

Source: U.S. Office of Personnel Management (OPM).

traditional undercounts of nontraditional households and populations in U.S. decennial censuses. They have also led to documenting the changes in family structure of marginalized or underdocumented groups (Schwede et al. 2006). The Bureau has used anthropological expertise to critique and improve its methods and approach to enumerating the national population, develop reliable methodologies for identifying marginalized and difficult-to-enumerate populations, including homeless, mobile populations (gypsies, migrant workers), urban American Indian households, and to recruit community-knowledgeable people to help conduct the census. The work of anthropologists and other social scientists within the Bureau (and contracted studies from outside) has led to the recognition that accurate enumeration is enhanced by local knowledge of communities and rural areas (see U.S. Census Bureau 2004).

The NPS (U.S. Department of the Interior) has developed long term, in-house expertise and programs with archaeologists and cultural anthropologists, particularly the use of ethnography and rapid appraisals to ascertain local views and voices of traditionally associated people who have lived in, near, or used a park's resources. The Ethnography Program was firmly based on statutory requirements from NEPA, American Indian Religious Freedom Act, Alaska National Interest Lands Conservation Act, and the National Historic Preservation Act (NHPA). The ethnography program includes park and regional ethnographers and a small staff in its Washington, D.C., headquarters. Anthropologists in regional offices and parks do research to ensure that program planning and park management respond to the voices of traditionally associated peoples and that national parks interpret the cultural meanings of park resources in appropriate ways. In addition, the NPS is also the cornerstone for the robust federal archaeology program—see the Archaeology/CRM section below. The NPS programs are among the most visible to anthropologists because of the long-term commitment of a number of individuals and the development of many training workshops, partnerships and networks of affiliates, contractors, and grant recipients, who share resources and views (Crespi 1999; NPS 2003; Schafft 2004).

The NMFS (National Oceanic and Atmospheric Administration [NOAA]) has established a strong corps of social scientists including many anthropologists in regional and headquarters offices in addition to the more traditionally recruited economists and fishery biologists. The goal is to improve the ability to predict social and cultural impacts of alternative fishery management policies and actions on fishing families and communities. Like the NPS capabilities, NMFS's social-analytic strength has developed through the perseverance of a number of individuals who have systematically supported the need for more social science data in planning documents, directives, and annual plans. In addition, NOAA has funded many anthropologists through universities on research and extension efforts (Fiske 1990, 1999). A boost to the NMFS program occurred when the 1996 Sustainable Fisheries Act included amendments mandating that NMFS take into account the effects of fishery management alternatives on fishing communities' "sustained participation" in the fishery, and to minimize adverse effects on the communities to the extent possible (Clay and Olson 2007). Funding for the growing network of anthropologists and social scientists in regional offices and science centers was at last included in the FY2001 budget (Colburn et al. 2006).

The mission of the CDC, located in Atlanta, Georgia, is to develop and implement programs for disease prevention and control, environmental health, and general health promotion and education. The agency's mission expanded as the nation's health profile changed from its early work on insect-borne diseases in WWII, to infectious diseases, chronic, and noninfectious conditions. More recently, the agency has taken on environmental health issues, as well as injuries and homicides. There are about 45–55 anthropologists working for the CDC, including contractors, student interns, postdocs and others who are not FTE (full time permanent) civil servants. About half to two-thirds are FTEs. The number of anthropologists at the CDC has increased steadily since 1992, as have the areas of specialization where they are hired. The historical base for anthropologists at the CDC has been in the Division of HIV/AIDS Prevention, but anthropologists now work in prevention research and methods, tuberculosis, diabetes, immunization services, health communications, and environmental hazards divisions, among others.

The CDC is a case where a critical corps of anthropologists developed without a national legislative mandate for social impacts (such as NEPA), in concert with public health issues and agency's mission to promote health. The behavioral and social sciences at the CDC have had a notable impact on the public health agenda and programs in the United States (see Fiske 2007a).

USAID has developed a critical mass of anthropologists since the early 1970s. To date the majority of them work as institutional contractors, contractors in consulting firms, or NGOs. A handful of anthropologists have reached senior executive levels at USAID in both the civil and foreign service. A conservative estimate would be that there are 25 to 30 people with advanced degrees (Ph.D. or master's) in anthropology who are USAID direct hires. In addition, there are an estimated 100 to 200 anthropologists on contract at any given time (Atherton, personal communication, May 2005). USAID is unique among federal agencies in the extensive use of contractor hires. Since 1992, the change in the direct-hire workforce, in both USAID Washington and overseas, has declined by about 1,000 positions (500 positions each), or a 31 percent decrease in Civil Service and 29 percent in foreign service positions (USAID, Quarterly Workforce 2006). Anthropologists tend to work in areas such as rural and agricultural development, as contract officers, in program evaluation, women's initiatives, governance and democratization, and as mission directors in the foreign service, as examples.

WHAT TYPES OF CAREERS CAN ANTHROPOLOGISTS EXPECT IN THE FEDERAL GOVERNMENT?

I considered two ways to approach this question: by federal agency and by specialization. Hopefully the most informative and least confusing is to talk about federal careers by specialty such as development assistance, natural resource management, or cultural resource management.

In gathering information for this article, I conducted in-depth interviews with eight anthropologists about their careers working for the federal government. My hope is that including cameos of their work and lives as anthropologists working for the federal government will put a face on the diverse ways that anthropologists have developed careers in the federal government. This chapter also includes insights from my 24 years of experience in the executive and legislative branches of government, as well as with local and national professional associations.

Careers in International Development

Most anthropologists who want to do applied work have aspirations of working abroad in some aspect of international development or assistance. Following are two cameos illustrating different approaches to careers in international development and assistance, both of whom consider themselves to be working for the federal government.

International Development as a Government Employee. USAID comprises two different services, the civil service and foreign service. The majority of anthropologists have appointments in the foreign service, but Joan Atherton is a career direct hire (FTE) at USAID, who started at USAID in 1979. She has over 25 years of experience in rural development and agricultural policy, the Africa Bureau, and central policy units in the Office of the Administrator at USAID.

Joan joined USAID at a time when the agency was particularly receptive to anthropologists after a series of influential IPAs (rotators from academic positions) had laid the groundwork for an *ex ante* social analysis and impact evaluation program—both of which benefited from anthropological knowledge and ethnographic grounding. A number of anthropologists were hired at that time, most of whom were in the foreign service. All have risen to senior levels in USAID. Joan worked for ten years in the rural development office of USAID's policy bureau on issues such as land reform, integrated rural development, and pastoralist development. She spent another dozen years in the Africa region office, first in the planning office and then managing a field program from Washington, D.C., involving the nine Sahelian states in West Africa. She was recruited in 2006 into the central policy office and is now working across U.S. agencies involved in development assistance to improve U.S. coordination with other donors of foreign aid, including nations, the World Bank, and other multilateral organizations.

Her advice for job seekers for foreign service or civil service portions of USAID is to have a substantive specialty that supports the USAID's mission. USAID doesn't hire anthropologists as an occupational specialty. An anthropologist might be hired, for example, as an *agricultural officer,* but not as an anthropologist per se. "Anthropology is valued because working cross-culturally is an important value in USAID, but a mission-specific, secondary field is important."

Joan points out that once hired, anthropologists have been very successful as direct hires: "A number of them have become Mission Directors, which is the top job in any [assisted] country where they have a lot of decision-making authority and they can inject an anthropological perspective into anything they do. Some of them have also fairly senior positions in the Washington hierarchy. But [anthropologists] have to be willing . . . to trade off their niche of being a technical expert for actually moving into senior management."

International Development as a Contractor. John Mason, formerly Executive Associate at Development Associates, Inc., based in Arlington, Virginia, developed a successful career working for the federal government while never actually being a direct hire with the federal government. He calls his current work "AID-linked," meaning the government is the client. "So it is government work . . . the critical part is 'paid for by the government.'" John has a Ph.D. in Anthropology from Boston University, uses Arabic and French professionally, and specializes in the Arab Middle East and sub-Saharan Africa. He has worked for almost four decades in international development, including over a decade overseas in Arab, African, and Caribbean countries. He worked for six years in evaluation research and four years in disaster management for an institutional contractor, placed inside USAID in their offices. Prior to and following those posts, John worked for a number of different consulting firms on USAID contracts. Notably, he was project director for the monitoring and evaluation of the USAID-funded economic growth strategy for Egypt, including a $400–$500 million budget per year.

He chose this career path (consulting versus permanent government employment) because being a contractor allows the anthropologist to keep his or her specialty, and practice hands-on development anthropology more directly. As he explains it, "it is not that USAID does not look for specific skills in direct-hires. The fact is that they do not end up using them very much over the course of a career (except perhaps in navigating the bureaucratic culture of the agency), and they [the skills] therefore fade." For example, John noted, "I kept my Arabic up because I use it in my work. Would USAID people keep up their Arabic? Less than likely—they do not get back out to the same countries. They're assigned worldwide, and you do not always have your choice."

John's advice to graduate students is to "study those things that you really like to study. Do not necessarily aim for a specific job or career, but see where it takes you. Be sure to master a language—that's invaluable." John was able to make the consulting world work for him and his family, and was able to maintain his specialty, the Arab Middle East, which kept his interest and allowed him to keep his skills in an area that he loved.

Archaeology and Cultural Resources Management (CRM)

By far the largest number of anthropologists hired by the federal government are archaeologists—approximately 1,153 archaeologists compared with 144 general anthropologists (see Table 1). This does not even include the vast number of archaeologists who have made careers working in CRM as contracting archaeologists in firms that work primarily with federal (but often state or private) funding through contracts and grants, or those archaeologists who are hired part time. Also, the majority of the archaeologists' jobs are not in Washington, D.C., but in regional or district offices in western states where there is vast acreage of public lands under the management of the U.S. Forest Service (USFS), Bureau of Land Management (BLM), NPS, the Department of Defense (DoD)—military reservations and in the Corps of Engineers (ACOE)—and other land management bureaus and agencies.

The successful growth in the number of federal archaeologists can be traced in part to the cumulative effect of legislative statutes, executive orders, and specific agency directives that mandate preservation and conservation of historic resources; the early existence of the archaeology job series; and the gearing-up of federal agencies to meet the preservation and environmental requirements mandated by laws, especially the Antiquities Act of 1906, NHPA and its amendments, and NEPA (1969).

The employment trends are positive and dramatic. In 1989, it was estimated that there were 300 to 400 FTE archaeologists. "The biggest employer of archaeologists is the BLM of the Department of the Interior with 120 full-time archaeologists (plus 60 or so part timers) and the Forest Service of the USDA with 100" (Gyrisco 1989:109). Eighteen years later, the Department of the Interior is still the largest federal employer of archaeologists, increasing to 512, and the USDA Forest Service is second with 446. The DoD—the ACOE and other branches—is third, at 177 archaeologists. Each federal department and agency is responsible for ensuring that its actions, or those it permits, licenses, or funds, do not destroy significant archaeological resources—without some mitigation of the adverse impacts.

The NPS internal and external programs, the USFS, the Advisory Council for Historic Preservation, and the Smithsonian Institution all have significant numbers of archaeologists, primarily in the management and technical assistance areas. The NHPA has spawned state-based offices, the State Historic Preservation Offices (SHPOs), which are funded through federal appropriations and state contributions. As federal agencies hired professional archaeologists in the 1970s to meet their legal requirements, this

> eventually led to the hiring of professional archaeologists by state agencies and private firms that found themselves required by federal agencies to carry our necessary cultural resources studies. By the end of the 1970s, federal and state agencies had developed a network that included hundreds of professional archaeologists filling positions in headquarters, regional and local offices, undertaking a variety of activities to implement CRM laws, policy regulations and guidelines. [McManamon 2000]

This helped establish a national network of professionally qualified archaeologists in the public sector in states across the nation (McManamon 2001; NPS 1994, 1998).

Looking to the future, McManamon observes that archaeological retirements in NPS and other land management agencies are reaching critical proportions. The NPS will likely lose individuals with hundreds of years of experience in the next five years. Unfortunately, the trend is not to advertise and refill the positions. The positions are being filled by bringing in temporaries, junior people on detail, or creating shared positions. This personnel strategy leaves a huge gap in institutional and specialized knowledge in public archaeology programs (McManamon, personal communication, May 2007).

Kate Winthrop is Acting Federal Preservation Officer at Bureau of Land Management (part of the Department of the Interior) while her supervisor is detailed on another assignment. Kate's Ph.D. is from the University of Oregon. She and her husband started their own CRM contracting firm in Oregon for the first ten years of her career, contracting primarily to the federal government. When a friend told her that he was leaving his job with the BLM in Oregon, he urged Kate to apply for the job of District Archaeologist. Kate found that working in a district office provided a great deal of scheduling flexibility in a family-friendly atmosphere: "The pay is good, you get your benefits, you have a lot of control over your schedule, you're doing interesting work, you have a career path that you can progress along. If you come in as a GS-7 or GS-9, you can work up to a 9, 11, or 12; so I think it is a good option for women." She worked in a district office doing identification of historic and archaeological properties, evaluation, mitigation of impacts—basic compliance work for Section 106 of the NHPA.

In 2000, a BLM archaeologist who was liaison from BLM to the Army Environmental Center in Maryland was retiring and asked Kate to apply. The timing coincided with flexibility in family responsibilities. The job was a two-year detail to the Army, but her FTE transferred from Medford, Oregon, to Washington, D.C. When the detail ended, she reported to the Washington office as a staff archaeologist. Now that she is based in Washington, D.C., Kate does very little fieldwork. "What I do, generically, is provide technical assistance and guidance to people in the field. Field offices cope with many different issues and situations. Our job in the Washington office is to assist with these issues and to ensure compliance with laws, regulations, and policies, and provide consistent guidance to the field." She gives the example of archaeologists with training in Native American sites, who then find themselves assessing historic buildings, and need help finding appropriate expertise.

Kate's job in Washington, D.C., also includes dealing with policy: "Policy starts in Washington, and it is part of the job staff specialists to make sure their program's interests stay on the radar screen of policy-makers and that policies are appropriate and conform to law and regulation."

Overall, Kate's feeling is that the federal government can provide a very satisfying career for archaeologists. She strongly recommends getting a background in GIS—something she didn't have. On standards or certification for archaeologists, DOI uses the Secretary of the Interior's standards and anyone, including contractors who want to be hired by the Department of the Interior, must meet these standards. The Secretary of the Interior's Standards and Guidelines for "Professional Qualifications Standards," developed by the NPS, is available at the website http://www.cr.nps.gov/local-law/arch_stnds_9.htm.

Careers in the Legislative Branch

The Legislative Branch includes the U.S. Congress (the offices of Members, Congressional committees, and the administration of Congress) and organizations that provide analyses, briefs, projections, and advise Congress on the operations and performance of programs funded by the federal government—the Government Accountability Office (GAO); the

Congressional Research Service (CRS); the Library of Congress; and the Congressional Budget Office (CBO). There are anthropologists who work in three of the legislative branch organizations, but the total number of anthropologists is less than 15. Most are social science analysts, program evaluators, methods specialists, or specialists in an area of interest to Congress.

The GAO is the largest of the legislative agencies and has regional offices outside the Washington, D.C., area. Phillip Herr is a Ph.D. cultural anthropologist from Columbia University who has worked for GAO for 17 years, starting as a GS-12 social science analyst in 1989. He has recently been selected as a candidate for the federal government's top echelon of professional managers, the Senior Executive Service (SES). After a rotation on the Hill, a rotation to Harvard's Kennedy School of Management, and the World Bank, he will likely become director of the International Affairs and Trade Division, which works on USAID, State, U.S. Trade Representative, United Nations, and multilateral issues. His work as a division director will involve the management and production of reports for 10–12 active projects staffed by senior-level GS-15s—about 25 to 30 staff. His job will be to make sure the reports come together, and that the data are good, accurate, complete, and well argued. At the end of the day he ends up with a written report, a briefing. He will be the one giving testimony to Congress in Congressional hearings.

Phil thinks of GAO as an "applied research job." "Congress needs numbers, context, objectives, and help in answering the questions, 'Does it work?' and 'How can it be improved?'" Originally hired as a social science analyst and promoted to senior evaluation analyst, the fact that GAO does not hire anthropologists as a professional category does not bother him—he observes that economists and attorneys are the only ones who wear their professional "stripes."

He's satisfied with GAO work because "you get to make a difference. You are objective in your work, and you are respected for it. You are not in anybody's back pocket, like a contractor. You are not beholden to anyone. As a taxpayer, we deserve good value for our money. Government oversight is an important role—it is checks and balances. It is important to answer the question: 'Is this a good investment for our $100 million?' that Congress asks GAO to investigate."

Natural Resources Management and the Environment

Natural resource management includes national forests, national parks, wildlife, rangeland resources, oil and gas, marine resources such as fisheries, and environmental health among many areas. Anthropologists work for the USFS; the Department of the Interior Bureau of Land Management (BLM), Minerals Management Service, and NPS; at NMFS in both Washington, D.C., and regional offices; and the Environmental Protection Agency, among other environmentally focused agencies. Two examples of anthropologists follow—one was hired as an anthropologist, and the other as a senior social scientist. Also see Gilden in this volume, who provides insights from an anthropologist working in a NMFS regional office.

Mark Schoepfle is Park Ethnographer in the Park Ethnography Program, in the NPS's Washington, D.C., headquarters. Mark is a Ph.D. cultural anthropologist with theoretical and methodological roots in ethnoscience and cognitive anthropology from Northwestern University. Mark's first jobs were working for the Navajo Nation, instilling ethnographic skills among Navajos conducting ethnographic research among their own communities. He begins his count on his "federal career" when he arrived in Washington, D.C., to work for the then-General Accounting Office (GAO) in 1990, and moved to the NPS in 1998 as a coordinator and implementer of a database that was a key component in the development of the Parks' Applied Ethnography Program. He has just completed a draft Park Ethnography Manual, now under review, pursuant to Director's Order 28B, which "promotes a common management framework for planning, reviewing, and undertaking ethnographic research." It provides comprehensive guidance to the Service on topics such as defining characteristics of ethnography and ethnographic research, minimal standards of ethnography, and the competencies needed for cultural anthropology and ethnography.

Rob Winthrop is the Senior Social Scientist in the Division of Planning and Science Policy, BLM, DOI. He is a cultural anthropologist with a Ph.D. from the University of Minnesota. Rob joined the federal government in 2003, after being a successful owner of his own consulting firm in Oregon.

Rob was hired to improve the quality of social science work in the BLM, although his duties are broad. Rob's core responsibilities include an initiative to stem an apparent slow drain of social scientists from BLM. Agency data indicate that since the late 1970s and early 1980s, there has been a decline in the number of social scientists in state, district, and federal offices. Rob suspects the decline suggests "the general diagnosis that management has not perceived what social science staff provide as being critical to their decision-making responsibilities."

As part of his assessment of the issue, Rob was tasked to develop and manage an outside assessment team to advise BLM management on quality and need for social science data. Other duties included defining the scope of work and reviewing the social and economic impact assessments that are required by NEPA under the Energy Policy Act of 2005. The BLM lands are prime lands for oil shale development and other oil and gas development, and social and economic impact assessments must be completed by the federal government prior to taking action on permits.

> We do not have as specific mandates as MMS or NMFS—they have fairly specific language in their organic act. BLM has fairly general language; NEPA says you have to look at the social as well as the environmental impact; and BLM's organic act, the Federal Land Policy Management Act, has similar language, broadly, but nothing comparable to the Endangered Species Act, or the NHPA. Because we have NHPA, we have about 160 archaeologists, and we have less than 16 FTE social scientists—mostly economists, with two anthropologists and two social scientists. The social types, sociologists and anthropologists, are definitely the minority. Working on issues that involve all three disciplines is a plus in this position.

Rob's assessment of his job is that while his responsibilities are particularly programmatic or mission driven, there is a great deal of opportunity to get involved in cutting-edge issues where anthropology can make an important contribution, such as valuation of nonmarket goods and developing indicators of sustainability for rangeland systems. "And that means economic and social indicators. One of the things we are looking at is what factors promote land fragmentation."

Military and National Security

Defense and intelligence agencies are again interested in anthropology in the aftermath of the invasions of Afghanistan and Iraq. According to the OPM data, 40 anthropologists and 177 archaeologists work in the DoD (see Table 1). The large number of archaeologists in DoD can be explained by the historic preservation and NEPA needs of military bases and ACOE; however, increasing numbers of cultural anthropologists are working for the Defense Department in the post-September 11, 2001 (9/11) days. A GAO study on federal ethnography, for example, describes the use of ethnography by the Defense Human Resources Center to supplement their Youth Attitudes Tracking Study (YATS) to understand factors affecting youths' propensity to join the military and strengthen recruitment (U.S. Government Accountability Office 2003). Other anthropologists are studying organizational culture and behavior in the defense and intelligence agencies in order to understand and improve military recruitment and training, and intelligence analysis (e.g. Johnston 2005). A number of anthropologists work for war colleges, either on contract to them or on loan from a university, and at least one anthropologist works as an advisor to the top leaders of the Pentagon.

Much of the interest, ironically, is because of anthropology's success in marketing what it does, which is to provide nuanced information about cultures and behavior in the context of rapidly changing global and state circumstances through ethnography and other methods. The defense and intelligence community's interest is largely generated by needs that developed after the tragedy of 9/11 and the ensuing war on terrorism and Iraq. The DoD apparently realizes the shortcomings of lack of knowledge about Iraq and Afghanistan for troops in the field, the inability to predict the insurgencies in Iraq, and the failures of reconstruction efforts in Iraq and Afghanistan. They believe they need to incorporate anthropological insights and approaches to training, decision making, and preparing troops for deployment.

The surge of interest, and the conditions under which anthropologists produce information for the military and intelligence sectors, is once again the topic of intense scrutiny by the anthropology community and the two national associations to which most cultural anthropologists belong—the AAA and the Society for Applied Anthropology (SfAA). Requests by the CIA to advertise job positions for anthropologists were denied by the Executive Boards of both organizations. This stimulated a debate and actions on the ethics of anthropological engagement with the two "communities" and the assessment of "the varied roles practitioners and scholars are playing in intelligence and national security agencies" (Fluehr-Lobban and Heller 2007). The AAA established an Ad hoc Commission on the Engagement of Anthropology with U.S. Security and Intelligence Communities, and reported its results in November 2007.

As reported in the *New Yorker*, anthropologist Montgomery McFate, a consultant to the Pentagon, believes that "the American government needs 'granular' knowledge of the social terrains on which it is competing" (Packer 2006). According to the article, the Army is launching an initiative known as Human Terrain Teams, for which they are actively recruiting social scientists. The teams go to "Iraq and Afghanistan with combat brigades and serve as cultural advisors on six-to-nine-month tours" (Packer 2006; see also Stannard 2007). The initiative has been criticized by the AAA and other groups because of concerns about breaching professional ethics regarding transparency, lack of informed consent, and inability to prevent doing no harm to the community under study, in addition to jeopardizing the profession of anthropology.

I interviewed a Ph.D. cultural anthropologist in the Intelligence Community (IC), who declined to be identified. His background includes working for the Institute for Defense Analyses (IDA) for 13 years, a federally funded Research and Development center, located in the Office of the Secretary of Defense. In the IDA, employees work for an independent not-for-profit contractor, funded by the federal government. Most of his work was organizational analysis related to personnel and readiness, internal organizational studies preparing DoD armed services employees for deployment. He worked on assessments of training needs, organizational change, group behavior such as building team cohesion, and live war games. During this period he also did a detail (rotation) at NASA to work on group behavior.

He currently works for the IC as a Lessons Learned Program Manager and is working on "Corporate Lessons Learned," which can be life-saving tips, or problematic military issues such as integrating armed service reserves with active forces, tactical to organizational. Much of current research agenda for behavioral and social scientists derives from the recommendations of the 9/11 Commission.

He observes that the concept of anthropology "making spies" is an erroneous assumption, and is not a contemporary military model. DoD's main purpose in engaging anthropology is to "protect people so they do not do 'stupid things.'" In Somalia, for example, "they found that Marines at check points were misreading body language, facial expressions, tones and inflections . . . and getting killed." McFate notes a similar situation in Iraq: "a gesture—arm straight, palm out—that means 'stop' in America but 'welcome' in Iraq. That difference translated into Iraqi families driving blithely toward a seemingly welcoming American soldier at checkpoints until shot as a presumed suicide bomber" (Stannard 2007).

Would he recommend working for the military or intelligence communities to grad students? He makes it clear that his choice was based on his experience and that he would *not* recommend it to all graduate students. For a graduate student to pursue a career in these sectors, "they have to want to believe in the value of helping to improve the military or intelligence services." He stated that he gets "hate mail" from other anthropologists, primarily "older" anthropologists.

I (the author) recommend that if you choose to pursue a job in this line of work, you be fully conversant with the issues and ethical choices involved, and the relationship your knowledge will have on the people you are studying or the analysis you undertake.

Robert Albro, in a recent *AN* article (2006:5), points out that the discussion often turns on how research practice is conducted—the degree of "classified-ness" or secrecy of the work that is undertaken, including the public dissemination of results. The current AAA code of ethics states that anthropologists should engage in "appropriate dissemination of results." Other concerns are whether embedding anthropologists with combat troops (in human terrain teams) breaches anthropologists' code of ethics, particularly informed consent, transparency, and the ethical code to "do no harm" to the people we study. Anthropology as a discipline has an extremely uneasy relationship with the "exercise of power," and particularly military power, and arguments are made that anthropologists working with the military are tacitly approving violence and hegemony of U.S. military and intelligence efforts. On the other hand, Montgomery McFate takes the view: "I see there could be misuse. But I just cannot stand to sit back and watch these mistakes happen over and over as people get killed, and do nothing" (Packer 2006).

Forensic and Physical Anthropology

The Smithsonian Institution is not technically a federal agency, although it is argued that it is a public institution, receiving nearly 70 percent of its revenue from funds appropriated by Congress. Most anthropologists work in the Smithsonian's National Museum of Natural History or the Folklife and Cultural Heritage Center, including at least 40 anthropologists that span specialties of forensic anthropology, cultural anthropology, archaeology, physical anthropology, and museum curation. The Museum of Natural History's Department of Anthropology includes programs in Arctic Studies, American Indians, Latin American Archaeology, and Ethnology. The Division of Physical Anthropology, Human Origins, and Repatriation has a critical mass of well-known forensic and physical anthropologists (Fiske 2007b). For a description of the history and work of forensic anthropologists working in the Smithsonian, I recommend an excellent summary article by David Hunt (2006). The Smithsonian Center for Folklife and Cultural Heritage, which produces the Folklife Festival, Smithsonian Folkways Recordings and other programs, is headed by a cultural anthropologist (Kurin 2002).

HOW DO I APPLY FOR A JOB WITH THE FEDERAL GOVERNMENT?

The AAA, SfAA, and the Washington Association of Professional Anthropologists (WAPA) routinely offer workshops dedicated to finding a job with the government. WAPA was a pioneer in this effort, offering the very first workshops on "Building your 171," the standardized form used for applicants to the civil service at the time. One of the best descriptions for finding employment has been written by Robert M. Wulff (1989), in *Stalking Employment in the Nation's Capital* (Koons et al. 1989), and the strategies are still excellent advice.

Job Announcements and Where to Find Them

The job announcement is an official request for applications published by a government agency. It specifies application procedures, deadlines, and defines the professional background from which the applicants must come. The most comprehensive listing of government jobs is the website of OPM, which provides employment information through USAJOBS, the federal government's employment information system (www.usajobs.opm.gov).

Jobs can also be found by going to specific agencies' websites, like the CDC, NPS, or USAID, and looking at their openings (co-listed on the OPM site). Searches can be conducted by federal agency, geographical location, job series (GS-190, GS-193, or GS-101), or grade level. Most master's level jobs begin at GS-9 or GS-11; and most Ph.D.-level jobs begin at GS-12–14.

The USAID Careers Website has (1) the USAID GS Vacancy Announcements, (2) the USAID Business Opportunities page, which is where the contracts are listed, and (3) information on the foreign service opportunities. Of note is a Junior Officer (JO) program, launched in November 2006, to address the Agency's need for middle managers, replacing the former New Entry Professional and International Development Intern recruitment programs. All new recruitment advertisements will be issued under the JO program according to the USAID (www.usaid.gov/careers/).

The Smithsonian Institution's job announcements are at www.si.edu/ohr/. They are simultaneously posted at the OPM's USA jobs website.

Job Applications and Forms

OPM has a "forms page" on their website (www.usajobs.opm.gov/forms.asp), and you can find the OF 612 there, along with advice on other specific forms that may be required. OF 612 is the Optional Application for Federal Employment form. It is labeled *optional*, but good sense tells you that you should use it. OF-612 has blocks to fill out your work experience and history, including your job title, employer's name and address, and space to describe your duties and accomplishments, among other things. The blocks of work experience should be tailored to the job's requirements, so that a supervisor reading an applicant's work experience can see a clear translation to the job announcement's responsibilities. Job announcements will specify what forms are needed, and if a resume is needed in addition to the OF-612.

Most vacancy announcements will require a statement of KSAs—Knowledge, Skills, and Abilities required by the job. KSAs are usually taken from the position description for the job. An applicant should describe how his or her experience, education, or other factors provide the knowledge, skills, and abilities to qualify for the position. KSAs are so important to federal job applications that an entire industry is devoted to coaching people through the drafting process. Web searches can be very useful in finding help for drafting successful applications, all for free. Two websites, managed by the Center for Disease Control, and the University of Delaware, turned out to be very helpful (www.cdc.gov/hrmo/ksahowto.htm; www.udel.edu/CSC/KSAs.pdf).

The following recommendations and lessons learned are based on cumulative, collective experiences and observations of the author, supplemented by the insights from the interviewees, as quoted.

(1) *Have a secondary specialty*: For cultural anthropologists in all federal agencies, but especially in international development, it is highly recommended to have a secondary specialty, which becomes a de facto marketing tool. It might be methodological, such as evaluation research, or qualitative methods; or it might be a substantive specialty such as public health, agriculture, public lands and resource management, housing policy, or any number of mission-related fields or analytic approaches.

(2) *The importance of the "experience factor" for USAID hires and how to get it*: Having or getting the experience factor is a critical part of one's preparation for development assistance jobs. According to Joan Atherton, "It is difficult to come direct from grad school, and be a viable candidate for a USAID job; even being an institutional contractor is very competitive, unless you can arrange an entry level or very junior job. Your fieldwork *might* get you there, but a lot of fieldwork is so theoretical, and not terribly pragmatic about actually running something, that I am not sure that [dissertation fieldwork] substitutes." Joan suggests that if you have a degree and some amount of experience abroad, you might look for a job with an NGO, "but most of the institutional contractors, because they're bidding on jobs, they want to demonstrate that their people have experience." One option that Joan noted is to get a position as an administrative type—managing from the home office—and work your way into more field experience. "So the best potential for starting, if you have only a degree and no experience, is working for an NGO. They do not pay much; they are willing to take a risk, and it can work as a way of gaining international experience."

(3) *Get methodological and statistics training*: Most anthropologists wished they had taken or been offered additional training in graduate school to prepare them for a career in practice. Most mentioned the need for training in quantitative methods and research design, statistics, economics, applied research methods such as program evaluation, or GIS. I (Fiske) found that a familiarity with research design and methods were critical to me as a policy analyst and later as an anthropologist and program officer in NOAA. As Atherton puts it, "If you are commissioning studies and reports, the one job you do as a direct-hire is act as a quality control—you have to know whether you're getting garbage or you're getting something worthwhile. So I would say not to neglect the behavioral science side for the humanistic, and not focus entirely on the more qualitative methods, but learn the quantitative, too." On the positive side, most anthropologists reported that they felt they received a very solid set of skills in interviewing and observation, and found those skills extremely useful in practice.

Many feel that familiarity with statistics is important. "You do need inferential stats, at least a semester, and a year is better. You need to know what a multiple regression is . . . and the same thing about non-parametric stats, those come in handy. You should be able to read an article and not be intimidated when people start using all that jargon, and you should be able to tell your thoughts to someone who hasn't had any background in it, what's going on" (Schoepfle).

(4) *Utilize internships, fellowships, and networking*: Internships provide a foot in the door, and an opportunity to learn the needs of an organization or agency. Take advantage of them if they are part of your graduate degree work, or use fellowships if you are post degree and want to enter the federal sector. They allow you to get into the agency and make ties and networks that ultimately are critical to job seeking. Networking is a lifelong skill that helps you make employment contacts and get information. Join interagency groups, professional groups, and local practitioner groups.

(5) *Prepare with training specific to government work*: The author and others recommend training in federal laws (NEPA, etc.) applicable to your specialization. In addition, there is often a history of the use of social science and anthropology in a federal agency—it is useful to be familiar with it. I found that public administration skills such as understanding the federal regulatory process and U.S. Code, the civil service rights and responsibilities, and practical skills such as how to read and interpret the federal budget and the budgeting process were extremely useful. Most are learned on the job; but often you can find workshops, classes, or courses on these topics.

CONCLUSION: WORKING FOR THE FEDS—VIEWS ON ENGAGEMENT

Working for the Feds—is it an opportunity for anthropologists or is it working as a hired hand? An exciting career option or work as a desk-jockey? "Working for the Feds can be frustrating because you have the built-in dynamics of any large organization, and you add to them the scrutiny and oversight that a government entity is susceptible to. And you end up with a great deal of time that appears to be spent on things other than your core responsibilities. That's as nice as I can say it. And it takes a lot of patience to do that, and not everyone wants to put up with that" (Winthrop).

In truth, there is probably a little of both—some drudgery and adversity; but overall, a great deal of opportunity to be involved, make a difference, and work on program and policy issues using anthropology. Archaeologists have successfully developed a strong professional presence in managing federal archaeological and cultural resources, which has dramatically affected the theory and practice of archaeology. Cultural anthropologists have an increasing role and presence in federal agencies and policy, from directing overseas missions for USAID to developing programs of research and lines of investigation in a surprisingly large number of cabinet-level agencies on domestic issues.

As a participant and analyst of the unfolding scenery during the last 20 years in the nation's capitol, I am impressed by anthropology's opportunities and successes. I urge anthropologists to engage outside the academy—in our roles as advisors, evaluators, decision makers, managers of studies, producers of critical knowledge, improvers of policy or process, providing voice for those with less access to policy and decision making. All of these are reasons to work for the Feds and have cumulative value. What we have to say is worth acting on, and working for the government is a commitment to social and institutional change—from within the bureaucracy and often in a participatory way with communities. I would argue that we can and need to be a part of improving health care, avoiding undercounts, or ensuring equitable allocation of resources. The mark of a mature, professional discipline is its ability to intersect with ideas, policy, and issues in a constructive way. My hope is that this chapter will be of assistance to students and others in thinking about a career in the public sector and acquiring professional skills and perspectives to influence public policy through careers outside of academia.

INTERVIEWS

I greatly appreciate the time each person took to speak with me, their willingness to share their insights, and their editing of the cameos. In alphabetical order:

Joan Atherton, Senior Policy Advisor for Aid Effectiveness, Bilateral and Multilateral Donors Division, Office of Development Partners, USAID. November 8, 2006.

Charity Goodman, Ethnographer/Senior Social Science Analyst in the Applied Research and Methods Group, GAO; now a health policy analyst, Substance Abuse and Mental Health Services Administration, Department of Health and Human Services.

Phillip Herr, SES Candidate and Acting Director, Financial Markets and Community Investment, Governmental Accountability Office. October 24, 2006.

John P. Mason, Director, JMason and Associates, Colesville, Maryland. October 25, 2006.

Mark Schoepfle, Headquarters Ethnographer, Park Ethnography Program, National Park Service, U.S. Department of the Interior. November 2, 2006.

Kate Winthrop, Acting Federal Preservation Officer, Federal Preservation Office, Bureau of Land Management, Department of the Interior. November 10, 2006.

Rob Winthrop, Senior Social Scientist, Division of Planning and Science Policy, Bureau of Land Management, Department of the Interior. September 26, 2006.

NOTE

1. Several website URLs are listed in this article. Over time their accuracy will diminish, so readers will need to turn to search engines more frequently to find the resources noted.

REFERENCES CITED

Albro, Robert
  2006 Does Anthropology Need a Hearing Aid? Anthropology News 47(8):5.
Clay, Patricia M., and Julia Olson
  2007 Defining Fishing Communities: Issues in Theory and Practice. NAPA Bulletin 28:27–42.
Colburn, Lisa L., Susan Abbott-Jamieson, and Patricia M. Clay
  2006 Anthropological Applications in the Management of Federally Managed Fisheries: Context, Institution History, and Prospectus. Human Organization 65(3):231–239.
Crespi, Muriel
  1999 Seeking Inclusiveness. Theme issue, "Stewards of the Human Landscape," Common Ground. Fall 1998/Spring 1999 issue. Washington, DC: National Park Service Departmental Consulting Archaeologist and Archaeology and Ethnography Program.

Fiske, Shirley J.

　1990 Anthropology and Marine Extension. Theme issue, Practicing Anthropology 12(4).

　1999 Value of Ground Truth. Theme issue "Stewards of the Human Landscape," National Park Service. Washington, D.C., Common Ground (Fall 1998–Spring 1999).

　2007a Anthropologists and the Public Health Agenda. Institutional Practitioner Profile: Dr. James Carey. Anthropology Newsletter 48(6):51–52.

　2007b Work in Repatriation. Practitioner Profile: Dr. Dorothy Lippert. Anthropology Newsletter 48(4):41.

Fluehr-Lobban, Carolyn, and Monica Heller

　2007 Ethical Challenges for Anthropological Engagement. Anthropology News 48(1):4.

Gyrisco, Geoffrey

　1989 Archaeology. In Stalking Employment in the Nation's Capital: A Guide for Anthropologists. Adam Koons, Beatrice Hackett, and John P. Mason, eds. Pp. 109–117. Washington, DC: Washington Association of Professional Anthropologists.

Hunt, David

　2006 Forensic Anthropology at the Smithsonian Institution. AnthroNotes 27(1):6–12. Washington, DC: Smithsonian Institution Press.

Johnston, Rob

　2005 Analytic Culture in the US Intelligence Community. Washington, DC: Central Intelligence Agency.

Koons, Adam, Beatrice Hackett, and John P. Mason, eds.

　1989 Stalking Employment in the Nation's Capital. Washington, DC: Washington Association of Professional Anthropologists.

Kurin, Richard

　2002 The Silk Road Festival: Connecting Cultures. Anthropology Newsletter 43(6):47.

McManamon, Francis P.

　2000 The Protection of Archaeological Resources in the United States: Reconciling Preservation with Contemporary Society. In Cultural Resource Management in Contemporary Society, Francis P. McManamon and Alf Hatton, eds. Pp. 40–54. London: Routledge.

　2001 Cultural Resources and Protection under United States Law. Connecticut Journal of International Law 16(2):247–282.

National Park Service (NPS)

　1994 Archaeology and the Federal Government. Cultural Resource Management 17(6). Washington, DC: U.S. Department of the Interior.

　1998 The Power to Preserve. Public Archeology and Local Government. Cultural Resource Management 21(10). Washington, DC: U.S. Department of the Interior.

　2003 Muriel "Miki" Crespi. National Park Service Chief Ethnographer. Her Professional Contributions to the National Park Service. Washington, DC: National Center for Cultural Resources, Archaeology and Ethnography Program.

Packer, George

　2006 Knowing the Enemy: Can Social Scientists Redefine the "War on Terror?" New Yorker, December 18: 60–69.

Schafft, Gretchen

　2004 Miki Crespi and the Applied Ethnography Program of the National Park Service. Theme issue, Practicing Anthropology 26(1):2–6.

Schwede, Laurel, Blumberg, Rae Lesser, and Anna Y. Chan, eds.

　2006 Complex Ethnic Households in America. Lanham, MD: Rowman and Littlefield.

Stannard, Matthew B.

　2007 Montgomery McFate's Mission: Can One Anthropologist Possibly Steer the Course in Iraq? San Francisco Chronicle Magazine, April 29:11–16.

U.S. Agency for International Development [USAID], Quarterly Workforce

　2006 Profile Report, March 31. Washington, DC: USAID.

U.S. Census Bureau
    2004 Census 2000 Topic Report No. 15 (TR-15). Census 2000 Ethnographic Studies. Washington, DC: U.S. Department of Commerce.

U.S. Government Accountability Office (GAO)
    2003 Federal Programs. Ethnographic Studies Can Inform Agencies' Actions. General Accountability Office Report number GAO-03-455. Washington, DC.

Wulff, Robert M.
    1989 Government Executive Branch Agencies. *In* Stalking Employment in the Nation's Capital: A Guide for Anthropologists. Adam Koons, Beatrice Hackett, and John P. Mason, eds. Washington, DC: Washington Association of Professional Anthropologists.

APPLIED ANTHROPOLOGY AND EXECUTIVE LEADERSHIP

BARBARA L.K. PILLSBURY
Medical Service Corporation International

Executive leadership is about mobilizing, managing, inspiring, and empowering others to achieve goals greater than what can be accomplished through individual works. Leadership flows from but is more than management and administration. Leadership can be learned—and typically is learned over time. This article presents a "hierarchy of executive capabilities"— from Highly Capable Individual, to Contributing Team Member, to Competent Manager, to Effective Leader, to Executive. The central message is that anthropologists, like all technical specialists who contemplate moving into management and up the ladder to executive leadership, must recognize that it will not be possible to stay on the cutting edge of their special area of knowledge and must be willing to give up being "the expert" in that area. This is illustrated through the careers of three anthropologists as they transitioned from traditional areas of anthropological knowledge into management and executive positions of increasing responsibility. The article discusses rewards but also assesses losses that occur along the way. It identifies the skills needed as one transitions up the management ladder and summarizes advice to anthropologists interested in executive careers. It also discusses ways in which a background in anthropology assists or may hinder in executive leadership. The context is primarily the world of international development assistance. Keywords: management, executive leadership, vision, skills development, international development

I did not set out to be an executive or a leader. I did not even set out to be an anthropologist. Yet in 2003, I found myself in Washington, D.C., managing a $48-million U.S. government-funded program and a staff of 36, providing services to the U.S. Department of State, the U.S. Agency for International Development, UN agencies, and countries around the world. Was I hired because I was an anthropologist? No. Did my training as an anthropologist serve me well in the challenges of this position? Yes.

It was a set of impulses that led me into anthropology, which eventually led me into this position. It was never a goal nor a plan. Just that set of impulses.

In fact, to be an effective leader, one must be driven by impulse that solidifies a commitment to a vision and set of values. In today's world, to be an effective executive means connecting that vision and the values to a position of responsibility for *executing* a program—that is, managing personnel, time, budgets, and ideas to achieve, and better yet surpass, expected objectives. While greed and ego-driven executives do exist (e.g.,

NAPA BULLETIN 29, pp. 131–151. ISBN 9781405190152. © 2008 by the American Anthropological Association. DOI:10.1111/j.1556-4797.2008.00010.x

Enron), principles of anthropology accord with "principle-centered leadership" (Covey 2003). In the words of one executive colleague, "[The] key is to have a passion about making a certain thing happen. Then work toward that goal without letting your ego get in the way of managing toward the goal. This is not about you—fame, glory or whatever. It is about achieving that goal."

This article begins with a personal journey illustrating how one anthropologist came into executive positions of increasing responsibility and challenge. It identifies a critical turning point from being a good anthropologist to becoming a competent manager. It evaluates the rewards and losses that occur along the way and discusses ways anthropology assists in executive leadership. Two other executive anthropologists are also profiled. Finally, the chapter summarizes with advice to anthropologists interested in executive careers. The context is primarily the world of international development assistance.

LEADERSHIP, MANAGEMENT, AND ADMINISTRATION

These terms—as well as *leader, manager, director,* and *administrator*—take on different meanings in different contexts. Managers are found at all levels. So long as one is managing other people or systems and processes within an organization, one is a manager. A director is typically a higher-level manager. In some contexts, "administrator" denotes responsibility for the day-to-day unglamorous but essential operations (finance, payroll, etc.) that keep an organization running. In other contexts, *administrator* is the title of the highest-level leaders. In some government agencies, for instance, this title designates the head of the agency.[1]

Leadership is leading others. Many great leaders are not executives or do not derive their leadership from holding an executive position, but lead through their ability to inspire others. Martin Luther King, Jr. is a prime example. While some people are "born leaders," leadership can be learned. Typically, leadership is learned over time. Current organizational theory teaches that all employees should be trained and inspired to demonstrate leadership at whatever level they work, be it at the top, leadership of one part of an organization, or just of certain processes.[2] Management and leadership are closely entwined. In management, the goal is to be a "manager who leads." The nuances of difference are illustrated in Figure 1.[3]

PATH TO EXECUTIVE LEADERSHIP: A PERSONAL EXAMPLE

Discovering Anthropology

Some people are motivated from early age to "be" something: a teacher, an architect, a doctor or a veterinarian, for instance, and go straight through school to the professional training that launches them into that career. Others only find their forté along the way. I was among the latter. It was "the times" that resulted in my getting a bachelor's degree in home economics, that next made it possible to hitchhike safely around Europe, which led

Managing	Leading
Plan	Scan
Organize	Focus
Implement	Align/Mobilize
Monitor and evaluate	Inspire

FIGURE 1. "Practices of Managing and Leading."

to a master's degree in languages, and then sheer luck that brought me to a wise man who advised a career (with Ph.D.) in anthropology. Never in my early years had I ever thought of becoming either an anthropologist or an "executive." Yet anthropology was the perfect, although eventual, fit for me. It is for this reason that I urge all college graduates unsure of their life's calling to take off time from school and work until something calls, until a vision emerges and it becomes clear what additional chunk of schooling is right.

Growing up in small-town northern Minnesota in the 1950s, eight of us graduated from high school as National Merit Scholars. The six boys went off mainly to East Coast schools: Harvard, Dartmouth, and Yale. However, for girls of that era in small-town Minnesota, the primary vocational choices ranged only from being a secretary or beautician to—more aspiring—a nurse, teacher, or home economist. Thus, for the two of us girls who were National Merit Scholars, going to the University of Minnesota, in big-city Minneapolis–Saint Paul, was very special and adequate indeed. My mother had gone there, majoring in home economics. That was the course I followed as well.

By the time of graduation from "the U" in 1964, however, I was eager to experience what the world was like outside Minnesota and headed off on a one-way ticket to Europe. I found work first in Sweden, then tried Paris, next Munich. In each country, while looking for work, I first found a language class and set immediately to learning Swedish, next French, then German. While in Sweden, a Russian émigré, Svetlana, wanted me to join a student trip to Russia in order to take news and gifts to her family in Leningrad, and she insisted on cramming enough Russian into my head for me to get around and successfully make my way to her family. Hitchhiking through Europe, it became apparent that picking up even a few courtesy phrases in the local language or dialect immediately led to rapport and valuable experiences one would never have had speaking only English. Naively I concluded that, if people could only speak each others' languages, we could have peace in the world.

It was this vision that, after about three years in Europe, compelled me to return to the United States to seek graduate training in linguistics. Wanting to experience what the United States was like outside of Minnesota, I had sent off applications to universities in major large cities. Returning to the United States, I went first to Harvard where I interviewed with the head of its Linguistics Department. It was 1967. He praised Harvard's linguistics program, emphasizing its preeminence in having access to computers (still a novelty then) at MIT for analyzing phonemes and morphemes. "What about the people who speak those languages?" I asked. "We are way beyond that," came his answer. That was hardly my vision.

Heading down to New York, my interview at Columbia University with the head of its Linguistics Department, Professor Robert Austerlitz, was totally different. He asked why I wanted to study linguistics. He did not laugh at my account of what I had experienced speaking other languages in Europe nor at the pouring out of my hopes of bringing peace in the world. Rather he responded, "I come from Hungary and Romania, I speak 13 languages and I understand exactly what you mean. I'd like to help you find what you really want." It was late and he invited me to continue discussion over dinner at a nearby Hungarian restaurant. "It is not linguistics you want," he said, "but anthropology." Until that moment, anthropology had never entered my mind. "There are four sub-fields in anthropology," he explained, "one of them being anthropological linguistics." Because I had never considered either anthropology or investing years of study for a Ph.D., he suggested I apply for the one-year M.A. program in applied linguistics at Columbia University Teacher's College. "Then, as an elective, sign up for Culture and Communication, taught by Margaret Mead in the anthropology department at Columbia."

It was the perfect advice and Margaret Mead hooked me into anthropology. Among her unique approaches to effectively teaching large numbers of students with a personalized approach was her requirement that any of us who wanted more than a B in the class, an automatic okay to see her during office hours, or ever a letter of recommendation from her, needed to fill out a 5 × 7 card with all our basic information plus write a cultural autobiography. This cultural autobiography was to include the cultural forces that made us who we are today: the ethnic heritage, the family dynamics in which we grew up, the values (religious and otherwise) that parents sought to instill, the neighborhood in which we grew up, and how we acquired knowledge about cultures outside our immediate own. It was a brilliant exercise (which I later used in my own teaching). New York City, however, was reverse culture shock for someone having grown up in "Minnesota nice" and having experienced friendships throughout Europe. Finishing the M.A. program, it was time to head overseas again. The program had conferred a degree in teaching English as a foreign language. I applied and was accepted to teach English—and study anthropology—at the American University in Cairo, Egypt.

Epiphany

Some people speak of having had an "epiphany" in their lives, some singularly major turning point. For me this came while hitchhiking through Turkey. Having arrived on a Greek boat at the then rather sleepy fishing village of Kusadasi, I and my travel companion headed up the coast toward Istanbul. Hospitality to visiting foreigners was still a common norm and along the way we were invited to stay with a Turkish family. There, in this land where squat toilets were still the norm, in their modest home, which had no running water, was a Western porcelain toilet sitting prominently in the living room. With a little prayer rug over the seat and a plastic rose and miniature Quran propped up on the back, it was simply a decorative piece, proclaiming modernity. In the next village up the road was a similar scene. I was told these toilets were a gift from the American government. Later, at the U.S. Embassy in Ankara, I was told these toilets were part of a sanitation program run by USAID, sent by bureaucrats in Washington, D.C., who had little understanding of the true conditions in these parts of the world. I concluded that what this USAID needed was someone like me who could design programs that would fit local circumstances.

During winter 1968, I plunged into the doctoral program at Columbia, believing that a Ph.D. in cultural anthropology would provide me the tools I needed to work for USAID and bring about socioeconomic development and reduce poverty in the world. This was the belief that motivated me for the next three decades. It was the same desire that would lead me to executive leadership, although I had no vision of this at the time. I never thought of becoming "an executive" but simply of using the tools—the knowledge and insights—of anthropology to make the world a better place.

Fieldwork and Teaching

My fieldwork was path-breaking research among Chinese Muslims, who number some 20-plus million but had never been documented by any Western scholars. During that challenging two years among the Chinese, I benefited again from another technique that Margaret Mead (who had become one of my advisors and a member of my doctoral committee) used for giving personal attention to her advisees. Like all anxious graduate students longing for guidance from a professor, I wrote to all of mine. Only she answered. Back came my letter to her with a note attached: "Dr. Mead asks that you re-type your letter triple-spaced with one-inch margins all around so that she can more easily respond." I did. And so, promptly, did she, with notes between lines and in the margins such as "Is this the idealized or the real behavior?" "What about intermarriage?" "Yes, focus on the pork taboo."

Finishing my dissertation, I was ready to head into applied anthropology, aiming for USAID. However, Mead urged otherwise. "Barbara, you must teach first," she boomed in that characteristic voice of hers. "If you do not, your colleagues will say 'She can't teach.' But if you teach first, they will not know if you can or cannot, and then you can go into practice. It's like a doctor needing to do an internship and residency before hanging up a shingle and going into private practice." At that time, in the early 1970s, this was good advice. The *practice* of anthropology had not yet become established as a truly respectable option for anthropologists and the National Association for the Practice of Anthropology (NAPA) was yet to be conceptualized, not established until ten years later.[4]

So I taught for four years. The teaching experience proved valuable grounding for my subsequent work as a practicing anthropologist and, eventually, as an executive. Teaching at a state university in southern California sharpened my understanding of world realities. Not an elite research university, San Diego State University had few students with heads in theoretical clouds. Rather it was courses I taught such as Urban Anthropology, Medical Anthropology, and Anthropological Research Methods that excited the students—and me. These were pragmatic hands-on courses with mainly middle-class and poorer students going out into the community and studying the realities of the Latino, Asian, and other cultures mixing there. For me, managing their experiences, many of them personally challenging, was training that would stand me in good stead decades later when I found myself managing a staff of employees coming from all corners of the world.

Practicing Anthropology: Stepping Stone to Executive Leadership

In 1977, I was fortunate to be granted tenure and also to connect with Dr. Peter Benedict, an anthropologist working in the Near East Bureau of USAID. I expressed interest in working there. Peter encouraged me to write a proposal on a topic about which I could produce useful guidance to USAID drawing on my anthropological knowledge and experience in Egypt. With his astute guidance and generous mentoring, this led to a six-month contract for applied research and the monograph, *Traditional Health Care in the Near East: Indigenous Health Practices and Practitioners in Egypt, Afghanistan, Jordan, Syria, Tunisia, Morocco, and Yemen* (Pillsbury 1978). This stimulated discussion of change in the prevailing paradigm in which doctors still were seen as the main providers of health care, even in developing countries. It also led to my being hired full time by USAID as Behavioral Science Advisor in the Bureau for Program and Policy Coordination (PPC). Specifically, my position was as medical anthropologist in the Studies Division of PPC, located in its Office of Evaluation.

In USAID's Studies Division, I applied my *technical* knowledge and skills gained through anthropology. At first I stayed relatively close to traditional anthropological domains, producing a publication that promoted the argument that USAID should not look to doctors as major providers of health care in developing countries but rather should bring in, appropriately, the indigenous health practitioners on whom poor people in those countries already rely (Pillsbury 1979). The head of the Office of Evaluation was Robert Berg, a strong supporter of bringing anthropology and social science to solving problems of development. Bob suggested I take leadership for USAID on the topic of female circumcision/female genital mutilation, a whispered health issue that had not yet come into open discussion in the halls of Washington, D.C., We formed a task force and brought forward the negative short- and long-term consequences, physiological and psychological, of the various forms of female genital cutting/mutilation, proposing strategies that USAID might pursue. Soon thereafter, Bob's suggestion that our office conduct a high-level series of impact evaluations was accepted by Doug Bennet, the Administrator (head) of all USAID.

Moving Slowly into Management

This launched the highly visible "Administrator's Impact Evaluation Series." I was put in charge of evaluations in the health sector and suddenly found myself managing not only technical but also political processes. The overseas missions (offices) of USAID in the individual developing countries were happy to identify various projects they had been implementing as "successes." When they learned, however, that our office intended to send out an evaluation team to study these bases of success, the walls went up. Timing was not convenient; there had recently been too many visitors; a flood had just washed out major roads; violence was threatened in that part of the country; perhaps next year. No longer was I dealing with traditional topics such as village midwives, but I was forced to expand my anthropological understandings of human behavior to understand the politics of a major government agency and to manage processes so as to work around obstacles and accomplish objectives. An important learning was that virtually all processes that challenge or in any way bump up against the authority of anyone else in the bureaucracy are political. Throughout, an exciting challenge was to analyze these experiences, as an anthropologist, and to share them with other applied and practicing anthropologists (Pillsbury 1984a, 1984b). It was a thrill to be recognized with a U.S. Department of State Award: "Certificate of Appreciation—For High Professional Contribution Which Helped to Establish the Studies Division."

From there I was hired into a position of increased management responsibility: Chief for Research and Evaluation for the Asia Bureau. This role had much less to do with traditional anthropological knowledge and much more to do with managing processes, the politics that went along with the processes, and managing a team—my staff of three. I was responsible for reviewing research agendas and contracts with the U.S. Bureau of Census and with various university-based agricultural research programs. I was responsible for developing the annual schedule for all evaluations that would be conducted of USAID programs and projects in the eight USAID-assisted countries of Asia. I was also responsible for organizing and managing, in each of the eight countries, an "Evaluation Workshop" consisting of evaluation training and technical assistance for USAID staff and their host-country counterparts in all sectors (agriculture, rural development, health and population, etc.). Finally, as part of the Asia Bureau management team, I was regularly required to advise on the soundness (or lack thereof) of projects being designed in all those sectors.

A then-unusual and not insignificant fact was that I and the other three of my team were all female—this at a time when sexual harassment had not quite come onto the agenda of U.S. government agencies. Our boss was Robert (Bob) Halligan. We were thus often referred to by male colleagues as "Bob's bunnies," "Halligan's honeys," "Halligan's harem" and other such labels. We knew better than to protest but to take it in stride and rise above silliness. We were committed to making a difference: not letting poorly designed projects get approved by people who either didn't know better, didn't care, or thought it would further their career. I was still motivated by those toilets in Turkey. For our efforts, our team received a "U.S. Department of State Unit Award for Outstanding Service," recommended by the head of the Asia Bureau, Dr. John Sullivan.

At this point I was clearly applying anthropological insights to management and decision making, believing I could make a difference in the world (Pillsbury 1986). My role was not really considered *executive,* however. I had to oversee some budgets, true, but it was my boss with whom the buck stopped, who walked the tightrope of success and failure.

Executive Leadership: Onto the Tightrope of Success and Failure

In 1980, Ronald Reagan was elected president, declaring that priorities for USAID would shift immediately from poverty reduction and development to containing communism and advancing U.S. commercial interests. Shortly before that a very special man had proposed we get married, start a family, and that I move to California where he was a professor at UCLA. My biological time clock was ticking. Did I want to stay in Washington, D.C., implementing Reagan policies? It was not a hard decision.

In Los Angeles, while mothering one daughter and then a second, calls came from Washington, D.C., asking me to do short-term consultancies. This, rather than full-time employment, proved an excellent way to engage professionally for several years while still spending major time with my daughters. In Los Angeles were other women like myself who had moved from positions of responsibility on the East Coast and were doing similar consulting work. We often shared experiences, finally asking ourselves "Why are we working for these male-headed organizations based in Washington, New York, London, and Geneva?"

This led to our cofounding the Pacific Institute for Women's Health. It seemed to us there was a crying need on the West Coast of the United States for an organization that could bring together the talent of the many women from San Diego to Seattle who had skills in areas related to women's health but who, like ourselves, were not full-time academics or who were academically based but seeking ways to make a difference in the world outside academia. This we saw as a rich, underutilized network of talent and energy that could benefit women and families in the United States as well as internationally, including those countries from which many of the West Coast's immigrants had come. Fortunately, this vision appealed to many foundations and other funders as well.

We created the Pacific Institute under the umbrella of California's long-established Public Health Institute so that we would not have to hassle with IRS and legal requirements but could instead plunge full-steam into developing our technical program and raising funding for it.[5]

We adopted a rather novel management model of codirectors. My initial responsibility, in addition to overall vision and leadership for the new organization, was primarily with developing a program of reproductive health services and advocacy and writing proposals to foundations for funding. Our first support came from the Rockefeller Foundation, which enabled us to hold a first fund-raising event, a showing of the documentary film of Maya Lin's design of the Vietnam War Memorial, then up for an Academy Award. We were fortunate to subsequently receive the support of the Packard, Hewlett, Ford, Summit, Compton, and Gates foundations, among others.

At first we were essentially a mom-and-pop shop (minus the pop). We all worked as volunteers from our living rooms and kitchen tables, juggling family responsibilities. As foundations began to invest in us, however, we rented a small office space, hired a receptionist followed by other paid employees, rented larger space, and began to pay ourselves.

Soon we were on the tightrope of success and failure. We needed to show our funders that we were achieving what we promised in our proposals. We needed to continue bringing in funds to pay the growing staff. We needed to continue giving value to our network of women, and a few good men, San Diego to Seattle, who were collaborating with us as "affiliates," some with monetary gain and others as volunteers. It was not easy.

This was my first true position of executive leadership. I was responsible for raising and stretching money to cover my staff and programs, and for keeping people under me happy or content with their work. Some of our ideas for activities were successful. Others didn't go far. We had certain unavoidable clashes of opinion on how to move ahead. It was very much a tightrope of success or failure as we sought to establish our organization as a major player in the field.

The Critical Turning Point to Executive Leadership

As I sought guidance from the plethora of books on management and leadership, the critical answer came from a weekend seminar, "How to Solve the Dilemmas of a Technical Person in a Management Position." Brilliant as the Peter Druckers and others of the management world may be, their advice never seemed to get at my particular issues. This seminar did it.[6]

During my years as a consultant and in launching the Pacific Institute for Women's Health, I had developed an expertise and some renown as an expert in reproductive health and women's empowerment, including women's health, family planning, gender, and empowerment. I was frequently sought out on these issues, both for public speaking engagements and for consultancies with international organizations (including WHO, UNFPA, UNICEF, and the World Bank in addition to USAID). But at the Pacific Institute, given the demands to write winning proposals, develop and balance budgets, manage programs, and satisfy staff and affiliates, the day did not have enough hours to also do the technical work that had brought me such satisfaction.

"How to Solve the Dilemmas of a Technical Person in a Management Position." The essential and most important learning for an anthropologist moving into management and executive leadership is what this seminar taught: that one can no longer stay on the cutting-edge knowledge of one's special subject while moving into management and executive leadership. "Let go! Let go! Let go!" asserted the seminar trainer. If you cannot let go of being the technical expert on your special topic, do not stress yourself trying to make it in executive management. Stay with the technical role. Only if you are willing and able to let go of the technical *expert* role will you succeed as an executive. Yes, you can continue to stay informed of the most important developments in your technical area, but you can no longer be *the* expert. In retrospect, this seems so simple. But until that seminar I was straining to do both, feeling I was not doing well at either. An anthropologist moving into executive leadership must learn how to let go of the technical and make the transition, coping with emotional and psychological loss and challenges this may present.

Executive Leadership in the Big Time

As my youngest daughter was preparing to go off to college, East Coast headhunters were contacting me about positions back in Washington, D.C. One position especially attracted me. The AIDS epidemic was killing millions in developing countries, devastating families, communities, and countries. Would I be interested in taking leadership of a USAID project called Synergy, created to coordinate the work of 60-plus organizations funded by the U.S. government to tackle HIV/AIDS in developing countries? Trusted friends advised against it, saying the management challenge was so great that it would be nearly impossible to succeed.

For many years I had participated in Los Angeles' fund-raising AIDS Walks. Two next-door neighbors had died of AIDS. At the Pacific Institute I had designed and overseen programs to help women's organizations in Latin America and Africa tackle AIDS. I had African women colleagues who were coping with HIV-positive husbands or struggling to raise children orphaned by AIDS. I was eager to make a more substantial contribution to fighting the epidemic globally than I felt I could do in California.

I thus accepted the East Coast challenge and, in 2003, moved back to Washington, D.C., as director of the $48-million USAID-funded Synergy Project. Now I was truly on the tightrope of success or failure. This was no longer women working together with good will at a women's organization in California. I was now responsible to both the firm that hired me and to USAID, not on the basis of good will but with the expectation that I could pull the Synergy Project through some serious doldrums and meet a set of demanding objectives. I was responsible both to layers of superiors in the firm as well as to a demanding professional in USAID's Office of HIV/AIDS, who was responsible for making sure that I did what was needed to transform the Synergy Project into a reliable, high-performing entity. If I failed, I would be fired.

Initially, there were far too many 80-hour work weeks. In the wake of recent staff turnover, more than a dozen staff were reporting directly to me, yet I hardly knew their names let alone their exact responsibilities. Major reports were due imminently; others were long overdue. I set modest, obtainable objectives for the first months. As I succeeded in filling the vacant deputy and middle-manager positions, the work hours went down to 70 a week and even 60. After nine months I could even take a very short vacation. In all these weeks, however, did I ever write a professional paper? Go to an anthropology meeting? Spend more than a few minutes here and there reading professional material not demanded by my work? Certainly not. That weekend seminar back in California, "How to Solve the Dilemmas of a Technical Person in a Management Position," had prepared me well for knowing my time needed to be totally devoted to the challenges of executive management and decision making.

Reward for my efforts was acclaim from many that I had dramatically turned the project around and was an effective leader. Concrete testimony was the fact that I had brought the project's annual "performance rating" from a low of 45 percent when I began to 90 percent two years later, a rating that brought an award of slightly more than $500,000 to our firm. Even in not-for-profit work, quantification of results is important.[7]

PROFILE OF ANTHROPOLOGISTS AS EXECUTIVE LEADERS

Executive status and positions are often measured by the size of staff and budgets one manages. The careers of two other anthropologists—who managed thousands of staff and budgets in the billions—provide further light on anthropologists in executive leadership.

Dr. Peter Benedict, USAID Mission Director

Peter Benedict is one of the anthropologists to have achieved highest-level positions in the field of international development and *the* anthropologist who has held the highest executive positions at USAID. Most notably during his illustrious career, Benedict served as Mission Director, in four countries, for USAID, the foreign aid arm of the State Department, rising to the rank of Career Minister in the Senior Foreign Service, the equivalent of a two-star general. In addition, he held executive and leadership positions in the Ford Foundation, the United Nations, a major nonprofit organization, and a leading consultant firm. He directed large, multisectoral offices in the United States and abroad and managed relations with the U.S. Congress, multilateral and bilateral agencies, senior host-country officials, and many foreign nongovernmental organizations.

Benedict received a Ph.D. in economic anthropology from the University of Chicago in 1970 following six years in Turkey, where he conducted field research, taught at universities in Ankara and Istanbul, and coauthored three books in Turkish and English. He thereafter moved quickly into management positions in the Ford Foundation (1970–76), becoming Ford Foundation Country Director in Turkey, where he directed the Foundation's programs in secondary school development, business management, population studies, and English language teaching. He then advanced to become the Ford Foundation Regional Social Science Advisor, based in Lebanon and then in Egypt. In that capacity he developed grant programs for universities throughout the region in economics, the social sciences, and business administration, managed programs in Egypt and Sudan and funded a regional association of scholars. From Ford, he was detailed to UNICEF to design and manage innovative Funds-in-Trust programs in Iran, Iraq, and the United Arab Emirates.

For 23 years (1976–97 and 1999–2001), Benedict held executive positions in USAID. As four-time Mission Director—in Mauritania, then Niger, Cameroon and Zimbabwe—Benedict managed budgets up to $100 million and U.S. and local staff up to 175. He developed, managed and oversaw innovative programs ranging from policy, finance, trade and legislation reform; public–private cooperation and local government strengthening; to agriculture and agricultural research; food security, famine and drought relief; environment and rainforest research; maternal health, family planning, HIV/AIDS, and child-survival immunization and diarrheal disease control; and housing. He coordinated annual multidonor relief efforts involving food, water, medical supplies, and nutritional surveillance, and launched programs that became models for the region.

Benedict's achievements were recognized by superior-performance awards from both the U.S. and African governments. At USAID in Washington, D.C., Benedict served as Assistant Administrator (chief executive) of the Food and Humanitarian Assistance Bureau; Director, Office for the Middle East/North Africa Affairs (coordinating with the Department of State, the National Security Council, and the Office of Management and Budget); and Director, Office of Budget and Development Planning, Asia and Near East Bureau (supervising budget formulation, accounting controls and presentation to Congress for a $3.5-billion annual program).

Along the way, Benedict honed leadership skills through training in the International Senior Management Executive Program of Harvard Business School (1990) and the International Monetary Fund Institute (1991). Most recently, he held executive positions with the firm RTI International (2003 to 2006). There he was Chief of Party for RTI's $236-million Local Governance and Democracy project, Senior Program Director and Country Manager for Iraq, and then director of RTI's Conflict Management, Mitigation, and Reconstruction group. Sadly, Benedict's achievements were cut short by cancer in 2006. A seasoned leader in international development assistance wrote of him:

> Peter represented a kind of golden age of good sense and care. When Peter moved from his role of social scientist to being an executive, I felt that this was the best possible sign, a significant breakthrough, and that social science would be permanently embedded in USAID's woodwork. Peter led thoughtfully and with greatest commitment for those USAID was trying to help; he debunked nonsense constructively, he encouraged good people, he obviously had his priorities straight. If we had a history of USAID's sharing and spreading of ideas, Peter's work would have a nice and deserved place. Perhaps the soft power contributions we make—and that Peter so well made—are the really enduring contributions.[8]

Dr. Tony Barclay, President and CEO

Barclay has the current distinction of being the only anthropologist heading up a major firm in the international development field. The firm is Development Alternatives, Inc. (DAI), with headquarters in Washington, D.C., and some 2,000 staff in 60 countries around the world. Being a chief executive officer (CEO) was never something Barclay envisioned early on or that he consciously prepared for.

Barclay's trajectory began with a bachelor's degree in African history and service as a Peace Corps Volunteer teaching school in rural Western Kenya. That experience inspired him to enroll in the Applied Anthropology doctoral program at Columbia University Teachers College under professors Lambros Comitas and Joan Vincent and to return to Western Kenya for his doctoral fieldwork. Research on the environmental and social impacts of the sugar industry (Ph.D., 1977) was the stepping stone that led him to work at DAI, which then, in 1977, was a small, informally managed startup organization focused on developing innovative approaches to help small farmers. Founded by three friends in 1970, DAI had achieved modest annual revenues of about $600,000 when Barclay joined. Initially, Barclay was traveling about six months a year, conducting studies and providing technical assistance in rural development, primarily in Africa. In 1979, he stepped in to manage the organization for a two-month stint while its president was away. Barclay did well in that role and found he enjoyed it. Also then in the new role of father, it made sense to spend more time in Washington, D.C.

As DAI expanded its technical range and grew during the 1980s, the need to develop systems was clear. Mentored by DAI's founder and president, Donald Mickelwait, Barclay took lead roles in developing the systems and strategies. He benefited "enormously" from three short courses to which DAI sent him, clearly grooming him for higher responsibility: a two-week executive short course at Stanford University's Business School; a financial management course at MIT's Sloan School; and a program in finance, marketing and organizational issues given by the American Management Association. In 1990, Barclay became president of DAI, and in 1999 its board advanced him to the additional role of CEO.

In addition to the valuable learning from these management courses, Barclay also identifies as "extremely important" his participation in a membership group of trusted peers. Called Vistage, this is a group of about 12 CEOs who meet for one day a month, spending half the day with a guest speaker and the other half in problem sharing and solving. None are in the development field, but all share similar problems of executive leadership. Barclay recommends to anthropologists looking for an executive career to find such a group of "trusted colleagues who hear you out as you wrestle with problems."

Of his role at DAI, Barclay says "The growth of the company has depended on bringing together the pieces. Anthropology helps in this by making you look below the surface." He urges reading The Living Company: Habits for Survival in a Turbulent Business Environment (de Geus 2002).

MOVING UP THE LEADERSHIP LADDER

As illustrated by these three careers, there are typically four management transitions in moving up the leadership ladder. In each, being a "manager who leads" requires seeing yourself as someone who mobilizes and empowers others (Galer et al. 2005).

Level One: Becoming a First-Time Manager, and Leading a Team: Before this transition, your success was measured by the quality and timelines of your own work and on having positive interactions with others. Now your success is measured by the success of your entire team. Essential skills include planning and organizing the work of the team, delegation, mentoring, managing interpersonal relationships, and supporting the needs of the team. Your time frame centers around "this week," "next month." With considerable crisis management, a year is probably luxurious thinking.

Level Two: From Managing a Team to Managing Other Managers: Now you need to develop the skills to support other managers as they go through their first transition. Your frames of reference become broader (e.g., a whole department) and time frame extended, planning for activities and results further into the future. You are now responsible for the performance of a department or other entity that requires several functions that may be completely new to you (e.g., human resource management, financial management, and public relations). Your time frame has probably extended now to six months, even two or three years.

Level Three: Becoming a Senior Manager: Your attention to strategic issues now must exceed your area of technical expertise. You need to educate yourself quickly about issues that other people managed before. Within the organization, you have to continue facilitating the development of managerial and leadership talent. Essential skills include strategic thinking, coaching, managing consultants, and managing conflict. While you still do shorter-term crisis management, your time frame probably extends two to five years into the future.

Level Four: Leading and Managing at the Top: You are now responsible for the organization's success into the future. You must pay attention to the success of *all* the different divisions and programs that comprise the organization and do everything you can to help them be successful. You are also responsible for cultivating and maintaining good working relationships with key stakeholders. A measure of your success will be succession management, effectively managing leadership transitions at all levels, including your own replacement. Your time frame likely ranges three to ten years into the future.

These transitions—from functioning as a "capable individual" to leading as an executive—are also referred to as a "Hierarchy of Executive Capabilities" (Collins 2001; see Figure 2).[9]

Level 5: *Executive*. Builds enduring greatness through a paradoxical blend of personal humility and professional will.

Level 4: *Effective Leader*. Catalyzes commitment to and vigorous pursuit of a clear and compelling vision, stimulating higher performance standards.

Level 3: *Competent Manager*. Organizes people and resources toward the effective and efficient pursuit of pre-determined objectives.

Level 2: *Contributing Team Member*. Contributes individual capabilities to the achievement of group objectives and works effectively with others in a group setting.

Level 1: *Highly Capable Individual*. Makes productive contributions through talent, knowledge, skills, and good work habits.

FIGURE 2. Hierarchy of Executive Capabilities.

To reiterate, the farther up the ladder you proceed, the more you need to let go of your technical aspirations. A manager and leader typically experiences technical "joy" and achievement only vicariously—through his or her people. To succeed, you must always be reminding yourself that those people you manage are needed and must be supported to do their jobs. You must be willing (and will find it pays) to spend time on *them*—choosing them, guiding them, motivating them—and have the confidence they will do the job.[10] You will also have to be quick to spot failure although, as a good manager, you will not go out looking for it.

ANTHROPOLOGY: HELP OR HINDRANCE?

A background in anthropology is definitely an asset for executive leadership. It is especially valuable when the focus of the work is international or intercultural. There are many reasons this is so. First and most obvious, anthropology conditions one to understand and work with difference. Beyond cultural differences, it prepares us to understand and work with difference in general—class, professional training, personality, work style, and others. Second, we know that each organization has its own culture and we are more likely than most to understand the specific organizational culture and to be able to look beyond the surface manifestations of what appears to be going on (Miller 2003). Third, being holistic, anthropology conditions us to integrate disciplines, bringing together the parts of a solution. Fourth, anthropology has trained us to communicate with people of diverse backgrounds and statuses, including stakeholders, and to understand how various forms of communication function in organizational interaction.

Coming from anthropology, however, may also hinder us. First and most importantly, placing too much emphasis on cultural differences may slow processes beyond what is optimal or even acceptable in today's fast-paced world. I tended, for instance, to be overly tolerant of certain idiosyncrasies of staff coming from other cultures, not pushing them hard enough toward higher standards of productivity. A seasoned development specialist and major supporter of bringing anthropologists into USAID expressed this more forcefully:

> A major issue that I found in the anthropological community is this. Anthropologists are so seriously trained to honor their particular community. Without that, so many cultures and groups simply would be submerged in an "average" description. It is a major strength of the professional contribution of anthropology and, of course, sets the field far apart from sociology. But in big organizations working across multiple cultures, you simply have to focus more broadly. You can't get a big network (e.g., Congress) to take the time to read up on 50 cultures. So you need to find larger prescriptions within which you can implement locally valid solutions. Most anthropologists are extremely uncomfortable with this approach as it runs exactly counter to their ethos and training. . . . Those who succeed in large organizations must learn to articulate sensitive generalizations, broader views that can inform, move issues forward, while not stumbling over local truths. It is such a hard

task to unlearn and accommodate, but if one cannot find the larger picture, there is no future for an anthropologist in such settings.[11]

Second, anthropology also inclines many of us to be more participatory than an M.B.A.-trained executive or than a fast-paced milieu will tolerate. The participatory elements in my anthropological worldview and natural management style fit well earlier with the values of a small NGO. However, in executive management in Washington, D.C., I was criticized for being too participatory. "The staff want you to lead," I was told. "Do not ask them to be involved in so many decisions. They want you to know the answers, to have the vision, to show the way." This took major effort to reshape my management style to provide the leadership and direction without being overly directive (bossy). Third, anthropology does not provide most of us with specific skills and knowledge in management and budgets that executive leadership requires. The anthropologist who has included economics in his or her training (as did Peter Benedict, above), had training in statistical methods, or complemented anthropology with M.B.A. or business-skills coursework, is likely to have an easier time as an executive than a cultural anthropologist without such complementary training.

SKILLS-BUILDING ADVICE TO ANTHROPOLOGISTS ASPIRING TO EXECUTIVE LEADERSHIP

Is executive leadership the career path for you? If so, you want to be developing and practicing now the essential skills and habits you will need for success. Interrelated, these may be summed up as follows:

- Matching passion and place
- Managing time
- Setting and meeting priorities
- Being an effective communicator
- Being proactive
- Developing and demonstrating leadership

Matching passion and place: Clarify your passion and vision and be in a work setting that supports this passion. This includes both colleagues who share your vision and a setting where you see opportunities for growth.

Time management: Consider time your most precious commodity. Efficient time use will be one of the greatest challenges in your executive role. Read up on time management advice and develop a personal strategy that works for you, enabling you to be most effective while also achieving a good work–life balance.[12] Be familiar with the often-cited and important "Time Management Matrix" (see Table 1); share and discuss it with coworkers and analyze where you spend most of your time and where you need to change. On any project, "begin with the end in mind." What do you want to achieve? Now, what

TABLE 1 Time Management Matrix[13]

	URGENT	NOT URGENT
Important	**I** **Quadrant of Necessity** (Urgent and important) (MANAGE) • Crises • Medical emergencies • Pressing problems • Deadline-driven projects • Last-minute preparations for scheduled activities	**II** **Quadrant of Quality & Leadership** (Important, not urgent) *—Where we should work most of the time—* (FOCUS) • Preparation/planning • Production capability activities • Prevention • Recognizing new opportunities • Values clarification • Relationship-building • True relaxation; exercise
Not Important	**III** **Quadrant of Deception** (Not important, seemingly urgent) *—Where we tend to work the most—* (AVOID) • Interruptions, some calls • Some mail, some reports • Some meetings • Proximate "pressing" matters • Many popular activities	**IV** **Quadrant of Waste** (Not important, not urgent) (AVOID) • Trivia, busywork • Some mail, junk mail • Some phone messages/email • Time wasters • Escape activities • Viewing mindless TV shows

are the steps, and ministeps, to get there? Being wise, you will not plunge headlong into an activity without doing this task analysis first.

***Setting and meeting priorities*:** While this is part of time management, it is so important that it needs special emphasis. Learn to set goals and priorities and make a realistic plan to achieve them. If you're not progressing, examine the plan to see what change is needed. Remember to "Put First Things First" and "Begin with the End in Mind" (Covey 2001; Wadsworth 1997).

***Being an effective communicator*:** Good communication skills (oral, but written too) are a sine qua non for leadership. Assess your strengths and challenges and take steps to improve; seek opportunity to benefit from a public speaking or presentation skills class. Learning effective negotiating skills will also be beneficial (Fisher et al. 1991). Finally, you may be able to make valuable contributions to your organization by assessing its communication use and patterns and suggesting appropriate measures for improvement—always needed (Roebuck 1998).

***Being proactive; be a proactive doer (see below) and also a proactive learner*:** Get guidance; find mentors. Your immediate superior will usually be a first source of guidance.

Other long-timers and superiors with whom you succeed in establishing a relationship of trust may also provide important guidance. Look for mentors who can provide insight into the organization and your role in it and coach you in problem-solving and building effective relationships. Reading about coaching (e.g., Media Partners Corporation 1997) will help you understand the sorts of guidance you can expect and seek from your supervisors. Look across the organization to maximize connections with other relevant skill and knowledge sets; learn from colleagues.

Think "professional development." Find out about professional development opportunities your organization offers and take advantage of them. If there is no professional development program, think about what you need for professional development and ask to be given this opportunity. If between jobs, use the time to take a short course (e.g., that public speaking course) to equip you with needed or potentially useful new skills and tools. As you move into management, ask to participate in management training, eventually executive training, and know the time may come when you should ask to have an *executive coach*.[14] Along the way, consider whether finding and working with a *life coach* would benefit you.

Develop and demonstrate leadership: Observe leaders and study leadership. Then be a proactive doer and practice leadership in all your work activity. You will do this appropriately and tactfully in accord with your current position and the principles of organizational learning. Organizational learning, following Peter Senge (1990), generally comprises five learning disciplines: systems thinking, personal mastery, mental models, shared vision, and team learning. You will be wise to consult the ever-growing literature advising on how to manage and lead successfully. You are likely to be spending hours in airports where the display table in airport bookstores presents the latest and hottest management books and affords you a time-efficient opportunity to quickly browse through them to see which might best address your current challenge. Some of these how-to guides are written specifically for executives. A good example is *Execution: The Discipline of Getting Things Done* (Bossidy and Charan 2002). Others are more general personal growth books that also provide good advice, because much of being an effective executive leader has to do with managing relationship issues and related personnel conundrums. *Difficult Conversations: How to Discuss What Matters Most* (Stone et al. 1999) is a good example, as is John Gray's *How to Get What You Want and Want What You Have* (2000).

Take short-term management courses (even by video or DVD). If possible, get an external advisor who coaches you. Develop a group of peers with whom to discuss and find solutions to workplace and career challenges.

Finally, as a young professional, you have an advantage in that you are likely to be on the cutting edge of change, technological and otherwise, in today's fast-paced world. You will also want to remember, however, the importance of balancing work and personal quality time. And you will always think "Win–Win."

The following wisdom, attributed to Lao Tzu in the *Tao Te Ching*, captures an ideal in leadership that rings especially true for anthropologists:

Go to the people

Live among them

Learn from them

Love them

Start with what they know

Build on what they have.

But of the best leaders

When their task is accomplished

Their work is done

The people all remark

"We have done it ourselves."

NOTES

Acknowledgments: The author expresses her sincere appreciation for the careful and thoughtful reviews of the manuscript by Prof. Robert Berg, Dr. John H. Sullivan, and Dr. Joseph Westermeyer.

1. For example, the head of USAID has, for most of its years, been the Administrator, USAID. Below him or her are Assistant Administrators (e.g., the Assistant Administrator for Africa or the Assistant Administrator of the Global Bureau).

2. See especially *You Don't Need a Title to Be a Leader* (Sanborn 2006); also Bennis and Nanus (2003); Byham (1998); Kouzes and Posner (1987); Wagner and Harter (2006).

3. Management Sciences for Health (Galer et al. 2005:8).

4. In the 1970s, most applied anthropologists of any reputation were university-employed professors who *taught* about applied anthropology. Applied anthropologists who worked outside of academia were usually looked on as people who couldn't get an academic position. When I was elected to serve on the American Anthropological Association's Executive Board (1982–86) it was on the platform of "anthropological practice." This led to the creation of the National Association for the Practice of Anthropology (NAPA) as an organization that would support anthropologists who desired to make *careers as practitioners,* distinct from the *study* of applied anthropology. I was honored to become the first elected president of NAPA in 1984.

5. This included using the IRS 501(c)3 designation of the Public Health Institute, then known as the Western Consortium for Public Health. Several years later, when our Pacific Institute program was well established, we went through the procedures of getting our own 501(c)3.

6. Peter Drucker (1909–2005), long regarded the world's foremost management theorist, made famous the term "knowledge worker" and is believed to have ushered in the knowledge economy. His prolific body of work has been considered the preeminent management thinking for most of the 20th century and into the 21st. See Drucker (2001, 2002a, 2002b, 2004) and Drucker with Senge (2001).

7. For further insights into leadership and management in the global health field see Foege and colleagues (2005).

8. Robert Berg, personal communication, May 26, 2006.

9. Presented in *Good to Great* (Collins 2001:20).

10. See especially *Motivating and Rewarding Employees: New and Better Ways to Inspire Your People* (Hiam 1999).

11. Robert Berg, personal communication, September 26, 2007.

12. Preeminent among anthropologists who have turned their lens on executives and leadership is B. Eugene Griessman, now a much-in-demand consultant and motivational speaker. His *Time Tactics of Very Successful People* (1994) identifies important strategies and is a good place to start.

13. Adapted from Covey and colleagues (1994), and Paauwerfully Organized (www. DeclutterYourLife.com).

14. Executive coaching provides individual leaders with the candor and objective feedback needed to nourish their growth. Data often come from a "360" survey of people who work most closely with that leader: boss, peers, and direct reports. Executive coaching integrates personal development with organizational needs and fosters cultural change for the benefit of the entire organization (Sherman and Freas 2004:85).

REFERENCES CITED

Bennis, Warren, and Burt Nanus
   2003 Leaders: Strategies for Taking Charge. 2nd edition. New York: HarperCollins Business Essentials.
Bossidy, Larry, and Ram Charan
   2002 Execution: The Discipline of Getting Things Done. New York: Crown Business.
Byham, William C.
   1998 Zapp! The Lightening of Empowerment: How to Improve Productivity, Quality, and Employee Satisfaction. New York: Fawcett Books.
Collins, Jim
   2001 Good to Great. New York: HarperCollins.
Covey, Stephen R.
   2001 The 7 Habits of Highly Effective People: Powerful Lessons in Personal Change. New York: Simon and Schuster.
   2003 Principle-Centered Leadership. New York: Free Press.
Covey, Stephen R., A. Roger Merrill, and Rebecca R. Merrill
   1994 First Things First: To Live, to Love, to Learn, to Leave a Legacy. New York: Simon and Schuster.
de Geus, Arie
   2002 The Living Company: Habits for Survival in a Turbulent Business Environment. Boston: Harvard Business School Press.
Drucker, Peter F.
   2001 The Essential Drucker: The Best of Sixty Years of Peter Drucker's Essential Writings on Management. New York: HarperCollins Business Essentials.
   2002a The Effective Executive: The Definitive Guide to Getting the Right Things Done. Rev. edition. New York: HarperCollins Business Essentials.
   2002b They're Not Employees, They're People. Harvard Business Review, Reprint 20202E.
   2004 What Makes An Effective Executive. Harvard Business Review, Reprint R0406C.
Drucker, Peter F., with Peter Senge
   2001 Leading in a Time of Change: What It Will Take to Lead Tomorrow. New York: John Wiley and Sons.
Fisher, Roger, William Ury, and Bruce Patton
   1991 Getting to Yes: Negotiating Agreement Without Giving In. New York: Penguin Books.
Foege, William, Nils Daulaire, Robert E. Black, and Clarence E. Pearson.
   2005 Global Health Leadership and Management. San Francisco: John Wiley and Sons.
Galer, Joan Brager, Sylvia Vriesendorp, and Alison Ellis
   2005 Managers Who Lead: A Handbook for Improving Health Service. Cambridge: Management Sciences for Health.
Gray, John
   2000 How to Get What You Want and Want What You Have. New York: Perennial.
Griessman, B. Eugene
   1994 Time Tactics of Very Successful People. New York: McGraw-Hill.
Hiam, Alexander
   1999 Motivating and Rewarding Employees: New and Better Ways to Inspire Your People. Avon, MA: Adams Media.
Kouzes, James M., and Barry Z. Posner
   1987 The Leadership Challenge: How to Get Extraordinary Things Done in Organizations. San Francisco: Jossey-Bass.

Media Partners Corporation
  1997 The Practical Coach: Inspiring, Encouraging and Challenging Your Team. Seattle: Media Partners
        Corporation.
Miller, John G.
  2003 QBQ! The Question Behind the Question. New York: G. P. Putnam.
Pillsbury, Barbara
  1978 Traditional Health Care in the Near East: Indigenous Health Practices and Practi-
        tioners in Egypt, Afghanistan, Jordan, Syria, Tunisia, Morocco and Yemen. Washington,
        DC: USAID.
  1979 Reaching the Rural Poor: Indigenous Health Practitioners Are Already There. USAID, Bureau
        for Program and Policy Coordination. Program Evaluation Discussion Paper, 1. Washington, DC:
        USAID.
  1984a Anthropologists in International Health. *In* Training Manual in Medical Anthropology. Carole E.
        Hill, ed. Pp. 84–110. Washington, DC: American Anthropological Association.
  1984b Evaluation and Monitoring. *In* Training Manual in Development Anthropology. William Partridge,
        ed. Pp. 42–63. Washington, DC: American Anthropological Association.
  1986 Making a Difference: Anthropologists in International Development. *In* Anthropology and Public
        Policy, Special Publication 21. Walter Goldschmidt, ed. Pp. 10–28. Washington, DC: American
        Anthropological Association.
Roebuck, Chris
  1998 Effective Communication: The Essential Guide to Thinking and Working Smarter. New York:
        Amacom.
Sanborn, Mark
  2006 You Don't Need a Title to Be a Leader. New York: Doubleday Currency.
Senge, Peter
  1990 The Fifth Discipline. New York: Doubleday.
Sherman, Stratford, and Alyssa Freas
  2004 The Wild West of Executive Coaching. Harvard Business Review 82(11):82–90.
Stone, Douglas, Bruce Patton, and Sheila Heen
  1999 Difficult Conversations: How to Discuss What Matters Most. New York: Penguin Books.
Wadsworth, Walter J.
  1997 The Agile Manager's Guide to Goal-Setting and Achievement. Bristol, VT: Velocity Business.
Wagner, Rod, and James K. Harter
  2006 12: The Elements of Great Managing. New York: Gallup Press.

CREATING YOUR OWN CONSULTING BUSINESS

CARLA N. LITTLEFIELD AND EMILIA GONZÁLEZ-CLEMENTS
Littlefield Associates and Development Systems/Applications International, Inc.

As academic positions become more competitive, many anthropologists are exploring the possibilities for creating their own consulting businesses. However, entrepreneurship is not a topic usually taught in graduate anthropology programs. In this article, two anthropologists provide advice on starting and operating a consulting business. The purpose of this article is to acquaint the budding professional with the basics of starting and operating a small business based on the skills, educational background, and experience of a professional anthropologist. The first part, Small Business Start-Up, describes the process of creating a business, from conducting a self-assessment to developing a plan to promote your services. The second part, Operating the Small Business, provides several frameworks for delivering good consultant services, from understanding the consulting process to an introduction to project management. Anthropologists are trained in data collection, analysis, and interpretation. We may also receive instruction on research design and how to conduct fieldwork and research. Our anthropological training in observing and understanding the beliefs and behaviors of groups, as well as seeing things from the client's unique perspective, gives us an edge as consultants. Our training helps us work in other cultural settings, and to work with different groups and subgroups. The authors emphasize networking as a fundamental promotion strategy that can take place at professional meetings (local, regional, or national) or with community organizations relevant to one's business (organizations, foundations, or coalitions). This article includes several useful websites for start-up topics and for networking with other anthropologists. Keywords: consulting business, applied anthropology, entrepreneurship, small business start-up, small business operation

As academic positions become more competitive, many anthropologists are exploring the possibilities for creating their own consulting businesses. However, entrepreneurship is not a topic usually taught in graduate anthropology programs. In this article, two anthropologists provide advice on starting and operating your own consulting business. Carla Littlefield started Littlefield Associates in 1989 and recently retired. Her business focus was grant writing, research, and community development. In the first half of this article, "Small Business Start-Up," she identifies the basic principles and tasks related to business start-up. In the second half of this article, "Operating the Small Business," Emilia González-Clements shares her experiences in operating her consulting business, Development Systems/Applications International, Inc., devoted to ethnographic applied research, policy research, strategic planning, and group facilitation. The overall purpose of this article is to acquaint the budding professional with the basics of starting and

NAPA BULLETIN 29, pp. 152–165. ISBN 9781405190152. © 2008 by the American Anthropological Association. DOI:10.1111/j.1556-4797.2008.00011.x

operating a small business based on the skills, educational background, and experience of a professional anthropologist.

SMALL BUSINESS START-UP

Myriad resources exist in the library and on the Internet to assist the entrepreneur with small business start-up. These include publications of the U.S. Small Business Administration as well as an extensive array of how-to books that can guide the professional toward success. The experts agree that many tasks precede rushing out and printing business cards.

Do a Self-Assessment. The first step is to assess whether you have the "right stuff" to be your own boss. Are you organized? The consultant must be a master of multitasking and keeping track of details, including keeping a schedule and being on time. Are you a self-starter? If you plan to work at home, a variety of distractions may prevent you from keeping on task. Walking the dog or watching TV may be more fun than analyzing client data. Do you have the physical and emotional strength to put in long hours required to meet client deadlines? Be honest about any behaviors that could interfere with your performance. If you have dependent family members, are they supportive of your decision to seek self-employment? Long hours or long absences in the field may take their toll on family relationships. How strong is your motivation? Initial doubts about starting your own business must be resolved before going forward. Your self-assessment may indicate areas that need attention before attempting to become self-employed.

Identify the Focus of Your Business. Anthropologists have found niches or significant roles in almost every area of employment. Your knowledge and skills in ethnography, advocacy, participant observation, qualitative and quantitative research, education, communications, and project coordination, to name only a few, can be applied to a variety of content areas. John van Willigen identified 27 such general areas (2002:8). The experience gained from completing your master's thesis or dissertation is an important starting point for deciding your business focus. Analyze the contacts, networks, and friendships formed during the thesis or dissertation process for their usefulness in your business start-up. You need a tickler file with the names, addresses, phone numbers, and e-mail addresses of these contacts along with a few key words. This file can be as simple as alphabetical cards or something more technical set up on your computer.

Some anthropologists come to the field with knowledge and practice in another field, for example, nursing, teaching, law, administration, information technology, community development, and marketing. Your education and training as an anthropologist can be applied to almost any field and enhance the toolkit of the practitioner. Perhaps you possess special skills, for example, foreign language fluency, computer expertise, photography, or videography. Fluency in Spanish may open doors in the United States, Mexico, and Central and South America. Fluency in other foreign languages may be the entrée to consulting with the federal government, as well as private companies and public organizations abroad.

Assess the Marketplace. Is there a market for what you have to offer and where is this market? You have knowledge and skills, but it is necessary to find out who will hire you. Remember the tickler file you started with names and contact information for people you interacted with in the past, people who may remember you from a recent project? Call them and set up appointments for the purpose of information gathering. You want to reintroduce yourself and find out if they have any projects that could benefit from your expertise. I used this tactic with the state migrant health program in a western state and immediately launched my consulting career with a successful special project.

Another source of information about the local market is your local network of practicing anthropologists, especially Local Practitioner Organizations (LPOs). Many LPOs meet monthly, quarterly, or semiannually. Meetings bring academics, practitioners, and students into regular contact. These same organizations may have web-based listservs that list job opportunities locally, regionally, nationally, or internationally. Most LPOs offer reduced membership dues for students and the unemployed. Go to your local anthropology department or academic library and ask to review their current issue of the American Anthropology Association's newsletter, *Anthropology News.* Note the job openings. Do not overlook the social science research firms operating in your area. While "cold calls" can be a lesson in rejection, sometimes they can work to one's advantage. Your goal is to get your foot in the door and find out what kinds of projects they are doing and whether there is a role for an anthropologist. Based on your assessment of the marketplace, you are ready to figure out how to structure your business.

Determine the Legal Structure for Your Business. Several options exist for a small business, including sole proprietorship, partnership, and corporation. An accountant can advise you as to which structure is best for you. Most small businesses start up as sole proprietorships. According to the U.S. Small Business Administration's website (2006), sole proprietorships have the advantage of being relatively easy and less expensive to organize than other business structures; as owner you have complete control and you receive all the income; and the business is easy to dissolve, if necessary. Some of the disadvantages of sole proprietorships are that the owner has unlimited liability; the owner is responsible for all debts; the owner's business and personal assets are at risk. These include your house, car, and savings accounts. Additionally, some employee benefits are not fully deductible from business income. Your accountant can help you assess these risks.

Another common structure for small businesses is the general partnership, whereby two or more people with similar or complementary skills share ownership of the business. Like the sole proprietorship, general partnerships are easy to organize, but the partners need to take the time to develop a partnership agreement. This legal document identifies how decisions are made, how disputes are handled, how the profits are shared, how new partners may be admitted, or how the partnership may be dissolved. The partners share in profits and losses as determined by the agreement. They also share unlimited liability. Other business structures that the entrepreneur may want to explore are limited partnerships, corporations, limited liability companies, and joint ventures, but are not discussed here. Use your accountant or attorney as your best guide when considering these options.

Choose a Name for Your Business. Select your business name carefully. You may have it for a long time. It should reflect who or what you are. It will appear on your business cards, telephone listings, correspondence, and publicity materials. If your name is known to potential clients, use it, for example, Littlefield Associates. If you do not have name recognition, try to convey the focus of your business, for example, Development Systems/Applications International. Check with the telephone book, the Internet, and the branch of your state government that registers trade or business names to make sure that no one else has taken your choice.

Write a Business Plan. Even if your start-up is a sole proprietorship, a business plan will keep you focused and serve as a guide to developing and managing the business. Business plans are usually required when applying for a business loan. However, if you do not intend to apply for a loan, consider doing a "plan for the business" (Stolze 1999:88–89), which is not as formal as a business plan. As the business evolves, this written document should be reviewed and updated periodically. Developing a plan for the business should force you to think seriously about the strategies needed to get going and the time frame for completion. A plan for a partnership or sole proprietorship should include the following:

- Present a description of the business and its services.
- Identify your goals for the business.
- Describe the market for your business as well as your existing competition.
- Include a marketing or publicity plan.
- Describe how the business will be managed.
- Present a realistic financial plan, including projected monthly cash flow for the first year.
- Include your updated resume and those of the partners. Emphasize skills and experience, but list relevant education.
- List your advisory group or board and determine how often the group will meet.

List the Equipment and Supplies You Need. Start-up will require equipment, some of which may entail a costly investment. Visit your local office supply store and apply for a business discount, which may include regular rebates. If you have decided on a partnership with leased office space, figure in the added expenses related to the lease and equipment and supplies for two persons. The following advice applies primarily to a home office for a sole proprietorship.

You will need a computer with ample memory along with the software necessary to conduct your business, for example, a word processing program, spreadsheet, and Internet access. High-speed Internet access is a decided advantage, especially when considering that the consultant's time is worth money. Explore the options available for protection against viruses and spying: never transmit viruses to your clients. Buy a computer monitor that is comfortable for your eyes; you will be spending a lot of time sitting in front of it. Consider a combination computer, printer, and fax machine, as well as a scanner. Your clients will want several options for staying in touch with you. At some point you may want to have your own website with details about your business. This venture could entail a fee for the development and maintenance of the website as well as an access fee.

In addition to the technical equipment and software, you will need furniture and office supplies. Look minimally for two sturdy desks, two comfortable chairs, a filing cabinet, a bookcase, and two desk lamps, all of which may be found at a used furniture outlet for significantly lower cost. Use one desk for the technical equipment, the other for working on a given project. Each project can have its own file folder and reside on a shelf of the bookcase. Within the file folder, separate the project components into manila folders, each marked clearly. You may create your own business stationery and business cards on your computer, or get an estimate from the professionals at your office supply store.

Consider opening a separate bank savings account, checking account, and credit card for your business. This could be helpful when doing your annual tax return. Provide all the detail in the check register and bank book necessary to identify the purpose of expenditures and the source of revenues. Get to know the people at your local bank; you may need a friend if revenues do not materialize when anticipated.

Determine Source of Start-up Money. Your list of office equipment and supplies should provide a rough estimate of how much it will cost to get going. This will determine whether you need to borrow money or whether you can cover the essential costs with your personal savings or credit cards. The latter may not be the best choice because of high interest rates. One strategy would be to prioritize your needs to spread out the expenditures for your most critical needs over several months. Your bank, credit union, or the Small Business Administration may be good resources for a short-term loan. Be prepared to present your business plan along with a proposal, which spells out the amount of the request and how it will be used.

As you consider your financial needs for start-up, factor in the monthly living expenses for you and your family, for example, rent, house payments, auto expenses, insurance, student loan payments, and food. If you have a working partner or spouse, these expenses may be shared. Another alternative is to keep your "day job" as you launch your consulting business. *Day job* is sometimes used for a full-time or part-time job that brings in a steady income while you lay the groundwork for what you really want to do with your education and experience.

Keep Good Records. Every business expenditure should be documented with a receipt and entry into an accounting system. Many resources exist in the library and on the Internet for examples of good record keeping systems. This can be as simple as a revenue and expense journal, which is used to record income and expenses (Pinson and Jinnett 2000:142). Expenses include checks written and credit card purchases. Revenues are payments from clients for your services. Keep a daily calendar with plenty of room for client appointments (who and where) and telephone calls. In your car, keep a travel log with starting and ending mileage for every business trip. If business or professional activities take you out of town, keep copies of your airline tickets, car rental, hotel, and food receipts. When you work on your annual tax return, you or your accountant will need all this documentation to determine your business deductions. It may seem a hassle to do the necessary bookkeeping on a daily or weekly basis, but it will take much more time at the end of the year to reconstruct past business meetings, income, and expenses.

Develop a Plan to Promote Your Business. To be successful, you must attract clients. You have a service for which you already determined a need. How will you let potential clients know that your service exists? The plan may start with a serious consideration of how you will price your service. What is the competition charging? Are you willing to price your service lower initially to draw clients? Another pricing strategy is to offer the first hour of consultation free to new clients. During this time, you listen carefully to the client's needs and determine what you could offer or make suggestions as to other approaches. This also allows you and the client to quietly assess whether you can work together. Leave your business card with the client and, if you really want the job, follow up a few days later to continue the promotion.

After you figure out how to price your service, start promoting your company. Start with your business card, which should include your name, degree, address, phone number, e-mail address, and website, if you have one. Also include three or four of the principal activities of your company, for example, community assessment, community development, research, training, and grant writing. Look at other consultants' cards for fresh ideas and formats. Always carry your business cards with you whether to client meetings, professional meetings, or social gatherings. An opportunity to present your business card may occur at any time. Be prepared.

Networking is a major promotion strategy. This can occur at professional meetings, including your local or regional practitioner organization. Let your colleagues know that you are in business. Join community organizations relevant to your business, for example, coalitions for the homeless, migrant health, migrant housing, and refugee services. These coalitions may bring together representatives from state and county agencies as well as private or nonprofit organizations. As you share your ideas at meetings of the group, you are also promoting yourself and your services. My own tactic was to join two coalitions of which the state migrant health program was a member. Within three months, I had my first contract to determine the feasibility of evening health clinics for migrant farm workers throughout the state, followed by a contract to set up the clinics.

Members of state and local agencies do their own networking. They keep each other informed of consultants to whom jobs may be successfully outsourced. My successful series of "special projects" for the migrant health program resulted in the director's recommending me for the research director position for the Task on the Medically Indigent. This activity led to other research projects, both with the migrant health program and other agencies at the state health department. Networking also may occur at the federal level. My work with the migrant health program in one western state led the regional federal office to recommend me to another western state to write a series of annual block grants to secure federal funds for maternal and child health programs.

Maintain Professional Client Relations. Clients expect the consultant to act in a professional and ethical manner. The first step in a client relationship is to establish a contract for a service or product, for example, a grant application, a research project, community needs assessment, or plan for community development. Contracts may be simple one-page documents, but each has critical components: a description of the consultant's responsibilities relative to the product, the client's responsibilities, the deadlines, the consultant's fee, additional expenses that may be billed (e.g., travel, mileage, postage, copying), and when payment of the billing(s) are due. Both you and your client sign the contract, and you both keep copies in case misunderstandings occur. Contracts are legal, binding documents, and you may want to check with an attorney before entering into a contractual agreement.

Business ethics is the topic of shelves of books in the library. Clients have the right to expect that the consultant will behave in an ethical manner. This includes trust and confidentiality, for example, not sharing any proprietary information with others, not revealing insider client "gossip" with others, and not sharing any client products with others without permission of the client. Such products could be grant applications or sections thereof, data generated by the client, and client correspondence to you or others. A contract usually implies that the product of the effort belongs to the client, so the client's permission is required before the consultant may share client products with others. Before reporting to professional colleagues on the results of a study funded by a client, ask the client for permission to make the report. The client may want to remain anonymous in the report or request that the study site be made anonymous.

In the following section, Emilia González-Clements discusses the principles of operating the small business. She draws on her experiences as chief executive officer of her own consulting business, Development Systems/Applications International, Inc., founded in 1984.

OPERATING THE SMALL BUSINESS

If you are considering becoming a consultant, read the material in Riall Nolan's (2005) excellent seminar for graduate students, "Work in the World: Advice on Non-Academic Careers" (see also Nolan this volume). You will find that your training in anthropology has given you a good toolkit to build upon as you plan your business. The process of creating a business is known as a "start-up." After creating your start-up, you are ready to tackle the hard work of operating your business on a day-to-day basis. You can find excellent, free advice on all aspects of start-ups at www.entrepreneur.com and at www.nolo.com. The former is the website for *Entrepreneur Magazine*; the latter offers legal information in everyday language.

Now that you have formalized your business, here are some suggestions for operating your newly-created consulting service. Developing ways to conduct your business is also part of your start-up.

Understand the Consulting Process. Your prospective client will have an idea or a need that requires a consultant. Organizations and companies hire consultants because their own staff may not have the particular expertise or contacts necessary for the task. Your marketing efforts will help get you in the door. Generally, you will have an initial contact with the prospective client and begin a negotiation process that, hopefully, results in a contract.

You may respond to a request for proposals (RFP) that explains the "scope of work" and the "project deliverables," or you may have to discuss these issues directly with a potential client. Either way, you and your client will need to be clear about what the project involves (scope of work) and what you will be turning in to the client (deliverables). Deliverables can be a research study report, a training session, or a grant application. Sometimes the methodology (how you will actually do the tasks) is specified by the client. Twice I have been requested by clients to use a specific technique or methodology. Generally, I design the research aspects of each project from my background and training in applied anthropology. I also have learned techniques and methodology for group facilitation, strategic planning, and public issues gathering. Some clients are sophisticated in methodology; others are not. However, very few are familiar with anthropology or know that we bring a flexible, reliable toolkit. I always explain to my potential clients that I am an applied anthropologist, which I define as someone with training in anthropology who helps groups or individuals solve problems by conducting applied research or designing and implementing projects. The reaction is usually the same: "Wow, I always wanted to be an anthropologist. Where did you dig? I didn't know anthropologists did this kind of work!"

Clients choose consultants who can get the job done, that is, provide the client the information he or she needs in a way that is useful. You will meet with your client and negotiate the assignment. One good way to organize your time and work is to follow a project management framework.

Follow a Project Management Framework. Project management has applications in many disciplines and is a skill that applied anthropologists will find useful. A project is a specific, time-, and resource-limited task, and project management is a process that guides the successful completion of tasks from idea to evaluation. One framework I like and use includes the following stages:

1. Visualize—create a project vision statement
2. Plan—break the project into manageable pieces
3. Implement—monitor and control—communicate, delegate, document
4. Close—evaluate the project
   [Snead and Wycoff 1997:115]

In the first stage, the consultant and the client discuss the intended work. This is a crucial stage because the resulting contract is based on the "deliverables" and "scope of work" agreed on at this early stage. You will negotiate the desired outcomes and then plan the project definition. The desired outcome is what the client wants. For example, when the client says she wants you to plan a research project, make sure you both understand what the client expects. You have an idea of what a research project entails; the client may be thinking of something entirely different. Be sure you understand what the client actually expects your work to involve.

In the planning stage, you will design the project. If a team is involved, the project manager decides who will do which task, by when, and with how much time and money. A consultant working alone will create a list of tasks and a timeline for completing each task. This is the project definition stage. For stage three and throughout the project, the consultant should communicate with the client, work on the tasks and document expenses and time.

Closing the project, stage four, often involves a report or presentation. I always keep notes about what I am doing, what works, and what does not. If you do not document your ideas and your expenses, it is very difficult to learn from the experience and to remember the costs you incurred and those that need to be reimbursed. The success of the project is defined by the client. On one project, my client did not like the findings. He found no fault with the work but did not want to use the report because it showed that the program was not meeting its goals. I pointed out that with the information, changes could be made to align the program with its stated goals. This was an evaluation project, which is a specialized type of consulting, and, in fact, one use of evaluation is to see if a project is being implemented correctly.

Develop the Characteristics of a Good Applied Practice. Following a project management process will help you organize and monitor your work. In an applied research project, when you report your findings, make sure you follow the characteristics of a good applied practice (van Willigen 2002:14), excerpted here:

- "First, knowledge should be provided in reference to areas where the client can act.
- Second, knowledge has to be provided on time.
- Third, knowledge has to be communicated in a way which facilitates action."

In other words, tell the client something doable, where he or she can take action. Provide the information by the agreed-on deadline, because some client actions may be time sensitive. Finally, present your findings as recommendations for action and explain your reasoning.

Write Clear, Brief Consultant Reports. Now that you have completed the implementation phase, you will need to report to your client. Here is an outline I use for the consultant's reports that I deliver to my clients:

1. Background
2. Purpose
3. Scope
4. Methodology
5. Major Findings
6. Recommendations

The background is a brief paragraph about why and how the project came about, and identifies who is involved. The purpose describes the actual project. The scope refers to the specific limits of the project. The methodology section tells about the techniques you used in implementing the project. The major findings section reports the outcome or findings, written in an organized way, summarized for rapid reading. The recommendations section lists the specific recommendations identified by the consultant.

I was recently asked to develop a three- to six-month strategic plan for a women's fund. The group was organized as a board of directors and had already raised substantial funds, and decided on a grant-making strategy to meet their goal of economic empowerment of women in their state. (This information went into the background section of the consultant's report.) They needed to identify and work on the next steps and priorities, including a mission statement and name. The purpose was to identify next steps and priorities, develop a mission statement, select a name, and write a strategic plan for the next three to six months. The methodology followed a standard strategic planning format in a conference room setting. The task of writing a mission statement required a specific process, the training of the group on the process, and facilitating the process to actually write the mission statement. The major findings were the new name, the mission statement, and the six strategic goals worked out by the group. In this project, the recommendations included the strategic goals, the working groups' assignments for each identified goal, and the specific objectives for each goal.

The 24-page report included copies of the agenda for each of the two days, summary worksheets, board roster, and other appendices. The first six pages comprised the consultant's report, including a formal, two-page strategic plan.

I have found that clients want reports that are brief, to the point, and specific. I often use bullets of the main points and try to keep the report to five pages. I also prepare a one- to two-page executive summary. The executive summary, in this case the strategic plan, is often the only part of the report that is actually read carefully and used. Other material, such as worksheets, lists of participants, and background documents should be included as appendices. Some projects, by their scope, complexity, and nature, result in a very long report. One statewide HIV/AIDS prevention intervention recommendations project yielded a 262-page report. I wrote a two-page executive summary and a ten-page consultant's report. The rest was the actual data, raw data, full findings, and appendices.

Ask Clients to Recommend–Refer Your Services. The HIV/AIDS project, based on the characteristics of a good applied practice, resulted in receiving contracts for three other major applied research projects. Remember that you will still be marketing while you are in the implementation stage of your current work. I always ask clients if they can write me a letter to mention to prospective clients and for permission to use their name as satisfied clients. As in good anthropological writing, I use quotes whenever possible. You can create a capability brochure that tells about you and your services, gives contact information, and lists the clients you have served. Here is where you would use the names (with permission) and the quotes.

Anthropologists as Consultants. Other consultants can conduct research, design programs, and perform services such as you might offer. What makes anthropologists good consultants? Why would a client particularly pick us over other social scientists? Obviously, you can compete if you have the necessary skills and knowledge; for example, how to conduct strategic planning, or topical expertise in HIV/AIDS at-risk populations. Skills refer to the ability to do something well, usually gained through experience and training. Knowledge includes information, facts, ideas, or principles, usually learned through education or study.

As anthropologists, we are trained in data collection, analysis, and interpretation. We may also receive instruction on research design and how to conduct fieldwork and research. Through undergraduate training in sociology, I learned survey skills that I still use today.

But I believe our anthropological training in observing and understanding the beliefs and behaviors of groups, to see things from their unique perspective gives us an edge as consultants. Our training helps us work in other cultural settings and to work with different groups and subgroups. In almost every consultant project, I have relied on my anthropological perspective to understand the client's context and the social organization issues relevant to the project.

Continue Professional Activities. Anthropologists who work in academic settings have professional activities and opportunities to interact with other anthropologists. As a consultant, you may work with professionals from many disciplines. It is important to maintain connections within the discipline, useful for networking, keeping abreast of new ideas, and learning from others. One way to stay connected is to join and participate in the various professional anthropological organizations, such as the American Anthropological Association (AAA; www.aaanet.org). An organization particularly suited for applied anthropologists is the Society for Applied Anthropology (SfAA; www.sfaa.net). Another is the National Association of Practicing Anthropologists (NAPA; www.practicinganthropology.org), which is a section of AAA. These groups hold annual conferences, publish journals, and provide many types of services to members, but most importantly, offer opportunities for you to network with other anthropologists.

Look also for Local Practitioner Organizations (LPOs), which are regional associations for academic and applied anthropologists as well as members of affiliated sciences. My coauthor and I are members of the High Plains Society for Applied Anthropology (HPSfAA; www.hpsfaa.net), centered in the Denver area but with members from other states. Although I have lived in Portland, Oregon, for over three years, I continue to attend and participate in High Plains events. Incidentally, I have been asked numerous times about how to form a consulting enterprise by members and students.

Consider presenting your own work at these conferences, ask for advice from members, and find others who work in your area of expertise or share your topical interests. As you expand your contacts, others will be learning from you. Also consider volunteer involvement on professional task forces, committees, and board work.

As you update your knowledge and learn new skills, you may find it useful to make arrangements to supervise an intern or two. You probably completed an internship and gained experience in work habits. Now you can "give back" to our discipline and pass along some of your knowledge and skills. In over 20 years of owning a consulting company, I maintained my connections with the local university, provided numerous internships, and attended seminars and presentations and worked with over 20 interns. Interns can help with everyday work tasks, answering the telephone, filing, copying, conducting research, and so forth. In exchange, they further their own career development by learning substantive skills from you, perhaps helping conduct a survey, or assisting with data analysis and interpretation. Do discuss the ins and outs of intern supervision and reporting with the university's office of experiential education. Interns want real-life experience and will often work for free. Make sure the student earns academic credit and, if at all possible, pay an intern stipend.

Starting a consulting business can be a straightforward decision, implemented with good planning. In my own case, I was a certified social worker with a brand-new M.A. in cultural anthropology, employed as an "ethnic outreach coordinator" in a comprehensive community mental health center in a small city in West Texas. Because the community had a large Latino and African American population, two new positions were created for providing culturally appropriate services to these minority populations. The laws were changed to require that mental health clients be placed in the least restrictive setting, meaning halfway houses or back in the community instead of in mental institutions. The agency was at a loss as to how to provide services to ethnic minority populations. None of the senior clinical staff were people of color or were familiar with other models of mental health perceptions, hence the two new positions, filled with a Latina social worker and an African American psychologist.

In case conferences where clients are assigned to professional staff, I immediately found myself trying to explain differing cultural beliefs and practices concerning mental health. After teaching a series of in-house sessions on cultural diversity, I was asked to train staff from other agencies. Soon, I was speaking to civic organizations and making presentations in local and regional professional organizations. Although I remained an employee and sometimes received honoraria (small token payments), I could have easily transitioned to a full-time consultancy position.

When I moved to the Midwest, I started my own company. I joined various community organizations that dealt with social issues and became a member of my church's social action committee. I became active and visible in my new home. I read many "how-to" books and made many contacts, including networking groups. I was asked to speak to school classes, civic groups, and professional association meetings. Through these exposures, I was invited to work as a consultant to the Cooperative Extension Division of the local land grant university to help communities prepare for the rapid changes in population driven by the newly expanding meat processing industry. In my new employment as the director of the city–county commission on the status of women, and through my work across the state with Cooperative Extension, my business grew. I became a full-time consultant when I was asked by the state health department to conduct a series of anthropology-focused research projects documenting perceptions of different ethnic groups on the causes and prevention of HIV/AIDS. The department had heard an anthropologist (Trotter et al. 2001) at a national conference present the results of a methodology for assessing, evaluating, and responding to increases of HIV infection. Because I always introduced myself as an anthropologist in my own presentations, the agency called me to do the job.

Meanwhile, I had become interested in environmental issues and had gained experience in strategic planning and public issues gathering, both sets of skills initially learned through civic involvement. Former clients referred me to potential clients. Word-of-mouth advertising resulted in my taking on various interns and part-time independent contractors (other consultants). The interns came from the local university, where I had taught applied anthropology.

I chose anthropology students because of their training in information gathering (literature research and fieldwork), their ease in working in different cultural settings, and their interests and expertise in a wide range of topics and areas. Good work habits and consultant skills can be learned. Through working with me in a variety of projects, interns learned practitioner habits and skills. Most of my former interns and employees have gone on to provide consulting services of their own.

CONCLUSION

Anthropology encompasses a very broad range: human societies across time and space. Applied anthropology focuses on helping solve human problems. Consulting anthropologists, therefore, are engaged in providing services in many domains of application (Kedia and van Willigen 2005). Most professional colleagues of the authors teach in universities or work in government and nonprofit agencies. Almost all the professors who are members of the authors' LPO also work part-time as consultants in their areas of expertise. A few provide solely consulting services. The topics and services include global change, grant-writing, sustainable development, science education, health, minority education, Native American resource management, HIV/AIDS prevention, program development, evaluation, and community development.

Consultants are judged by their clients based on their performance of the task at hand. It is important to develop a good reputation for delivering results in a timely and useful manner, ask for client referrals, maintain visibility, and continue networking. Through networking and contacts, González-Clements worked as an evaluator of a federal program in Hawaii, designed a development program in the Dominican Republic for a U.S. university, helped create a local working group to implement good foster care policy in Peru, facilitated the development of a strategic plan for a tribal council in the Midwest, and assisted communities in adapting to population change in Nebraska. While these projects seem very different from one another, they all have four commonalities. They are (1) grounded in anthropology, (2) focus on facilitating social change, (3) rely on a flexible toolkit developed over time, and (4) were implemented with good consultant practices. Establishing yourself as a consultant will take time and effort, and the financial compensation may not be huge, but the satisfaction of developing solutions for human problems is why we chose this path.

REFERENCES CITED

Kedia, Satish, and John van Willigen, eds.
　2005 Applied Anthropology: Domains of Application. Westport, CT: Praeger.
Nolan, Riall W.
　2005 Work in the World: Advice on Non-Academic Careers. Purdue University: Center for Career Opportunities.

Pinson, Linda, and Jerry Jinnett
  2000 Steps to Small Business Start-Up, 4th Edition. Chicago: Dearborn.
Snead, C. Lynne, and Joyce Wycoff
  1997 To Do Doing Done: A Creative Approach to Managing Projects and Effectively Finishing What Matters Most. New York: Fireside Simon and Schuster.
Stolze, William
  1999 Start Up: An Entrepreneur's Guide to Launching and Managing a New Business, 5th edition. Franklin Lakes, NJ: Career Press.
Trotter, Robert T., II, Richard H. Needle, Eric Goosby, Christopher Bates, and Merrill Singer
  1999 A Methodological Model for Rapid Assessment, Response, and Evaluation: The RARE Program in Public Health. Field Methods (13):137–159.
U.S. Small Business Administration
  2006 Starting Your Business. Electronic document, http://www.sba.gov/starting_business/startup/guide2.html, accessed October 3, 2007.
van Willigen, John
  2002 Applied Anthropology: An Introduction. 3rd edition. Westport, CT: Bergin and Garvey.

USING ANTHROPOLOGY OVERSEAS

RIALL W. NOLAN
Purdue University

Applied anthropologists commonly work overseas, particularly in the areas of international development and humanitarian assistance. The competencies or skill sets they bring to this work make them exceptionally well-suited to succeed. At the same time, their training does not fully prepare them either to compete successfully for international assignments with other nonanthropologist candidates, or for some of the challenges they may face in the field. This article outlines the qualifications needed for employment in international development and humanitarian assistance, and breaks down these qualifications into categories. I then look in detail at how students, even in a very traditional anthropology program, can prepare themselves for employment as practitioners in the international arena. The article provides an outline of the structure of today's "development industry" and describes how develop-ment organizations identify and hire candidates. I describe how to use a simple Strengths, Weaknesses, Opportunities, and Threats (SWOT) technique to establish one's own areas of particular strength before entering the job market. I then describe a simple and straightforward approach to job-hunting, interviewing, and evaluating job offers. Throughout this article, I stress that although the strength and quality of anthropology's contribution to overseas work can be considerable, academic preparation alone is not enough—anthropologists who work overseas in development or humanitarian assistance must have more to offer than research skills alone, and must be able to work effectively with others, many of whom will come from different cultural and/or disciplinary backgrounds. I conclude by reminding practitioners in the field to maintain strong connections with their academic roots and to contribute to the transformation of anthropology from a discipline into a true profession. Keywords: applied anthropology, development anthropology, overseas work, networking, careers

THE NATURE OF OVERSEAS WORK

For most applied anthropologists, international engagement means either development work or its close cousin, humanitarian assistance. This article will talk about how to prepare for, and secure employment in, this type of activity. The first issue to address, however, is the "so what?" question. Why should someone with a degree in anthro-pology consider working overseas, in often difficult, sometimes dangerous, and always challenging situations?

There is a simple answer: it is an opportunity to become part of one of the most exciting and important enterprises of our time. Through international development (and I include

---

NAPA BULLETIN 29, pp. 166–180. ISBN 9781405190152. © 2008 by the American Anthropological Association.
DOI:10.1111/j.1556-4797.2008.00012.x

here, and throughout this piece, humanitarian assistance as a form of development work), we are attempting to create the future that our children will inherit. The world's problems—and the world's opportunities—are now our problems and opportunities. By using what we know as anthropologists, and by working in collaboration with others around the world, we can achieve far more than any of us could manage to do on our own. In fact, anthropologists excel at development work.[1] And the demand for what anthropology can bring has never been greater. As one observer, Ahmad Sadri, commented, "Never before have so many lived so closely to so many of whom they know so little" (Becker 1994:165).

Although development priorities and paradigms come and go, the challenge of the work remains what it has always been: using human intelligence and compassion to find common ground on which to base real and sustained collective improvement. How people from different backgrounds learn to work together is the human resource challenge of our time.[2] This is both a goal and—perhaps most importantly—a process.

HOW ANTHROPOLOGY CAN CONTRIBUTE

Anthropologists are well suited to development work for several reasons. We are locally centered, focused on local ways of seeing and describing the world. We are inductive in our methods and our thinking, good at building a picture of reality from the ground up. We are very good at eliciting local data, making sense of it, and using it, rather than relying on theoretical constructs from outside. And, in the process, we are not threatened by ambiguity, contradiction, or discrepant information. We may take these attributes largely for granted, but they are not shared by everyone in the development enterprise, as practitioners quickly discover.

At the same time, however, we need to recognize that our training also gives us a few handicaps. One is a fixation on research. Although data collection and analysis is something we pride ourselves on doing well, it is not the only thing that development work requires, and indeed, it is often not the main thing. So although it is a useful and powerful component of our skill set, it probably will not be enough by itself to get an anthropologist a job, as we will see a few pages later on.

Most anthropologists are trained as lone-wolf operatives, and this is embedded in the nature of the graduate school experience. My program, my research, my dissertation, my grant, my publications, all of this tends to reinforce the individual, but it may not encourage or even permit the type of multidisciplinary teamwork that is part and parcel of development work. If there is one main skill that anthropologists need to develop to do development work successfully, it is that of collaboration with differently minded others.

Finally, we often lack skills and experience in constructive application. Many of us have been trained to be "critical," which often means looking at something that someone else has done and finding the flaws in it. Like research itself, this is a useful skill, but it is not always what is needed. Telling others what is wrong with a development project is not nearly as helpful as being able to figure out what to do to make it better. In development work, anthropologists are valued not so much for what they know but for what they can do.

GETTING PREPARED

Although each development job will have specific needs and requirements, all development anthropologists need a similar set of threshold qualifications to enter the market. There are four of these:

1. Academic background
2. Workplace skills
3. Cross-cultural experience
4. Language proficiency

Let's look briefly at each one.

Academic Background

Although for some jobs—particularly of a highly complex nature—a Ph.D. is necessary, the M.A. is sufficient for many entry-level jobs in international development. Make sure you have taken courses that complement your anthropology (in, e.g., management, economics, or area studies). Make sure, too, that you have research or project work, preferably of the collaborative type, in your background.[3]

Language

If you can speak the specific language or dialect of the area where you are working, so much the better, but any language beats no language every time. Knowing another language gives you insight into how others see the world, and if you can learn one language, you can learn another. Five major world languages are important in development work: English, French, Spanish, Arabic, and Portuguese. Many other regional languages are also highly useful, of course.

Cross-Cultural Experience

Employers are taking an enormous risk every time they send someone overseas. By insisting on some type of previous international experience, they minimize the risk that you will crash and burn overseas. Study abroad is a good qualification; Peace Corps or similar volunteer experiences are even better. Even purely domestic experience will qualify, however, if it required you to develop cross-cultural sensitivities and skills.

Workplace Skills and Competencies

Skills are things you know how to do, and are divided into three broad categories (see Table 1):

1. *Self-management skills* are the basic attributes of an employable person: punctuality, neatness, sociability, politeness. They are not normally taught in school. Few employers, obviously, are interested in training you to be on time for work, or to be considerate of others. In the professional world, these things are simply a given.

2. *Functional skills* are those that help you do a variety of jobs. They are similar in outline across a range of industries and occupations, although the way they are done in each may vary. You can learn many of these in school.

3. *Technical skills* are highly specific to a particular field, profession, or situation. These skills are usually learned in school or, later, through on-the-job experience. Your anthropological training has given you some of these skills, but your employers will teach you others.

TABLE 1 Categories of Skills

TECHNICAL SKILLS	FUNCTIONAL SKILLS	SELF-MANAGEMENT SKILLS
Using statistical programs	Negotiating differences	Managing time and priorities
Speaking Swahili	Planning a project	Communicating effectively
Coding a Federal Form SF-171	Meeting facilitation	Managing conflict
Interviewing	Preparing a presentation	Making decisions
Designing a social survey	Writing a report	Flexibility and tolerance
Outlining kinship structures	Writing a proposal	Cooperativeness and sociability
Multidisciplinary teamwork	Editing/revising a document	Punctuality and reliability

Competencies are simply collections of skills. The competencies needed for international development work include these in Table 2.

TABLE 2 Competencies for Development Work

COMPETENCIES OR SKILL SETS	APPLICATIONS
Finding out things	Survey design; literature research; interviewing; needs analysis
Analyzing things	Data analysis; statistics; summarizing documents, findings, and reports
Communicating things	Presentations; report-writing; training; briefing constituents
Planning and designing things	Designing programs and projects; designing office procedures; handling bureaucratic requirements
Managing things	Working with other people; delegating and assigning; negotiating; monitoring and assessing
Judging things	Evaluating projects and programs; troubleshooting and fixing things; identifying strong and weak points

There are many different ways to use your time at a university to enhance your qualifications for international work. Even if you are in a very traditional anthropology program, in 12–18 months you can, with careful planning, equip yourself with:

- a solid academic background with coursework in areas directly related to international development work;
- an enhanced set of personal and functional skills (including grant and proposal writing), which can be applied to whatever job you take;
- one or more highly specific skills, such as statistical analysis, survey design, or project planning, which will be particularly useful in any development-related job;
- an initial set of contacts that you can use to begin the process of networking during your job search;
- a working knowledge of at least one vehicular foreign language; and
- some experience in working in other cultural settings, whether in the United States or overseas.

With this, you are ready to enter the job market.

TYPES OF JOBS: THE MARKET

The Development Industry

There are seven major types of organizations doing international development work today (see Figure 1):

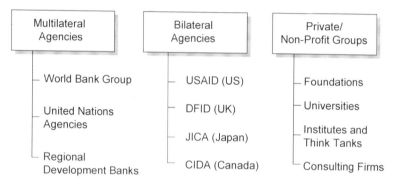

FIGURE 1. The Structure of the Development Industry.

1. Large *multilateral agencies* such as the World Bank, the IMF, and the United Nations
2. National *bilateral agencies* such as USAID in the United States or CIDA in Canada
3. *Nongovernmental organizations (NGOs)* in the United States and in other countries, such as CARE, Save the Children, World Vision, or Oxfam
4. *Foundations* in the United States and elsewhere with an interest in international development
5. *Universities* in the United States and elsewhere active in international development
6. Independent *institutes* and *think tanks* active in international development
7. *Consulting firms* in the United States and abroad that supply the development industry with specialists and managers

The industry is large, diverse, and interrelated in complex ways. It is also somewhat volatile, depending on yearly budget allocations, the demands of the moment, and political and economic currents from several directions.

Development agencies may compete with one another for predominance within a region or sector. In other cases, however, they collaborate, sharing project responsibilities, personnel, and funding. NGOs in particular may receive a major share of their funding from the larger agencies. NGOs, which typically do not have established or extensive bases of financial support, must raise funds in a variety of ways. Personal contributions account for a large portion of the working budgets of many NGOs, of course, but in addition to this, the organizations have found it expedient to partner with the larger development agencies to implement projects and programs in specific areas, and as a result, to claim a share of the budget for that. This fits in quite well with the desire of the larger agencies to delegate implementation tasks to subcontractors. Although some NGOs remain relatively independent from the larger agencies as a matter of principle, others have no problem with accepting funds from them, despite the fact that the funding often comes with certain constraints.

Of note here are the consulting firms that serve the development industry. Many do nothing but supply personnel to the larger agencies (World Bank, USAID, and the United Nations). As such, they provide a rich source of entry-level jobs. These firms typically work quickly, and have a number of projects in the pipeline at any one time. Typically, too, the process of project development requires approvals at a number of levels, here and overseas. One result of the cumbersome process of funding and authorization is that the persons originally slated to participate in a project are, as the process draws itself out, no longer available. Firms then search quickly for substitutes, and it is here that a newcomer with good threshold qualifications stands a good chance of being hired on a temporary basis.

The job market within the development industry differs significantly from the academic job market. There is no central listing of job opportunities, for example. Jobs may become available at short notice. Many jobs are temporary, and keyed to projects. Although the large bilateral and multilateral agencies are bureaucratic labyrinths, most of the other organizations (NGOs, consulting firms) are relatively small, with lean, flat structures. Turnover can be high in some agencies. None of this is necessarily bad news for newcomers: it means that there are a variety of opportunities at any one time, and these change fairly frequently.

Specialists and Managers

Job opportunities in the development industry are generally for either specialists or managers. Although these two roles overlap somewhat, job seekers should be aware of the differences and what they imply for recruitment and career patterns. The development industry needs *specialists* with specific sets of technical skills in a wide variety of areas. Although they may be full-time organization employees, specialists are more likely to be engaged as short-term or part-time employees, often on a consulting basis.

Anthropologists hired as specialists often tend to work on aspects of data collection and analysis. Sometimes, they are experts on a particular area, language, or group of people. They might be specialized in pastoral land use systems, cross-cultural survey design and analysis, or technology transfer, to cite only three of many possibilities. Their involvement is often temporary, and they serve as consultants or advisers for part of a project or a policy study. Anthropologists are frequently hired to perform social impact analyses, for example, to do evaluation reports, or to design sections or parts of a project. There is a relatively high likelihood that an anthropological specialist will be recognized and referred to as an anthropologist by his or her colleagues. Indeed, agencies often—although not always—issue job descriptions with the word *anthropologist* in the title, particularly if data collection or analysis is involved. You will also see the blanket designation "social scientist" used for these types of assignments.

Managers, on the other hand, are often considered generalists, even though they may have specialized degrees. They tend, on the whole, to find longer-term work within the agencies, as planners, analysts, project and program managers, and researchers. Often—although not always—the word *anthropologist* does *not* appear in the job title or terms of reference. In my own job experience, for example, I have been hired as a "social policy planner," a "project director," a "training manager," and a "policy advisor." None of these jobs was written specifically for an anthropologist, and all of them could have been filled by a nonanthropologist who had a grasp of training, policy, or project work, and who came with the requisite language and cross-cultural skills.

Managers deal not with one set of things, but with many. Managers usually oversee all or part of a program or project or serve as core staff in headquarters. Anthropologists tend to make good managers, particularly in multicultural situations. Although contract managers are sometimes hired only for the duration of a specific project, they are also in high demand as full-timers inside organizations.

The implications are straightforward. If you portray yourself as a specialist, then your data collection and analysis skills, your command of a foreign language, or your knowledge of a particular area may be very advantageous. But you will also be restricted to jobs that require those specific skills. These jobs will tend, for the most part, to be short-term assignments unless there is a high, continuing demand for your specialty.

It is somewhat harder to promote oneself initially as a manager. Although anthropology is very useful here, it is secondary to the broader work skills outlined earlier. Specialists tend to be put into the field fairly quickly, but managers will often begin work for an agency in the home office, learning the ropes, and writing reports or proposals. Only later will they be assigned to the field. Although this is not a rigid pattern, it is fairly commonplace.

Should you try for a technician's or a manager's job? In part, it depends on what you see yourself doing in the long run. It is difficult to sustain a career that consists of an endless succession of short-term assignments, and so at some point, most development people will seek to "go inside," that is, to join a firm or an agency on a full-time basis. Short-term field experience (probably in a specialist role) is highly recommended as preparation for the long-term and, in particular, for managerial roles. A stint in the field is the equivalent of starting on the shop floor, so to speak; you will quickly learn whether you like the development business or not, and you will develop a sense of how projects actually work in the field that is almost impossible to acquire in any other way. This is not to say that short-term overseas assignments are easy to get. Your employers will need to be assured that you can actually operate in a new cultural environment, and that you will be an asset to their work, not a liability. It is for this reason that previous international experience is so valuable to you.

So you may very well be offered an entry-level job at headquarters, backstopping field operations. Do not dismiss this opportunity: use it to convince your employers to send you into the field after a suitable period. One way or the other, if you want a long-term career as a manager in the development industry, you will need to have field experience, in just the same way as most academic administrators need to have had faculty-level experience to give them credibility.

BEFORE YOU START

Envisioning Your Job

Prior to starting a job hunt, take some time to think about what you want and why, in terms of three things: your values, your interests, and your skills. Your values are fundamental because they shape how you live and what you consider important in life. Your interests, however, define what excites your curiosity and summons your creative energy. Your skills, as we have seen, are about what you know how to do.

You have been trained in school to focus on knowledge and skills, but do not forget values and interests because they are a more integral part of who you are. Not every job that you are able to do will feed your soul or excite your passion. Your ideal job should be interesting, it should make use of your skills, and it should fit in with how you want to live your life. Why waste your time with anything else? It is useful to see overseas jobs in terms of four main components: a *base* of support; a *sector* of engagement; one or more *functions* performed within that sector; and a specific *location* (see Figure 2).

Base:	Sector:	Function:	Location:
Bilateral	Social services	Management	Africa
Multilateral	Public administration	Implementation	Asia
NGO	Agriculture	Design	Latin America
Foundation	Environment	Evaluation/assessment	Middle East
University	Manufacturing	Data collection/analysis	Europe
Institutes/Think- tanks	Health	Needs assessment	North America
Consulting firms	Education	Advocacy	
	Human Rights	Policy formulation	
		Training	

FIGURE 2. Components of an Overseas Job. *Adapted from*: American Anthropological Association 1982; Nolan 2003:8; Omohundro 1998:32.

If you can now define, in a general way, where you would like to start your involvement with development, you can start investigating the possibilities, prior to beginning a full-blown job search.

Networking

First, develop your professional *network*. Networking is a systematic method of making contacts and collecting information, and it will

- connect you with industry insiders;
- give you valuable information about the development industry and the opportunities it offers; and
- give you initial feedback on how your qualifications and experience match industry opportunities.

Simply put, networking will allow you to map the industry and identify places within it that are of particular interest to you.

To network, you will need a story; a story about who you are and what you are seeking. Because networking is a professional activity, and not simply chitchat, craft this story carefully. Develop several different versions: one to be delivered in approximately 20 seconds as you ride an elevator with someone, another of perhaps three to five minutes as you walk down the hall with someone, and a final, full-blown version of perhaps ten to 20 minutes, for those rare occasions when you can actually sit and talk at length with someone. As you network, you will be able to construct a more detailed and realistic vision for yourself of the job you want and start identifying organizations that are likely to have those jobs.

Informational Interviewing

Once you have identified a small set of likely employers, seek *informational interviews* with each of them. Try to talk to actual managers instead of people in the personnel office. The best way to identify the people to talk with, of course, is to ask your network.

An informational interview can be done on the phone, but it is much better done in person, during a focused half-hour, which is all you are likely to get at a busy office. You are not asking for a job, and you should make that clear in your request for the appointment; you are seeking information and advice. If people see you as a job applicant, they will be somewhat guarded in their responses and will be thinking, much of the time, about reasons not to employ you. Having you come as an information- and advice-seeker will put them more at ease and will result in better information. They know, of course, that you are—or will be—on the job market, but they will not consider this a job interview, which is exactly what you want.

You should try to learn four main things during your informational interview:

1. *What does this organization do and how does it do it?* What sectors are they involved in? What kinds of activities do they engage in? How are they funded, and what is their overall approach to or philosophy of work? Who are their clients or customers?

2. *What are the working conditions like here?* What are salary and benefit levels? How are these determined? What are the possibilities for promotion and advancement? What is a typical career path here?

3. *What qualifications do people need to be considered for employment by this organization?* What type of personality does well here? What skills or experience are people expected to bring when they are hired? What things are they expected to learn once they come on board?

4. *What are the procedures and criteria that this organization uses to hire people?* Where are jobs advertised? What application forms and documentation are necessary? Who makes hiring decisions, and how?

Be prepared to talk about yourself, if asked. Have a resume available, and ask, if appropriate, how it might be improved. Ask what suggestions, if any, they have for shaping your job search strategy. Before you leave, do not forget to ask for the names of other people you might contact, either in this organization or in another.

Determining Your Comparative Advantage

If you have done your interviews properly, you are now well acquainted with the types of organizations that do the work you want to do, and—most importantly—you have learned some valuable things about how your qualifications match what they are looking for.

Take the time now to carry out a quick strengths, weaknesses, opportunities, threats (SWOT) analysis, looking at external opportunities and threats, and your own internal strengths and weaknesses. Put all this together in a simple matrix, as illustrated in Table 3.

TABLE 3 Strengths, Weaknesses, Opportunities, and Threats (SWOT) Analysis Step 1

	Strengths	**Weaknesses**
INTERNAL FACTORS	What are my major internal strengths?	What are my major internal weaknesses?
EXTERNAL FACTORS	**Opportunities** What are the major external opportunities in my field?	**Threats** What are the major external threats in my field?

Then compare your strengths and weaknesses with the external threats and opportunities you have identified (see Table 4).

TABLE 4 Strengths, Weaknesses, Opportunities, and Threats (SWOT) Analysis Step 2

	EXTERNAL FACTORS	
INTERNAL FACTORS	Opportunities	Threats
Strengths Weaknesses	Comparative Advantage Investment/Divestment	Mobilization Damage Control

Typically, you will find that you are superbly qualified in some areas. This is your *comparative advantage*: where you really stand out. In other areas, however, you are going to need to do more work to develop skills or experience to match the requirements or the standards of the market. We will call these *investment areas*. In still others, you may need to improve or brush up existing skills—to *mobilize*—to meet market standards. And in a few areas, you are really unqualified—you simply do not have what it takes to get in the door. These are areas where you will have to do *damage control* if you want to be successful.

A SWOT analysis will provide both good and bad news. If you find that you have some serious gaps in your training, you should of course remedy these as quickly as possible. But it is highly likely that, as a result of networking and informational interviewing, you have targeted areas of practice where your existing skills are well-suited to the requirements of the hiring organization.

Now it is time to prepare a portfolio, keyed to your areas of greatest strength.

Creating Your Professional Portfolio

Your portfolio showcases your comparative advantage by highlighting your capabilities, your experience, and your accomplishments. Now that you know what your target organizations do, and what they look for in the people they hire, it should be relatively easy to highlight those areas of your background and experience that make you stand out. The portfolio has a number of basic items, including

- a resume,
- lists of people who can provide references for you,
- a 1–2 page career summary, and
- a list of publications, projects, assignments, or other accomplishments, and examples of the best of these.

The resume is the first thing that prospective employers will see, and it should connect you to the needs of the organization. A resume is *not* an academic C.V.; it is a much shorter document (2–3 pages at most) that summarizes your qualifications. A resume for international work should

- stress your language abilities;
- outline your cross-cultural experience;
- highlight any periods of travel or residence overseas;
- give details of the functional and job-specific skills you possess;
- show how these have been applied in the past to get things accomplished; and
- provide evidence of good self-management skills.

There are many sources of information about crafting resumes, but several books stand out as guides for people with academic qualifications who are interested in applying what they know to non-academic settings. These would include Susan Basalla and Maggie

Debelius (2007), Margaret Newhouse (1993), and Jan Secrist and Jacqueline Fitzpatrick (2001). Richard Bolles (2007) is, as always, an indispensable guide to job-hunting in general.

BREAKING IN: GETTING THAT FIRST JOB

Identifying Jobs

This is easier than you might think. Your network is your main tool here. In your discussions with people, you will have learned about how organizations recruit, where they advertise, and what criteria they use to screen applications. Use your networks now to advertise your marketability and to help you identify jobs. Firms and agencies use their own networks, of course, to locate suitable individuals quickly for assignments that come up, and if you are connected to these networks already, there is a good chance that you will be contacted.

Because landing the first job is often the hardest, you may want to opt for short-term assignments at first. A short-term assignment is an excellent way to learn quickly about the field, the work, and the organization. It establishes you as a successful professional, integrates you into a wider network, and provides you with an excellent reference for future work.

Short-term assignments may not be what you ultimately have in mind, of course. You may, for example, have your heart set on working full-time for the United Nations, USAID, or the World Bank. But the major agencies will have only a limited number of full-time positions open each year, and individuals who are already well-networked with a portfolio of relevant experience will be at an advantage.

People entering the market therefore stand a better chance of finding short-term assignments with NGOs or private consulting firms because turnover tends to be high, and there is a continuing need for qualified entry-level people. The nature of the development business creates conditions that favor people who are available when needed, as a consequence of the way projects and programs are developed. Here is how it works: An NGO may have bid on a government contract 12–18 months ago and only now has the contract been awarded. In the meantime, members of the team they originally proposed—containing many outside consultants—have moved on to other assignments.

Now the organization must find new team members, and fast. They will rarely have the time or the inclination to advertise these jobs; instead, they will go to their data banks and call members of their network, looking for qualified candidates. If you are already in their network, and if your resume is sitting in their data bank, you have an excellent chance of getting called. If you are well-qualified and are known to the firm through its network, you stand a very good chance of getting called for an interview.

Such assignments constitute excellent preparation for later, more permanent assignments. Initially, work may be limited to the headquarters office, but after an initial trial period, field assignments are likely, and these will provide extremely valuable experience.

Anthropologists tend to begin field assignments as collectors of data, eventually moving to planning and implementation tasks, and, finally, to management and policy work.

Interviewing

Regardless of the form or structure of an interview, and regardless of how many different people actually participate in the interview, the organization that is interviewing you essentially wants to know four things:

1. *Why are you here?* What are your motivations in seeking work in international development? What do you hope to gain from such work? Why did you come to us? What was it about the job that particularly attracted you, and why?
2. *What can you do for us?* What are your skills and abilities, and how will these be useful to us? What in your background or experience is particularly relevant to our needs, now and in the future?
3. *What will you be like as a colleague?* If we hire you, what will it be like to work with you? Are you a pleasant, mature person? What are your expectations, professionally and socially, of us? How are you likely to develop over time? Besides wanting a job, are there other agendas or issues that seem important to you here?
4. *What will it cost us?* What are your salary expectations likely to be (even though we might not discuss them in a first interview)? What other things do you want or need from us? Do we run any risks in hiring you? What changes in our present arrangements might we have to make if we hire you?

Throughout the interview process, you should return whenever possible to your comparative advantage; to the strong points that distinguish you from the crowd.

Evaluating and Negotiating Job Offers

The formal terms of an offer vary greatly from one organization to another. Some firms provide a very simple Memorandum of Agreement, while others will draft a long contract for you to sign. All such offers, however they are written, should contain specific language about four main things:

1. The *scope of work* or *terms of reference* under which you are being hired. This spells out the nature of the job that you are expected to do.
2. The *conditions* under which the work is to be performed. This includes information about your rights and responsibilities, reporting arrangements, timetables, locations, and other matters.
3. Any *special considerations* that will affect your employment or your performance under the contract. These might include the availability of project funding, security clearances, government approvals.
4. The *salary* and *benefits* that you will receive for performing the work.

Each of these aspects of an offer can be negotiated. Once you have given it your best shot, look at the offer, the firm, the assignment, and the location, in terms of these six considerations:

1. *Task*: Do you understand what is expected of you? Can you learn what you need to know fairly quickly, thereby having a chance to succeed? Do you like the work?

2. *Support*: Are there the resources to help you get the job done? Who controls these? What happens if they dry up? How crucial are resources to your own performance?

3. *Context*: Do the situation and the organization look stable? What are people like? Is the job where you want it? Is the company the kind you want to work for? Are the company's mission, culture, and reputation ones you like? Do you like and trust your colleagues and supervisors? Can you get along with your boss and your peers?

4. *Performance*: How are you going to be evaluated in this job? How will you be rewarded? Is there opportunity to grow in directions that you want to go in?

5. *Satisfaction*: Where does this come from on this job? Will the job provide you with the challenge you seek?

6. *Compensation*: Are you getting paid enough? Are your other benefits satisfactory? Can these be expected to improve over time?

If the answer to these questions is affirmative, then you have just landed your first assignment.

AFTER THE FIRST JOB

Managing Your Career

Your career will be a work in progress. You will undoubtedly change jobs several (perhaps many) times. In your first set of jobs, you should be focusing on performing well, learning as much as you can, and connecting with as many professional colleagues as possible.

Careers develop in many different ways, but they almost always involve accepting progressively responsible positions with impact on larger and larger areas of activity, and learning a wide variety of new skills to complement the ones you brought in with you. Each subsequent work experience will be a strategic opportunity to build skill, experience, and knowledge about how best to use what you know, and to do this, furthermore, across different types of projects, different regions, and different organizations.

Whether you stay in one job or change jobs at intervals, stay in the market, always. This means continuing to learn, to hone your skills, to network, and to seek professional challenges. It also means staying visible to others. As you gain work experience, develop your career vision still further, paying attention, as before, to your values and your interests to help guide the application of your skills. In addition to your networks, seek mentors who can help guide you and advise you. And, finally, stay active in professional groups.

Building an Anthropology of Application

Do not forget your discipline. Anthropology has a great deal to contribute to development work and humanitarian assistance, but the discipline has much to learn, as well, about the work of its practitioners in these fields.

One of your most important tasks as a practitioner, therefore, is helping your discipline grow and develop into a true profession. You can do this in any number of ways, but only if you are willing to engage with the salient issues of how anthropological knowledge is produced and used, and how the practitioner's perspective is communicated to the next generation of anthropologists.

International development is one of the most compelling and significant projects of our time, one whose outcome carries enormous implications for all of us. Anthropologists really have no choice about whether or not to be involved with combating poverty, sickness, and inequality—their only real choices are about *how* to engage. Our discipline has a crucial role to play here, if only we are strong enough and smart enough to play it.

NOTES

1. See Nolan 2001:6–26.
2. Julia Chang Bloch (Institute of International Education 1995:8).
3. More can be found in Nolan 2003:33–65 on how to use graduate school to prepare yourself for practice.

REFERENCES CITED

American Anthropological Association
    1982 Getting a Job outside the Academy. Washington, DC: American Anthropological Association.
Basalla, Susan, and Maggie Debelius
    2007 "So What are You Going To Do With That?" Finding Careers outside Academia. Chicago: University of Chicago Press.
Becker, Carol, ed.
    1994 The Subversive Imagination. New York: Routledge.
Bolles, Richard
    2007 What Color Is Your Parachute? Berkeley, CA: Ten Speed Press.
Institute of International Education
    1995 Investing in Human Capital: Leadership for the Challenges of the 21st Century. New York: IIE.
Newhouse, Margaret
    1993 Outside the Ivory Tower: A Guide for Academics Considering Alternative Careers. Cambridge, MA: Harvard University Office of Career Services.
Nolan, Riall
    2001 Development Anthropology. Boulder, CO: Westview Press.
    2003 Anthropology in Practice. Boulder, CO: Lynne Rienner Publications.
Omohundro, John T.
    1998 Careers in Anthropology. Mountain View, CA: Mayfield Publishing Co.
Sadri, Ahmad
    1994 Adjusting to the World According to Salman Rushdie. In The Subversive Imagination. Carol Becker, ed. Pp. 165–180. New York: Routledge.
Secrist, Jan, and Jacqueline Fitzpatrick
    2001 What Else Can You Do With a Ph.D.: A Career Guide for Scholars. Thousand Oaks, CA: Sage.

BECOMING AN INTERNATIONAL CONSULTANT

GISELE MAYNARD-TUCKER
UCLA Center for the Study of Women

The goals of this article are to give students advice related to entering the world of development and a clear view of the responsibilities and pitfalls that come along with the profession of international consultancy as applied anthropologists. In doing so, I discuss the necessary skills required, such as a background in research, knowledge of foreign and vernacular languages, and fieldwork experience. I also give some advice about contacting development agencies and preparing for overseas work. In addition, I comment on what to expect while working in developing countries in the field of public health. In order to illustrate some of the interventions, I have drawn examples from my own experiences in the field. Motivation is very important for this career and students must be aware that although the profession may be exciting, it is also difficult and demanding. Apart from giving counsel, I have attempted to show that being a consultant is a great opportunity to learn more about the human race and that the job is full of challenges and rewards. Keywords: consultation, development, fieldwork, careers overseas, applied anthropology

This chapter offers advice to students who want to enter the field of development as an international consultant. Over several decades, social scientists have contributed widely to projects involving agriculture, economics, health, nutrition, nursing, management, administration, education, and many other fields to improve the lives of populations. The role of the consultant has changed since the 1970s (Almy 1977; Belshaw 1974); donors and agencies are now focusing much more on the consultant as the key figure for rapid improvement of programs. The complexities and challenges in consulting, international aid, and the contributions of applied anthropology and sociology in development have been discussed in much recent work (Crewe and Harrison 1998; Justice 1989; Ledwith 1997, 2005; Sillitos et al. 2002). Practicing applied anthropology permits us to understand social and cultural change and becomes a useful skill to ease the change from traditional ways of living to modern life. The challenges of introducing modernity as an agent of change and the implication of policy and improving the life of the beneficiaries can be found in numerous studies (Barrow et al. 2001; Bhuha 2004; Clavi-Parisetti and Higney 2006; Duch 2005; International Monetary Fund [IMF] 2004; Mosse 2005; Stewart and Strathern 2005).

Becoming a consultant implies that one has acquired a general background in applied anthropology or other social sciences and has mastered a specialization. Students might want to choose a specialization from the fields of engineering, agronomy, ecology, education, computer systems, media, administration–management, medicine, or public

NAPA BULLETIN 29, pp. 181–194. ISBN 9781405190152. © 2008 by the American Anthropological Association.
DOI:10.1111/j.1556-4797.2008.00013.x

health because they are much in demand. There are many difficulties and rewards with this career, which will be addressed throughout this article.

For the purpose of this article, I focus specifically on the field of public health in developing countries because I have worked in this field for two decades as a research and evaluation consultant. I have conducted research and evaluation of health projects and programs about reproductive health, child survival, and HIV/AIDS prevention in several countries in Africa, Latin America, and Asia. Doing research or evaluating projects or programs in different countries is a challenge that is both exciting and intimidating. Usually, the consultant's expertise is tested by the approval or disapproval of suggested change granted by local authorities. Furthermore, the role of a consultant implies being a mediator among agencies and an agent of change for local authorities and beneficiaries. In the field, the consultant focuses on the people in a particular area of study and tries to determine how the project or program will improve their lives. At the same time, the consultant must follow the donor's terms of reference and examine the project's feasibility based on the human and material resources of the local authorities. It is a complex role dealing with different entities that are not totally united. Only through experience does the role of the consultant become easier.

The following sections will present the academic preparation that should facilitate development of the skills necessary for consultancy work. A section discussing the benefits and challenges of the profession and the lessons learned from the field will follow. In the final section I will examine the challenges and complexities associated with working in development and will look back on my experiences. Although this article provides students with some stepping stones for preparation, I would like to note that becoming a consultant is not easy, and one has to be willing to tough it out, to be flexible and willing to adapt to various situations, to be able to make decisions on short notice, and to be pragmatic and focused. As Matthew Bolton wrote: "An ability to compromise and diplomatically adapt to challenging situations is essential. Plans rarely work out perfectly" (2006:3). It should also be noted that development work is mostly focused on Third World countries, and these countries are characterized by complex and unequal social structures including great disparities in wealth and poverty, but because of the very nature of development work dealing with humanitarian issues, a consultant will mostly interact with the side where poverty reigns. In the following sections, I will present the basic elements for acquiring a solid background in research and international experiences.

ACADEMIC PREPARATION

Research

You can become a consultant with a master's degree and a specialization, or with a Ph.D. and a specialization. Some agencies require a Ph.D. while others accept an M.A. depending on the size of the project and the funding available. However, there is a difference in the fees between the two degrees. A background in research is very important because you must know what type of research should be used for each project. One must have experience in qualitative research, interviews, focus group discussions, in-depth interviews, exit interviews, group interviews, as well as with quantitative research survey techniques, sampling methods, and statistics (Bernard 1988, 1998; Krueger 1988; Maynard-Tucker 2000). Also important is to know how to compose instruments. This craft demands experience that can often be acquired only in the field. It is one of the most important elements of the research because if questions are not well formulated and then developed during the interviews or during focus group discussions, the data will not be substantial enough to analyze the problems, to suggest changes, and to formulate recommendations (Harrison and Bramson 1984; Tanur 1994). I suggest that students enroll in research courses and familiarize themselves with the art of interviewing, composing instruments, and developing questions. Many departments in sociology, public health, and anthropology offer such courses.

Students also need to become familiar with social policy and development by taking classes or reading on the subject because consultants work within governmental policies. Consequently, when studying public health issues, students should be aware of the state of policies concerning violence against women, policies about women's equity regarding ownership and a husband's authority within the context of the family, in addition to policies that might restrict the implementation of programs (Hall and Midgley 2004; Hoefer 2006; Partridge 1984).

Languages

Speaking different languages and learning one or two vernacular languages is also a great asset. If one speaks the language of the people, it is easier to make contact and to communicate, and people will trust a consultant more readily. When I was a doctoral candidate at UCLA, I decided to learn Quechua because the Quechua Indian women who were living in the highland Peruvian village where I had chosen to do my research preferred to speak Quechua instead of Spanish. Learning their language really opened their hearts to me and we became friends on a basis of fictive family ties as they asked me to become the godmother of their children. In addition, I was able to compose questionnaires and translate their answers without the need of a facilitator. A few years later, I also learned Haitian Creole during my long-term consultancy in Haiti, and this was invaluable for composing questionnaires and verifying the answers during the surveys. Spanish and French are two languages that are very popular and useful for working in Africa and South America. Knowledge of vernacular languages is an invaluable asset.

Field Experience

How does one get field experience? Students can get fieldwork experience by doing research for a master's degree, a master's in public health, or a doctoral thesis in a foreign country if they can get a scholarship grant to support their studies. Otherwise, they can do community work for a clinic, enlist in the Peace Corps, do a research internship for a national company, do an internship in a drug rehabilitation center, or conduct surveys and research for prisons or orphanages, among other possibilities. They might want to join various ethnic clubs for young people and learn about their cultures—immerse themselves in them and learn their customs and ways of life. Bolton (2006:4) emphasizes the importance of getting good international experiences. He suggests working for the Peace Corps or the Voluntary Service Overseas (VSO) as a first step because these two organizations will provide good training, support, and language classes (see also Calvi-Parisetti and Higney 2006). Likewise, development work is difficult at times and therefore is not for everyone; it would be advisable to test whether one is suited for the profession by doing internships abroad or enlisting in the Peace Corps. Most employers want to hire people with experience. They look for someone who has experience with a wide range of cultures and contexts and who is able to adjust to and perform in difficult situations.

I started to work in development in Haiti by answering an announcement published by the International Planned Parenthood Federation, Western Hemisphere Region (IPPF–WHR). The agency was looking for a family planning and research advisor. I was hired because I had experience in family planning, had worked in Peru for several years for my doctoral dissertation, and spoke French. Working in Haiti permitted me to extend and deepen my knowledge of research by working with the Child Health Institute while conducting several surveys and research studies on women's behavior and the use of contraception. The work was challenging and living conditions were difficult. However, I acquired experience and expertise that helped me find more consulting work after I left the island.

Specialization

Organizations hire experts because development projects are tied to financial investments, a structured bureaucracy with a limited schedule, and resources and the expectation of a good performance. When an organization is looking for a consultant, it sends out a document known as Terms of Reference (TOR). This document is usually one or two pages long and explains their research project and the work required from the consultant. A consultant is usually chosen because of his or her work experience and expertise on the matter. This is why a specialization is paramount. Research in development is extremely focused. The terms of reference are the core of the research; they are restricted and are constrained by several factors, including funding, time, and the brevity of the fieldwork (Macintyre 2005:133). By specialization, I mean the topic or area studied in addition to the general curriculum covered in graduate school. For example, a consultant might have experience in health, nutrition, children's health, education, reproductive health, HIV/AIDS prevention, or others (Hill 1991). Whatever a consultant's specific field, one must show that he or she has experience in the domain of specialization. When asked one's opinion about a project's proposal, a consultant must be able to develop a clear plan of research and strategy that can be used to collect the necessary data.

Knowledge about Development Projects

Agencies require strong analytical and writing abilities. The consultant must be able to analyze data and write reports (within a limited time period) that are going to be read by several key persons within the agency. The format and writing style for evaluating projects or programs or for research reports are different from academic writing and one should be aware of these differences by reading the organizations' publications. In addition, in order to be knowledgeable about the organizations' development projects, one should read their publications and learn their language, be aware of their writing style, the format of their reports, and the proper use of acronyms. Most publications are free or available for a small sum. All development agencies have a website, including the World Health Organization (WHO), United States Agency for International Development (USAID), the World Bank, the Joint United Nations Program on HIV/AIDS (UNAIDS), the United Nations Educational, Scientific and Cultural Organization (UNESCO), the United Nations Children's Fund (UNICEF), and the United Nations Population Fund (UNFPA), and they have their publications available there for download or for sale.

There are also nongovernmental organizations (NGOs) such as Cooperative for Assistance and Relief Everywhere (CARE), Oxford Committee for Famine Relief (OXFAM), World Vision (W-USA), and many others that are involved in community-based development, nationally and internationally. These NGOs are usually supported by private funding, charitable donations, and voluntary services, and sometimes get government grants (Fernando and Heston 1997). Doing an internship with an NGO would be ideal for a novice because NGOs work at the community level and are usually very dynamic in their approaches. Based on my own experiences, I found NGOs in the health sector more effective than the public sector because they are usually less limited by political constraints, are smaller and, therefore, generally more efficient than the public sector, are better organized, and work at the grassroots level.

Communication Skills

Taking a speech class will help a consultant with public debriefings. Debriefing is usually done at the end of the field trip in the country of the research in front of ministry officials, donor representatives, the director of the project, and the representative of the administrative agency. There are about 15 to 20 people attending this meeting depending on the project. During debriefing a consultant must report the findings and the audience will ask questions about them. Being able to communicate ideas clearly and authoritatively is essential. With great assurance, consultants must be able to report their findings and recommendations and explain why they will be able to improve the project or the program. The local experts will judge consultants' experience and expertise during these discussions. They will evaluate the consultant's recommendations and the changes suggested in their program, and they will defend their own ideas. Change is not always readily accepted because it implies new routines, new strategies, and new efforts, and because it suggests that the previous plans were not entirely effective. Ministry offices would almost always rather continue with their old routine and consultants must be able to convince them that their recommendations will improve their programs. However, if they know that they will get additional funding for two or three more years, they will make some efforts to implement the new recommendations in order to please the donor(s).

Types of Consultations

I now turn to consultations. More details about the different types of consultations can be found in various works (Moore 2001; Pillsbury 1991; Stirrat 2000). In the following section I will describe the types of consultations I have performed. Consultations are done under contract, and it is advisable to never get on the plane without a contract on hand. Pillsbury notes: "A contract should contain the scope of work, specification of salary or 'daily rate' and details concerning per diem or other reimbursement for expenses. All should be carefully but tactfully negotiated" (1984:56). A consultant's daily rate is based on one's experience. Therefore, it is important to show that you have acquired previous experience. However, when consultants are hired, they are given a topic and they must go along with the topic and develop the research from that point.

Lorenzo Brutti asserts, "In the context of a consultancy, you are 'framed' in different ways. You are given a topic of research by your employer and can choose to take it up or not, but there is very little you can do to modify the topic itself within the frame of the consultancy" (2005:107). This is very true. Research or evaluations are programmed and a consultant must follow the terms of reference; the consultant has no freedom to deviate from the original proposal unless it is authorized. On my part, I have been involved in two types of consultations. One type involved my individual work as a research consultant. For example, I was once asked to go to a country to examine why women were not using contraceptive methods even though they were aware of contraception through media messages that were transmitted through the radio. I prepared my research by reading materials on the topic, reading previous reports on the projects, and establishing a research plan. The plan examined how many women were going to be interviewed at the clinics or in their homes, how many members of the medical community were going to be interviewed, what the messages were on the radio, and so on. I analyzed the data collected, gave the recommendations, and wrote the report. For the second type of consultation, I was often asked to work with a team of social scientists in order to evaluate the performance of a project or program. For this purpose, a group of social scientists with a team leader are sent to a country and each member of the team has a defined role in collecting data, analyzing data, and writing the final report. Working with a team is challenging because one must work with several individuals, never lose the focus of his or her own research, add to the team's findings, follow the team leader's directives, and work efficiently for long hours. It is a very good experience because you learn to work in teams and get along with people from different backgrounds and with varying personalities.

Short- or Long-Term Consultancies

Development projects usually offer short- or long-term consultancies; short-term can be from one to three or more weeks, while long-term consultancies are often from two to five years depending on the length of the project. During these years abroad, the consultant immerses himself or herself in the intricacies of development, its problems, and challenges. I would recommend that a novice take this path because it is the breaking point of a person's career. By living abroad for a few years, a consultant can learn about the culture of that country more deeply, learn the language, and become an expert on the problems associated with development work. It is not always easy, but it has enormous rewards and benefits for one's career. In doing so, you acquire experience and expertise that can be used everywhere else in the development world because you will find that there are commonalities to the problems of poverty, violence, gender inequality, lack of resources, day-to-day living, and illnesses.

Personally, my first long-term consultancy experience in development took place in Haiti. I could not have chosen a more dangerous or more difficult place to work. My work took place during President Jean Bertrand Aristide's election year (1990), and there was daily political turmoil in the streets. In addition, Haiti is one of the poorest places on earth and a place where complex historical problems such as corruption and political extremism are entangled. I had unforgettable learning experiences about the complexities of development; corruption; the environmental problems related to logging and charcoal burning, water shortage, and lack of electricity; and the painful daily living of a population.

Contacting a Development Agency

How does one contact an agency interested in hiring applied anthropologists? To contact such an agency, a student should prepare his or her curriculum vitae specifically focusing on educational background and international experiences (fieldwork, internship, knowledge of languages, etc.). Then he or she will send it to various development agencies, followed by a phone call to introduce him or herself. Ideally, if one took a trip back East (because most development agencies are located on the East Coast), try to contact the human resources person and pay a visit. Administrators have a tendency to hire people they know. When presenting qualifications, one should be flexible, open-minded, and well motivated. A consultant should learn the jargon of the field by reading the reports, having curriculum vitae ready for review, and through discussing one's experiences in the field. The following sections address two important questions related to working in development: (1) what are the benefits, and (2) what are the constraints of the profession.

WHAT ARE THE BENEFITS OF THE PROFESSION?

Some of the benefits include being able to work independently, under contract, and being able to choose the country of work and the assignment; acquiring worldwide experience about different cultures and expanding your understanding of people's behavior within the context of culture are other advantages. Trying to improve people's lives and being able to travel and explore many parts of the world, including some remote faraway communities, are also benefits. There are no books or courses that can replace the experience of learning in the field, from living the lives, problems, and constraints of various ethnic societies, and from being part of their isolation, their marginality, and their distress. This experience expands one's understanding of the human condition and the complexities of human behavior that are often inexplicable for people from wealthier societies. Frequent contact with various ethnic groups permits a consultant to understand and better comprehend the large spectrum of complexities of human behaviors. Furthermore, fieldwork experiences do become a great asset for teaching students. Students love anecdotal stories about one's experiences working with various informants, describing their environment, beliefs, customs, and ways of life. Development work as a consultant opens doors for further careers and positions, and once one has acquired experience working in development, he or she can apply for positions within the agencies' offices and work their way up the ladder (Carland and Trucano 1996; Segal and Gross 1993). In addition, it is not unusual for a consultant to be able to also work at a research institution and teach.

WHAT ARE THE CONSTRAINTS OF THE PROFESSION?

Among the constraints found in this type of work, it is important to note that, as mentioned previously, most development agencies are located on the East Coast, usually in Washington, D.C., or New York. Living away from these cities is a great handicap because many contracts are based on personal relationships and social networking. It is much more difficult to be chosen from a consultant registry based on one's specialization than to be recommended by a friend. For consultants living outside these cities there are often gaps between contracts. Bolton writes: "It is essential to network and build contacts. Go to conferences, use mutual friends to get introductions, and save business cards" (2006:4). Another constraint that deals with the bureaucratic and programmatic set-up of development agencies is that a project can be evaluated only once by any individual consultant; for each following evaluation they must hire different consultants. However, some of us do not have the same ideas, and this is why the wheel is constantly being reinvented many times in development. Barbara Pillsbury (1984) wrote that there are various types of evaluations elaborated by the agencies and that some are better finalized than others, but in general it seems that they are elaborated by a majority of bureaucrats who have little field experience and where disagreement about evaluations and competition between staff sometimes leads to a standoff in a project.

On a different scope, most overseas work is very challenging and it often takes place in countries facing political turmoil. In my particular case (Bolivia, Haiti, Guatemala, Guinea, Peru, Madagascar, and Nigeria, to name a few), foreigners are usually targets because they are frequently associated with the international personnel working for companies that exploit the resources of these countries. For instance, in Nigeria it was not possible to leave the hotel after work for fear of being kidnapped, molested, robbed, or killed. International oil companies exploit the Nigerian oil resources without giving compensation to the communities contaminated by petroleum waste after oil extraction. In Haiti, one could get kidnapped or killed for ransom because Aristide's followers needed money to bring their leader back. Other dangers are car accidents because of bad roads and the excessive use of speed on highways. The highway from Rabat to Marrakech in Morocco is well known for numerous deadly accidents. Another more mundane problem that is often on one's mind is how to avoid a number of serious diseases that are common in many of the countries where development work takes place, such as malaria, tuberculosis, hepatitis, poliomyelitis, diphtheria, and many others. Hygiene and sanitation are nonexistent in many rural parts of the world, and water carries bacteria that are deadly to foreigners.

LESSONS LEARNED

Based on my development work and conversations with colleagues in the field, there are numerous lessons learned from working in development. One of the most important is the fact that a consultant needs to adapt to various ecological environments, cultures, and behaviors. A consultant needs to learn that people's beliefs are very strong, even when confronted with modern technology and an overall globalized world. For instance, many women in developing countries may use contraceptive methods but often do not understand the mechanisms behind them and have their own concept of the reproductive organs (Maynard-Tucker 1989). I learned that people's life priorities are established as a function of their poverty and their daily lack of resources, that family ties are a network of ready help in case of distress, that gender inequality favors males, and that women do not have any rights in some countries. I learned that some people's daily burden is simply to survive and that death is not a big deal to them. Working in the field and facing an informant's socioeconomic issues, health problems, cultural beliefs, customs, and religious beliefs can open one's understanding of what life is about, all of which expands understanding of the human race with its challenges and rewards.

However, development work is not perfect and is limited by funding and excessive bureaucracy. International aid is given to certain countries and for a limited time. For example, international health grants have goals to better the health of the populations through the improvement of the delivery of programs or projects, but these programs or projects are often channeled through the public health sector. In most countries, the public health sector's infrastructure is very weak because of a lack of human and material resources, and most international aid programs suffer from this weakness. In addition, once the funding ends, the local ministry of health usually has enormous difficulty in sustaining the program. Furthermore, beneficiaries do not understand how development works and why a program does not last forever. For instance, a family-planning program that offers free contraceptives for two or three years and then stops because the program comes to an end creates many difficulties among the women who are used to getting free contraceptive methods. At the end of the program they must change their methods or pay for the method that they were using. Sometimes they do not have the money to buy the pills and they do not want to change methods, so they abandon the contraceptive method and become pregnant. Development has created a dependency on international aid, and unfortunately the poorest people are often the victims. A major problem is that local governments wait for international aid and do not use their local resources to secure social and health benefits for the populations on a sustainable basis.

Another important skill I learned is to be able to mediate between three entities that are characterized by different socioeconomic levels: (1) the donor organization(s), (2) the administrative office in charge of project administration, and (3) the local government offices. Each one has different goals. Donors are investing money into programs that improve the life of the people, the administrative office has the responsibility for the project in the field, the government offices are interested in using the funds from their own perspectives, and the investigator's recommendations represent informants' needs. The consultant's mediating skills must include an understanding of the role and positions of the donor who has invested funding in a project with a concrete schedule and anticipated results. The administrative office works closely with the consultant in order to present a good report that would be pleasing to the donor, and the local government officials usually promise to follow the recommendations and make some changes in their programs in order to get additional international aid.

The role of the consultant is to mediate among these three entities and to articulate their common language into recommendations that would improve the lives of beneficiaries and satisfy the government offices and donors. The most difficult part is to convince the local ministry officials to promote changes in their programs. They are usually characterized by a large bureaucracy mostly centralized in cities, and officials generally have very little field experience and must deal with a shortage of human and financial resources. Most disconcerting is the fact that generally there is a lack of supervision in the rural regions, and poor communication between rural communities and central offices. Although it is a general constraint, the consultant should not be stopped by this but should take into account these problems in their recommendations. A person who wishes to become a consultant needs to understand these issues and be ready to accept that his or her recommendations and hard work might not be put to use because of the issues that I commented on above and that are beyond the control of the consultant.

CONCLUSION

A consultant is a researcher, evaluator, mediator, communicator, ethnographer, and informant to the development agency. As a mediator, the consultant must deal with ministry offices and have them approve his or her suggestions in order to realize some changes in their approaches. The consultant must take into consideration the feasibility of the activities, the costs, the impact, and the length of the project for a successful performance. One should always keep in mind the goals of the donors and the length of time available to accomplish the project. This mediating process is a learning experience and is always changing depending on the countries, the type of the research, and the findings. Some donors are very knowledgeable, others are more bureaucratic. On the one hand, all have definite goals for their projects and the consultant must execute them. On the other hand, administrative agencies are very helpful for report writing, formatting, editing, and for support. Doing cross-cultural fieldwork in development is a wonderful experience in expanding your understanding of different cultures, peoples' behavior, concepts, and communication. By the very nature of development work, a consultant has to navigate in the same day between two different worlds—the high society who live in a high-class environment, and your informants who live generally in the countryside and are very poor. Richard Scaglion wrote in his article, "From Anthropologist to Government Officer and Back Again," about how difficult it is not to lose the momentum with your informants when you are caught between two worlds. He explained that when he became a government officer, his informants did not accept him as a friend anymore but saw him as a Westerner working for the government; although he tried to be their advocate in his work with the government, he was never able to regain their friendship and trust (2005:60).

Because of my long experience in cross-cultural research, I have expanded my knowledge and understanding of people's behavior and needs, their constraints in many countries, and have come to realize that there is a commonality to their distress, which cannot be avoided because of our fast-encroaching technological world. Looking back at my work, I might have helped to somewhat improve the lives of my informants. But I have also learned that the challenges are enormous because of poverty, lack of resources, gender inequality, domestic violence, violation of women's rights, trafficking, lack of legislation and policies that protect women, lack of education for girls in male-dominant societies, health issues, and the HIV/AIDS epidemic.

To conclude, the goals of this article have been to give advice to students who want to embrace the world of development. In doing so, I presented what I consider the benefits and constraints of becoming a consultant based on my own experiences in the field of public health. Development work can be difficult, and one should look within oneself to be certain of his or her motivations and aspirations before entering this career. Do you feel that you have something to offer? If so, do you possess the right academic background and required international experiences to market yourself? Do not forget that your skills as an applied anthropologist are invaluable for the job along with a strong interest in humanitarian work and an interest in cross-cultural experiences. I have purposely presented the most critical problems in my field in order to demonstrate that development work, like employment in any other field, is not perfect. A novice should enter the profession knowing that there are pitfalls. Only through experience can one learn to avoid them. Mastering the difficulties of development work will give students the opportunities to challenge themselves physically and intellectually and to become more flexible about the complexities of living.

Finally, I want to emphasize the beneficial impact that development has had on the world's most needy populations. For instance, development in the health field has saved incalculable numbers of lives through its delivery of children's immunizations in rural areas and community outreach programs in which people did not have any health services, and in the worldwide distribution of antiretroviral therapies for those infected with HIV/AIDS.

In spite of the poor living conditions of populations where poverty and lack of resources prevail, development work has done much to further humanitarian relief to those in need and has paved the future for better programs to improve the life and health of the world's poorest populations.

Experience is a great teacher. After accomplishing your first assignment, you will be filled with excitement and reward, and with each project your interest in humanitarian causes will increase. Working in development you will soon realize how enormous is the task of improving people's lives and health, but also how equally valuable are the possible personal and professional rewards.

REFERENCES CITED

Almy, W. Susan
  1977 Anthropologists and Development Agencies. American Anthropologist 79(2):280–292.
Barrow, Ruth Nita, with Barriteau Eudine, and Alan Cobley
  2001 Stronger, Surer, Bolder: Ruth Nita Borrow: Social Change and International Development. Center for Gender and Development Studies. Barbados: University of the West Indies.
Belshaw, Cyril S.
  1974 The contributions of Anthropology to Development. Current Anthropology 15(4):520–526.
Bhuha, Zulfigar A., ed.
  2004 Maternal and Child Health in Pakistan: Challenges and Opportunities. Oxford: Oxford University Press.
Bernard, Russell
  1988 Research Methods in Cultural Anthropology. Newbury Park: Sage.
  1998 Handbook of Methods in Cultural Anthropology. Walnut Creek, CA: AltaMira Press.
Bolton, Matthew
  2006 Becoming an Aid Worker. Electronic document, http://www.transitionsabroad.com/publications/magazine/0409/becoming_an_international_aid_worker.shtml, accessed March 10, 2007.
Brutti, Lorenzo
  2005 Where Anthropologists Fear to Tread: Notes and Queries on Anthropology and Consultancy. Inspired by a Fieldwork Experience. *In* Anthropology and Consultancy: Issues and Debates. Pamela Stewart, and Andrew Strathern, eds. Pp. 106–123. New York: Berghahn.
Carland, Pinto, Maria, and Michael Trucano eds.
  1996 Careers in International Affairs. School of Foreign Service. 6th edition. Washington, DC: Georgetown University Press.
Clavi-Parisetti, Pietro, and Angela Higney
  2006 Working in International Development, Emergency Aid. Electronic document, http://www.gignos.ch/aidworker/uk/, accessed October 15, 2007.
Crewe, Emma, and Elizabeth Harrison
  1998 Whose Development? An Ethnography of Aid. New York: St. Martin's Press.
Duch, Helena
  2005 Consultation in International Development: the Case of Early Childhood in Maldives. School of Psychology International 26(21):178–191. Electronic document, http://spi.sagepub.com/cgi/reprint/26/2/178, accessed March 27, 2007.

Fernando, Jude L., with Alan W. Heston, and Abigail McGowan, eds.

1997 Annals of the American Academy of Political and Social Science. Thousand Oaks, CA: Sage.

Hall, Anthony L., and James Midgley

2004 Social Policy for Development. Thousand Oaks, CA: Sage.

Harrison, Allen F., and Robert M. Bramson

1984 The Art of Thinking: Strategies for Asking Questions, Making Decisions and Solving Problems. New York: Berkley Books.

Hill, Carole E., ed.

1991 Training Manual in Applied Medical Anthropology. Washington, DC: American Anthropological Association, Special Publication No. 27.

Hoefer, Richard

2006 Cutting-Edge Social Policy Research. Binghamton, NY: Haworth Press.

International Monetary Fund

2004 Health and Development: Why Investing in Health Is Critical for Achieving Economic Development Goals. A Compilation of Articles from Finance and Development. Electronic document, http://www.imf.org/external/pubs/ft/health/eng/hdwi/hdwi.pdf, accessed March 10, 2007.

Justice, Judith

1989 Policies, Plans and People: Foreign Aids and Health Development. Comparative Studies of Health Systems and Medical Care, vol. 17. Berkeley: University of California Press.

Krueger, Richard A.

1988 Focus Groups: A Practical Guide for Applied Research. Newbury Park, CA: Sage.

Ledwith, Margaret

1997 Participating in Transformation: Towards a Working Model of Community Empowerment. Birmingham, UK: Venture Press.

2005 Community Development: A Critical Approach. Bristol: Policy Press.

Macintyre, Martha

2005 Taking Care of Culture: Consultancy, Anthropology, and Gender Issues. In Anthropology and Consultancy: Issues and Debates. Pamela Stewart, and Andrew Strathern, eds. Pp. 124–138. New York: Berghahn.

Maynard-Tucker, Gisele

1989 Knowledge of Reproductive Physiology and Modern Contraceptives in Rural Peru. Studies in Family Planning 20(4):215–224.

2000 Conducting Focus Groups in Developing Countries: Skill Training for Local Bilingual Facilitators. Qualitative Health Research 10(3):386–410.

Moore, Sally Falk

2001 The International Production of Authoritative Knowledge: The Case of Drought Stricken West Africa. Ethnography Online 2(2)161–189. Electronic document, http://eth.sagepub.com/cgi/reprint/2/2/161.pdf, accessed March 10, 2007.

Mosse, David

2005 Cultivating Development: An Ethnography of Aid Policy and Practice. Anthropology, Culture and Society Series. London: Pluto Press.

Partridge, William, ed.

1984 Training Manual in Development Anthropology. Special Publication, 1. Washington, DC: American Anthropological Association.

Pillsbury, Barbara

1984 Evaluation and Monitoring. In Training Manual in Development Anthropology. William Partridge, ed. Pp. 42–63. Washington, DC: American Anthropological Association, Special Publication no. 1.

1991 International Health: Overview and Opportunities. In Training Manual in Applied Medical Anthropology. Carole E. Hill, ed. Pp. 54–87. Washington, DC: American Anthropological Association, Special Publication no. 27.

Scaglion, Richard

2005 From Anthropologist to Government Officer and Back Again. *In* Anthropology and Consultancy: Issues and Debates, Pamela J. Stewart, and Andrew Strathern, eds. Pp. 46–62. New York: Berghahn.

Segal, Nina, and Laurie Gross

1993 Careers in Consultancy. New York: School of International and Public Affairs, Columbia University, Association of Professional Schools of International Affairs.

Sillitos, Paul, Alan Bidker, and John Potter, eds.

2002 Participating in Development: Approaches to Indigenous Knowledge. ASA Monographs 39. New York: Routledge.

Stewart, Pamela J., and Andrew Strathern, eds.

2005 Anthropology and Consultancy: Issues and Debates. New York: Berghahn.

Stirrat, R.L.

2000 Cultures of Consultancy. Critique of Anthropology 20(1):31–46. Electronic document, http://coa.sagepub.com/cgi/reprint/20/1/31, accessed March 27, 2007.

Tanur, Judith M., ed.

1994 Questions about Questions: Inquiries into the Cognitive Bases Surveys. New York: Russell Sage Foundation.

FURTHER RESOURCES FOR CAREERS IN APPLIED
ANTHROPOLOGY

SCARLETT SHAFFER
School for International Training

This article is offers different resources related to career-building in the field of practicing anthropology. The information provided complements the insights and recommendations of the various authors featured in this bulletin. To begin with, a list of nongovernmental and governmental organizations that employ anthropologists and individuals with anthropological skills has been provided. Online job boards and an annotated bibliography on the subjects of career building in practicing anthropology are also included. In addition to these resources, this article seeks to connect the reader with other individuals involved in practicing anthropology to broaden their career opportunities through professional networks. For this purpose, there are links to community groups such as professional and local practitioner organizations. The sources offered are by no means exhaustive, but they are useful for widening the reader's knowledge, expanding their career opportunities, and generating ideas for furthered field experience in the realm of practicing anthropology. Keywords: Cultural resource management, governmental agency, local practitioner organization (LPO), non-governmental organization, practicing anthropology, professional organization.

NONGOVERNMENTAL ORGANIZATIONS

Because of the magnitude of the nonprofit sector, it is not feasible to provide a complete list. Instead, this article includes a list of a few major organizations. The four subfields of anthropology are represented by organizations that offer resources, employment, internships, and volunteer work related to the various specializations. The following organizations either employ anthropologists or individuals with related skills.

Social Service/Socio-Cultural Anthropology

Care

http://www.care.org

Care is an international nonprofit organization that fights global poverty. Care's work is primarily aimed at the empowerment of women. The efforts are community based and aimed at improving education, preventing HIV, increasing access to clean water and sanitation, expanding economic opportunities, and protecting natural resources. Care also offers relief and emergency aid to survivors of war and natural disasters.

Counterpart

http://www4.counterpart.org

NAPA BULLETIN 29, pp. 195–205. ISBN 9781405190152. © 2008 by the American Anthropological Association.
DOI:10.1111/j.1556-4797.2008.00014.x

Counterpart is an international nonprofit organization offering programs in humanitarian assistance, environmental protection, economic development, global health and child survival, food security, and sustainable development. The organization works at the local, individual, and institutional level to promote solutions to poverty.

Food First

http://www.foodfirst.org

Food First is an international nonprofit organization that fights injustices that cause hunger. The organization works to raise the awareness of the inequalities of those suffering from hunger. Through research, advocacy, and aid, the organization promotes both ecologically and socially just farming.

Heifer International

http://www.heifer.org

Heifer is an international nonprofit organization promoting sustainable community-based development through teaching environmentally sound agricultural techniques, donating livestock, training in animal management, microlending, and urban agriculture. The organization offers the opportunity to buy goats, cows, honeybees, or other animals that offer food or draft power to communities and families in economically marginalized areas.

Refugee International

http://www.refugeesinternational.org

Refugee International is an international nonprofit agency that works to provide humanitarian aid to displaced people surviving natural and human-made disasters.

Survival International

http://www.survival-international.org

Survival is an international nonprofit organization supporting the rights of tribal peoples worldwide. Survival is represented in 82 countries in the world.

UNICEF

http://www.unicef.org

UNICEF is an international nonprofit organization offering a wide range of services in the world's developing nations. Services offered promote health, education, equality, protection, and the advancement of women and children.

UNESCO (United Nations Educational, Scientific and Cultural Organization)

http://portal.unesco.org

UNESCO is an agency of the United Nations that promotes peace, security, and global solidarity through education, science, and culture.

Non-Human Primate Protection Agencies/ Physical Anthropology

The Diane Fossey Gorilla Foundation

http://www.gorillafund.org

The Diane Fossey Gorilla Foundation is an international nonprofit founded by Diane Fossey, advocate, scholar, and friend of mountain gorillas. The foundation was first established as The Digit Fund, a campaign started by Fossey to raise awareness and money to protect mountain gorillas against poachers. The foundation operates out of Atlanta and houses staff at Fossey's original field site in Rwanda.

The Jane Goodall Institute
    http://www.janegoodall.org
    Founded by legendary primatologist Jane Goodall, this organization promotes conservation and protection of nonhuman primates and their habitats. The Jane Goodall Institute also works to promote awareness about the need for primate protection. The organization is a nonprofit agency that also seeks to expand nonintrusive research programs dealing with chimpanzees and other nonhuman primates.

Cultural Resource Management–Archaeology

Center for Historical Archaeology
    http://historicalarchaeology.org/myweb/about.html
    The Center for Historical Archaeology is a nonprofit organization that promotes and houses archival research, maritime archaeology, and cultural resource analysis and conservation.

Language Preservation, Service, and Acquisition–Linguistics

Center for Applied Linguistics (CAL)
    http://www.cal.org
    The Center for Applied Linguistics is a nonprofit organization working to increase awareness and improve communication through cultural sensitivity. The organization does this through a wide range of activities and is headquartered in Washington, D.C.

U.S. GOVERNMENTAL ORGANIZATIONS

Listed below are U.S. governmental organizations that serve and protect various sectors of the U.S. and international community. The organizations provide work in areas related to all subfields of anthropology and offer employment and internship opportunities.

Agencies in the Department of Health and Human Services

Administration for Children and Families (ACF)
    http://www.acf.hhs.gov
Agency for Healthcare Research and Quality (AHRQ)
    http://www.qualityindicators.ahrq.gov
Indian Health Services (HIS)
    http://www.ihs.gov
Office of Women's Health (OWH)
    http://www.4woman.gov

The Office of Minority Health (OMH)
http://www.omhrc.gov

Agencies of the Department of Education

Office of English Language Acquisition (OELA)
http://www.ed.gov/about/offices/list/oela
Office of Innovation and Improvement (OII)
http://www.ed.gov/about/offices/list/oii

Agencies Dealing with Development

African Development Foundation (ADF)
http://www.adf.gov
Appalachian Regional Commission (ARC)
http://www.arc.gov
Office of Community Development and Planning (CPD)
http://www.hud.gov/offices/cpd
U.S. Agency for International Development (USAID)
http://www.usaid.gov
U.S. Department of Housing and Urban Development
http://www.hud.gov

Civil Rights Protection Agencies

Office for Civil Rights (OCR)
http://www.ed.gov/about/offices/list/ocr
U.S. Commission on Civil Rights
http://www.usccr.gov

Cultural Resource Management

National Park Service (NPS)
http://www.nps.gov

Environmental Protection

The Environmental Protection Agency (EPA)
http://www.epa.gov

Minority Protection Agencies

Bureau of Indian Affairs (BIA)
http://www.doi.gov/bureau-indian-affairs.html

Department of the Interior Indian Arts and Crafts Board (IACB)
    http://www.doi.gov/iacb
National Indian Gamming Commission (NIGC)
    http://www.nigc.gov
Office of Refugee Resettlement (ORR)
    http://www.acf.hhs.gov/programs/orr

PROFESSIONAL ORGANIZATIONS

The following major professional organizations are associated with four subfields of anthropology. The organizations' websites offer job boards, publications, conference and meeting dates, as well as technical information. These organizations suggest useful information and opportunities for professional exchange and networking. The organizations are a great resource to begin a job search, as they provide information about the numerous opportunities available in specific areas of interest and expertise.

Archaeology

Society for American Archaeology (SAA)
    http://www.saa.org
Society for Historical Archaeology (SHA)
    http://www.sha.org
Archaeological Institute of America (AIA)
    http://www.archaeological.org
Register of Professional Archaeologists (RPA)
    http://www.rpanet.org

General Anthropology

American Anthropological Association (AAA)
    http://www.aaanet.org

Linguistics

The American Association for Applied Linguistics (AAAL)
    http://www.aaal.org
The Linguistic Society of America (LSA)
    http://www.lsadc.org
The Society for the Study of the Indigenous Languages of the Americas (SSILA)
    http://www.ssila.org

Museum Studies/Cultural Resource Management

American Cultural Resource Association (ACRA)
   http://www.acra-crm.org
Council for Museum Anthropology (CMA)
   http://unparallel.com/cma
International Council of Museums (ICOM)
   http://icom.museum

Physical/Biological

American Academy of Forensic Sciences (AAFS)
   http://www.aafs.org
American Board of Forensic Anthropology (ABFA)
   http://www.csuchico.edu/anth/ABFA

Practicing/Professional Anthropology

National Association for the Practice of Anthropology (NAPA)
   http://www.practicinganthropology.org
Society for Applied Anthropology (SfAA)
   http://www.sfaa.net

Student Organizations

National Association of Student Anthropologists (NASA)
   http://www.aaanet.org/nasa

Local Practitioner Organizations

Local Practitioner Organizations (LPOs) are organizations that assist in professional networking and exchange and serve as employment resources. The LPOs included below offer the same services and resources of professional organizations but at the local, state, or regional level. The first website listed is an umbrella site that includes many LPOs for practicing anthropology. Provided below are also two major regional LPOs from the Midwest and East Coast.

List of Local Practitioner Organizations

http://www.practicinganthropology.org/lpos
High Plains Society for Applied Anthropology (HPSfAA), Midwest
   http://hpsfaa.org
Washington Association of Professional Anthropologists (WAPA), East Coast
   http://www.wapadc.org

Below are various online job boards. The job boards are organized by focus and are related to the four subfields of anthropology.

Anthropology/Humanities

AAA Careers in Anthropology
    http://www.aaanet.org/careers.htm
Anthrojob.com
    http://www.anthrojob.com
Anthrotech
    http://www.anthrotech.com/career
H-net (Humanities and Social Sciences) Job Guide
    http://www.h-net.org/jobs
NAPA Find/Post Job Site:
    http://www.practicinganthropology.org/employment
SfAA Employment
    http://www.sfaa.net/sfaajobs.html

Archaeology

Archaeology Fieldwork.com
    http://www.archaeologyfieldwork.com
SAA Careers, Opportunities, and Job in Archaeology
    http://www.saa.org/careers

Cultural Resource Management/Preservation

Employment Bulletin Society for American Archivists Online
    http://www.archivists.org/employment
Museum Employment Resource Center
    http://www.museum-employment.com

Nonprofit Sector

International Development Jobs and Consultancies
    http://www.devnetjobs.org
Ethical Performance, the CSR and CSI Recruitment Job Site
    http://www.ethicalperformance.com/recruitment/index.php
The Green Directory
    http://www.greendirectory.net/Jobs/latest.cfm
Nonprofit Network
    http://www.nonprofitcareer.com

The websites that follow are sites offering anthropology-related internship opportunities.
AAA Internship Opportunities

    http://www.aaanet.org/ar/internopps.htm

The Field Museum

    http://www.fieldmuseum.org

Idealist.org

    http://www.idealist.org

Intern Abroad

    http://www.internabroad.com

Serve Your World

    http://www.serveyourworld.com

BOOKS

The following section includes general sources and sources specifically written for practicing anthropologists and anthropology students. In addition, some of the resources present information on tips for writing a well composed resume and organizing a successful job search.

Anderson, Nancy

    2004 Work With Passion. Novato, CA: New World Library.

    This source is based on experiences the author, Nancy Anderson, has had with clients during the years she has spent as a career counselor. Anderson offers success stories and insight on how to discover and express one's individual passion and earn a living.

Ballard, Chris

    2006 The Butterfly Hunter: Adventures of People Who Found Their Calling Way off the Beaten Path. New York: Broadway Books.

    This book is a compilation of narratives from people who have sought and discovered fulfilling and inspiring work. Through the various narratives, the book offers insight into finding rewarding employment.

Banderjee, Dillion

    2000 So You Want to Join the Peace Corps: What to Know Before You Go. Berkeley: Ten Speed Press.

    The above work is an insider's guide written by a man who spent two years as a Peace Corps volunteer in Cameroon. Banderjee chronicles the trials and triumphs of life as a Peace Corps volunteer.

Bornstein, David

    2004 How to Change the World: Social Entrepreneurs and the Power of New Ideas. New York: Oxford University Press.

    This volume chronicles the work of various "social entrepreneurs," people working for large-scale "social profit" or change organizations. The book is intended for anyone looking for work within the nonprofit industry.

Bolles, Richard Nelson

2007 What Color Is Your Parachute? A Practical Manual for Job Hunters and Career Changers. Berkeley: Ten Speed Press.

This book contains guidelines for job hunting and career changes. It is written for a wide range of readers at various levels of their careers and educations.

Brophy, Paul C., and Alice Shabecoff

2001 A Guide to Careers in Community Development. Washington, DC: Island Press.

This instructive work is a guide for individuals interested in community development. It gives information on jobs in both national and international community development.

Camenson, Blythe

2000 Great Jobs for Anthropology Majors. Chicago: Contemporary Publishing Group.

This book gives the reader alternatives to academic anthropology. It discusses practicing anthropology and various other career opportunities dealing with anthropology.

Camenson, Blythe

2000 Opportunities in Museum Careers. Chicago: Contemporary Publishing Group.

This is a starting place for information on career opportunities within museums.

Camenson, Blythe

1997 Great Jobs for Liberal Arts Majors. Lincolnwood: NTC, Contemporary Publishing Company.

This work puts forward the value of a degree in the liberal arts. The author suggests various career paths for liberal arts majors and reveals information pertaining to the job search.

Eisenberg, Ronni

2000 Organize Your Job Search. New York: Hyperion.

This guide offers advice on how to organize a job search. The book gives advice pertaining to arranging job interviews, performing well in the interview process, and resume writing.

Giangrande, Gregory

1998 The Liberal Arts Advantage. New York: Avon.

This book contains insider information on career opportunities for individuals with liberal arts degrees.

Griffith, Susan

2005 Work Your Way Around the World. Guilford: Globe Pequot Press.

In this volume the author gives a collection of firsthand accounts from people who have worked in various enterprises around the world. The book offers a country-to-country guide with information on volunteer work and employment in grassroots organizations, wildlife conservation, and other opportunities. This book is ideal for the newly graduated student who wants to explore the world and its various cultures, as well as continue to build their resume.

Gurvis, Sandra

2000 Careers for Non-Conformists. New York: Marlowe and Co.

This is a resource for the individual who wants to break away from the nine to five routine. It presents 225 careers that cover an assortment of interests and education levels. The book also includes 30 career profiles.

Hamilton, Leslie, and Robert Tragert

2000 100 Best Nonprofits to Work For. 2nd edition. Stanford, CA: Thomson Learning.

This book offers profiles of today's best paying and most gratifying nonprofits for which to work.

Jebens, Hakley

1996 100 Jobs in Social Change. New York: Macmillan.

This volume gives a range of careers in social health, education, nonprofit, media, communication, and technology dealing with social change and advocacy.

King, Richard M.

2000 From Making a Profit to Making a Difference: How to Launch Your New Career in Non-Profits. River Forest: Quality Books.

In this guide Richard King puts forth an account of life and opportunities available within the nonprofit sector. The advice given in the book is specifically geared toward business professionals wanting to make a transition into the nonprofit sector, but it is also useful for anyone interested in working for a nonprofit organization.

Krannich, Ronald L., and Wendy S. Enelow

2002 Best Resumes and CVs for International Jobs. Manassas Park, VA: Impact Publications.

This is an instructive book for international resumes and CVs. It presents 86 sample resumes, tips on resume writing, and websites for international resume writing.

Landes, Michael

2005 Back Door Guide to Short-Term Job Adventures. Berkley: Ten Speed Press.

This book lists jobs that range from fruit picking in Europe to internships in nonprofit organizations. The book is a guide for recently graduated individuals who want to experience life and work outside of the United States.

Mannion, James

2004 The Everything Alternative Careers Book. Avon: Adams Media.

This volume presents a collection of nontraditional short-term and long-term jobs. It discusses organizations such as the Peace Corps and Habitat for Humanity. The book also provides information on grant writing and financial planning.

Nolan, Riall

2003 Anthropology in Practice: A Guide to Non-Academic Jobs and Careers for Anthropologists. Boulder, CO: Lynne Rienner.

This resource is a guide for individuals who want to pursue nonacademic careers in anthropology. It looks at differences between academic and practicing anthropologists. Along with sample resumes and cover letters, the author lists anthropology-related websites.

Powell, Joan

2003 Alternatives to the Peace Corps. Oakland, CA: Food First Books.

In this book Powell gives a list of one-hundred national and international organizations working in the civil service and nonprofit sector. Along with websites and books discussing various agencies, the book presents tips for evaluating organizations and budgeting funds.

Stephens, Richard W.

2001 Careers in Anthropology. Boston: Allyn and Bacon.

This book offers 16 real life stories and career profiles of people who have used their degrees in anthropology to find unusual work.

van Willigen, John

1993 Applied Anthropology. Westport: Bergin and Garvey.

This volume is an overview of applied anthropology and discusses the various areas in which an applied anthropologist can affect change. There is also a chapter on being able to support oneself financially as a practicing anthropologist.

van Willigen, John, Barbara Rylko-Bauer, and Ann McElroy, eds.

1989 Making Our Research Useful: Case Studies in the Utilization of Anthropological Knowledge. Boulder, CO: Westview Press.

The above is composed of case studies of various projects employing anthropological technique and perspective outside of academia.

Veruki, Peter

1999 The 250 Job Interview Questions You'll Most Likely Be Asked ... and the Answers That Will Get You Hired. Avon, MA: Adams Media Corporation.

This work is an instructive guide and gives information on interview preparation and strategies.

Wulff, Robert M., and Shirley J. Fiske, eds.

1987 Anthropological Praxis: Translating Knowledge into Action. Boulder, CO: Westview Press.

This source is written for the individual interested in learning more about the work and ideas behind practicing anthropology.

Biosketches of Authors

Shirley J. Fiske is a practicing anthropologist with 22 years of experience in the federal government (Executive and Legislative branches), including management, research, analysis, and outreach. She received her Ph.D. in cultural anthropology from Stanford University. She spent 16 years in the Executive branch with the National Oceanic and Atmospheric Administration (NOAA) in ocean and atmospheric policy and research affecting ocean and coastal resources and communities. She worked for the National Sea Grant College Program, a multidisciplinary research, extension, and education program working with communities and businesses along coastlines. Recently, she worked for Senator Daniel K. Akaka (D-HI) as legislative aide for energy, natural resources, oceans, and the environment. As president of the Washington Association of Professional Anthropologists (WAPA) and NAPA, she has worked to ensure that practicing anthropologists are represented and active in national associations. Currently, she is an independent (available) consultant and adjunct professor of anthropology at the University of Maryland. (shirley.fiske@verizon.net)

Jennifer Gilden received her B.A. from Vassar College in 1987, and her M.A. in environmental anthropology from Oregon State University in 1996. Her thesis focused on changing gender roles in an Oregon timber community. Later, she worked with Oregon Sea Grant, studying the lives of fishermen's wives, fishermen's attitudes toward salmon disaster relief programs, the social networks of watershed councils, public attitudes toward salmon restoration, and communication in fisheries management. The latter project led to her current position at the Pacific Fishery Management Council in Portland, Oregon, where she develops outreach and educational materials, contributes to social impact analyses and other social science efforts, staffs the council's Habitat Committee, develops the council newsletter, and works on enhancing the council's communication with constituents. Jennifer was a cofounder of the Institute for Culture and Ecology, a nonprofit research organization that studies the links between culture and environment. (jennifer.gilden@noaa.gov)

Emilia González-Clements is founder and director of the Fifth Sun Development Fund (FSDF), a private international development agency. She is currently directing a long-term sustainable mountain development initiative in northern Mexico with rural small producers. She has over 25 years of experience as an applied anthropologist, including assistant professor of applied anthropology, women's advocacy agency director, director of a Latino community center, and certified social worker. She has completed consulting projects in Mexico, Peru, Hawai'i, and with tribes in the United States.

NAPA BULLETIN 29, pp. 206–210. ISBN 9781405190152. © 2008 by the American Anthropological Association. DOI:10.1111/j.1556-4797.2008.00015.x

Her consulting company specializes in community-based and strategic planning, applied research and group facilitation. González-Clements is the former president of the High Plains Society for Applied Anthropology and is current chair of the Society for Applied Anthropology Public Policy Committee. She holds a Ph.D. in applied social anthropology from the University of Kentucky, an M.A. in cultural anthropology from Texas Tech University, and a B.A. in sociology/social work from Niagara University. (egc@fsdf.org)

Carla Guerrón-Montero is assistant professor of anthropology and Latin American Studies, Black American Studies, and Women's Studies at the University of Delaware. She received her M.A. (1997) in applied anthropology from Oregon State University and her Ph.D. (2002) in cultural anthropology from the University of Oregon. She has conducted ethnographic and applied work on development, globalization, tourism, and racial–ethnic and gender relations, particularly among Afro-Latin American populations in Panama, Ecuador, Grenada, Chile, and Brazil. She has participated on collaborative interdisciplinary projects on nutritional anthropology, and gender and development in Ecuador. Guerrón-Montero is author of several articles and book chapters published in the United States, Latin America, and Europe. She is a fellow of the Society for Applied Anthropology (SfAA) and the Salzburg Seminars. Guerrón-Montero has served on the executive boards of several sections and committees of the American Anthropological Association, SfAA, and the Latin American Studies Association. (cguerron@udel.edu)

Pissamai Homchampa is assistant professor and head of the Health Education Department (Faculty of Public Health) of Burapha University, Thailand. Her qualifications include a Ph.D. in biocultural anthropology from the University of Oregon (2001), M.Sc. in physical anthropology from the University of Oregon (1999), M.P.H. in rural health from the University of Philippines (1990), and B.Sc. in nursing from Khon Kaen University, Thailand (1985). Dr. Homchampa's work centers on the public health aspects of health behavioral modification and health promotion, as well as anthropology of health with a focus on gender and sociocultural determinants of health and illness and self-care practices, particularly among industrial workers, adolescence, and population with chronic illnesses (e.g., HIV/AIDS). In recent years, Dr. Homchampa has developed extensive experience researching, working, and training health personnel to enhance health and self-care capacities of people living with HIV/AIDS and health promotion– HIV/AIDS behavioral risk reduction of adolescence and couples. (phomcham@buu. ac.th)

Satish Kedia received his Ph.D. in applied and medical anthropology in 1997 from the University of Kentucky, where he also earned a certificate in medical behavioral science. He is currently Dunavant University Professor and associate professor of medical anthropology, as well as director of the Institute for Substance Abuse Treatment Evaluation (I-SATE) at the University of Memphis. His research focuses on alcohol and drug abuse treatment evaluation, caregiving and adherence to treatment protocols, HIV/AIDS in the United States, health impacts of forced displacement in India, and pesticide use in the Philippines. He coedited *Applied Anthropology: Domains of Application* with John van Willigen, has authored or coauthored numerous journal articles, book chapters, and encyclopedia entries, and has published more than 25 evaluation and policy reports. (skkedia@memphis.edu)

Luke Eric Lassiter directs the Graduate Humanities Program at Marshall University Graduate College in South Charleston, West Virginia, where he is also professor of humanities and anthropology. He received his Ph.D. in anthropology from the University of North Carolina at Chapel Hill in 1995. Lassiter is the author of several books, including *Invitation to Anthropology*; *The Chicago Guide to Collaborative Ethnography*; and, with Elizabeth Campbell, Hurley Goodall, Michelle Natasya Johnson, and Ball State University students, *The Other Side of Middletown*. He is a Fellow of the Society for Applied Anthropology and the recipient of the 2005 Margaret Mead Award. (elassite@earthlink.net)

Carla Littlefield received her Ph.D. in anthropology from the University of Colorado, Boulder in 1981 after ten years in nursing education. Her doctoral research on the health and nutrition of migrant farmworker children led to a consultant position with the Colorado Migrant Health Program, where she developed and implemented special projects, including a statewide survey of migrant health needs and a manual which was distributed nationally to assist migrant health centers in the delivery of culturally appropriate family planning services. She also served as research director for a statewide task force for the medically indigent. In 1989, she established Littlefield Associates, a general partnership that provides community assessments and grant writing for city, county, and state agencies in the Denver metropolitan area. Dr. Littlefield is a past president of the High Plains Society for Applied Anthropology and is a recipient of the Omer C. Stewart Memorial Award. (cnlittlefield@cs.com)

Gisele Maynard-Tucker is a research scholar at the Center for the Study of Women at University of California, Los Angeles (UCLA), and a medical and applied anthropologist. She holds a Ph.D. in anthropology from UCLA, and has worked as an international consultant since the 1980s for development agencies such as WHO, USAID, World Bank, European Union, POPTECH, Development Associates, Academy for Educational Development, and many others. She has conducted research and evaluation of health programs regarding family planning, reproductive health, maternal and child survival, and HIV/AIDS prevention in Africa, South America, Asia, and the Caribbean. She has published articles about the Quechua Indians of Peru and contraception, quality of care of services in Haiti, management of Acute Respiratory Infections (ARI) in Morocco, development of skills training for bilingual facilitators, women's empowerment in Madagascar, and AIDS prevention in the workplace in Nigeria. She is also part-time faculty member in the anthropology department at California State University, Northridge. (gmaytuck@aol.com; www.csw.ucla.edu/researchscholars)

Geraldine Moreno-Black is a professor in the department of anthropology at the University of Oregon and the cochair of the Lane County Food Policy Council. Trained as a nutritional anthropologist and human biologist, she is also a board certified nutrition specialist ([CNS] American Institute of Nutrition). Her research, which is located at the intersection of nutritional anthropology, human biology, and medical anthropology, has involved nutrition-related issues in Latin America (Bolivia and Ecuador), Southeast

Asia (Thailand and Indonesia) and the United States. Using a biocultural framework, she has addressed issues of childhood obesity, nutritional status, and hunger and food security. Professor Moreno is the recipient of research awards from the National Science Foundation, Social Science Research Council, Fulbright-Hayes and Wenner-Gren Foundation for Anthropological Research. She also received numerous teaching and curriculum grants. Her recent publications deal with the relationship of nutritional status to child growth, concepts of hunger and food security. (gmorenob@uoregon.edu)

Riall Nolan is associate provost and dean of international programs at Purdue University. He received his D.Phil. in social anthropology from Sussex University in the United Kingdom in 1975. His specialties include international development, cross-cultural adaptation, and applied anthropology. Dr. Nolan worked overseas—in Senegal, Tunisia, Papua New Guinea, and Sri Lanka—for nearly 20 years as a development project designer, manager, and evaluator. His experience includes grassroots community projects with the Peace Corps, project management with USAID, and policy analysis with the World Bank. He has also participated in numerous consulting assignments for both bilateral agencies and NGOs. He joined Purdue University in 2003. Prior to that, he directed international programs at the University of Cincinnati. He has also held administrative and teaching positions at Golden Gate University, the University of Pittsburgh, the School for International Training, Georgia State University, and the University of Papua New Guinea. (rwnolan@purdue.edu)

Barbara L.K. Pillsbury was the founding president of NAPA. She is a cultural anthropologist, specialized in the design and evaluation of health programs in developing countries. Following a Ph.D. from Columbia University on ethnicity and Muslims in China, she moved into international development, first as a foreign service officer with USAID. In 1988, she established and became president of International Health and Development Associates, a woman-owned consulting firm, through which she has carried out consultancies around the world for international agencies including USAID, WHO, UNICEF, UNFPA, the World Bank, and the Rockefeller, Ford, Hewlett Packard, and Gates Foundations. In 1993, she cofounded the Pacific Institute for Women's Health, working with women's NGOs around the world. More recently she was director of the $48-million USAID-funded Synergy Project, coordinating and reporting on outputs of the 60-plus organizations funded by you, the taxpayers, to attack HIV/AIDS globally. (bpillsbury@gmail.com)

Terry Redding is currently at work on a memoir about hitchhiking around the world and runs a small home improvement business. He is also the communications manager for Beta Social Research, a developing nonprofit organization based in Florida, and does occasional consulting in the Washington, D.C., area. From 2000 to 2005 he worked for LTG Associates as information resources specialist for POPTECH, a USAID-funded population technical assistance and evaluation project. In 1999, he was the editor for NAPA Bulletin 19, "Applied Anthropology and the Internet: Innovation and Communication," the first wholly online publication of the American Anthropological Association. He is a past president of the Washington Association of Professional Anthropologists (WAPA), and also a past local practitioner organization liaison for NAPA, and is on two

NAPA committees. He received an M.A. in applied anthropology from the University of South Florida in 1998, and has undergraduate degrees in journalism and sociology. (terrymredding@yahoo.com)

Scarlett Shaffer is a graduate student at the School of International Training (SIT) in Brattleboro, Vermont. At SIT, Shaffer is pursing an M.A. in sustainable development. Her current research interests include community-based sustainable tourism and long-term social and economic development in Latin America. Shaffer earned a B.A. in anthropology and Latin American Studies at the University of Delaware. As an undergraduate, she studied in Mexico and Spain, did preliminary research in Panama and Korea, and volunteered in Kenya. Enriched by her experiences abroad, she now hopes to explore and promote, through her scholarship, low-impact travel that encourages environmental, social, and cultural awareness and appreciation. In her future work, Shaffer hopes to participate in the advancement of the application of anthropological methodology and dialogue within the field of sustainable development. Shaffer's contribution to this *NAPA Bulletin* is her first publication. (phenox@udel.edu)

Peter Van Arsdale is senior lecturer at the Graduate School of International Studies at the University of Denver. Through 2006, he served as faculty advisor to its Center on Rights Development (CORD), a graduate student organization that sponsors human rights activities. Since 2007, he has been director of the school's new certificate program in humanitarian assistance. Trained as an applied cultural and medical anthropologist, with a subspecialty in refugee studies, Van Arsdale has conducted fieldwork in the United States, Romania, Bosnia, Indonesia, Sudan, Ethiopia, Guyana, Peru, and El Salvador, and has just helped initiate a program in East Timor with Nobel Peace Laureate José Ramos-Horta. He is a member of two national human rights committees and (among a number of publications) author of *Forced to Flee: Human Rights and Human Wrongs in Refugee Homelands*. He cofounded the Denver Hospice and the Rocky Mountain Survivors Center. (pvanarsd@du.edu)

Philip Young is Professor Emeritus of anthropology at the University of Oregon (UO). He received his Ph.D. (1968) in anthropology from the University of Illinois at Urbana. He has done ethnographic and applied research in collaboration with the indigenous Ngöbe in Panama. He has also worked in Mexico, Costa Rica, Honduras, Ecuador, Nepal, and the southern Sudan. In 1976, he worked for a Washington, D.C.– based NGO as project director in Panama of a nonformal education project for the Ngöbe. On his return to UO after this baptism of fire experience, he began to teach courses in applied anthropology. He worked for Development Alternatives, Inc. (DAI) in the Southern Sudan as a consultant to the Yambio Institute of Agriculture (1981–82), and as senior program manager for the Development Strategies for Fragile Lands in Latin America and the Caribbean (DESFIL) project (1989–92). His research interests include adaptive strategies of indigenous peoples and small farmers. (pyoung@uoregon.edu)